The Suicide of Reason

THE SUICIDE *of* REASON

Radical Islam's Threat to the Enlightenment

LEE HARRIS

BASIC BOOKS

A Member of the Perseus Books Group
New York

Designed by Timm Bryson

Library of Congress Cataloging-in-Publication Data

Harris, Lee, 1948-
  The suicide of reason : radical Islam's threat to the enlightenment / by Lee
Harris.
      p. cm.
  Includes index.
  ISBN-13: 978-0-465-00203-0
  ISBN-10: 0-465-00203-X
  1. Fanaticism--Psychological aspects. 2. Religious fanaticism--Psychological
aspects. I. Title.

  BF575.F16H27 2007
  303.48'2--dc22
                                                          2007009754

10 9 8 7 6 5 4 3 2 1

For Andy Fuson

Our fond hope is that by some accord of conscious purpose among the states of the world the passion to expand and master can be eliminated from the politics of men. But when we grasp the living quality of human societies, we realize that this is a vain, and, indeed, a perilous hope. Because they are living entities, not conscious associations, these historical societies unavoidably struggle with one another. We know from the nature of living things that they are certain to do so. We can anticipate the type of situation that must always develop between two societies as it must develop between two competing species. The details of such historical struggles, being among the societies of men, will not resemble the struggles of species of wild animals but the essential patterns will be the same. Each society will seek to live its life regardless of the welfare of others. We know historically that some societies have destroyed others, as some species have destroyed other species. We know also of societies that have existed together. But we know equally that no society has ever long existed through the forbearance and charity of another. Each that has survived has survived by its own material power.

LAWRENCE R. BROWN, *The Might of the West*

Nothing is easier than to admit in words the truth of the universal struggle for life, or more difficult—at least I have found it so—than constantly to bear this conclusion in mind.

CHARLES DARWIN

CONTENTS

Preface   *ix*

PART ONE

1   Fanaticism and the Myth of Modernity   3

2   The Denial of Fanaticism   15

3   Fanaticism and Resentment   29

4   The End of History?   39

5   Clash or Crash?   55

6   The Fanaticism of Reason   61

PART TWO

REASON, FANATICISM, AND THE STRUGGLE FOR EXISTENCE

7   Demystifying Reason   79

8   Thomas Hobbes and the Politics of Reason   105

PART THREE

THE ORIGINS OF POPULAR CULTURES OF REASON

9	Condorcet's Tenth Stage	137
10	Reason and Autonomy	157
11	Liberal Exceptionalism	165

PART FOUR

THE CHALLENGE OF ISLAMIC FANATICISM

| 12 | The Logic of Fanaticism | 205 |
| 13 | The Legacy and Future of Jihad | 215 |

PART FIVE

14	Can Carpe Diem Societies Survive?	241
15	Our New World Disorder	253
	Conclusion	265
	Index	281

PREFACE

Not so long ago, many intelligent men and women in the West thought that the world was approaching the end of history. Though it might not be quite the golden age of the starry-eyed socialist utopians of the nineteenth century, it would definitely achieve something of enormous value: The end of history would mean the virtual abolition of the law of the jungle as it applied to human affairs. The global spread of capitalism would relieve the poverty of the Third World—not immediately, of course, but, if given a chance, over the not too distant future. Western-style liberal democracies would replace the corrupt regimes that impeded human progress in so many parts of the world. Of course, there were bound to be skirmishes and conflicts, but these could be dealt with through international bodies such as the United Nations, backed, needless to say, by the awesome military might of the United States. After all, this multilateral approach had worked during both the Gulf War and the Balkan War. Certainly the same technique could be applied to any other situations in which the law of the jungle threatened to disrupt the rule of law that had come to govern the conduct of all civilized and reasonable people.

Yet today, brute force and atrocious violence increasingly shape the course of events. In spring of 2005, *Time* magazine displayed a cover captioned "People Power" that showed a jubilant scene of the Lebanese people celebrating what was called the Cedar Revolution. In mid-July of 2006, the cover of *Time* showed the bombed wreckage of Beirut. Meanwhile, in Iraq, once the promised land of Middle Eastern democratic reform, death squads murder in cold blood Iraqi boys who dare to wear shorts, and Iraqi barbers who sin against Islam by shaving off beards, while American soldiers are accused by their own government of brutalizing and killing innocent Iraqi women and children.

What went wrong? How could so many intelligent men and women have been so terribly mistaken about the future? Those who hailed the Cedar Revolution in Lebanon were no doubt completely sincere in their conviction that the withdrawal of Syrian troops would lead to the triumph of democracy in Lebanon. The American neoconservative intellectuals who planned the reconstruction of Iraq were just as sincere in their faith that Iraq would become a model of democracy, and they were equally convinced that other Muslim nations would be eager to imitate it. Yet all these intelligent men and women were not merely wrong, they were disastrously, mind-bogglingly wrong.

When the confident expectations of our leaders and opinion makers turn out to be so dreadfully off the mark, this is a signal that either they have drifted away from reality, or reality has drifted away from them. It is also a warning sign that those who are shaping our destiny may be the victims of their own wishful thinking and ideological enthusiasms, in which case we have just cause for alarm. Despite what our leaders tell us, we are not getting close to the end of history. We are not even confronting a mere clash of civilizations. Instead, we are facing something none of our leaders wishes to think about—the crash of civilization as we know it. The leadership of the West refuses to think the worst. But refusal to think the worst is the best way to permit the worst to come about. The historian Allan Nevins argued that one of the "causes" of the American Civil War was the general failure to imagine just how horrible such a war would be, and the same principle holds for many other historical catastrophes.

Therefore, it is urgently necessary for someone to think the very worst. That is why I have written this book.

Paradoxically, the source of our troubles is that we have been blessed to live during one of those rare and exceptional eras in which the law of the jungle *appeared* to have been repealed. In the modern liberal West, for the first time in history, something new came into the world: popular cultures of reason, and all of us in the modern liberal West are its beneficiaries. Before the Enlightenment, reason had been the preserve of privileged elites; but with the advent of universal secular education, undertaken by the state, the goal was to create whole populations that refrained from solving their conflicts through an appeal to violence and brute force. Instead, conflicts were handled through reasonable procedures—discussion, debate, arbitration, parliamentary routines, courts of law, international bodies. Vigilante justice was no longer accepted; mobs no longer rioted to get their way; there was no need for the vendetta and the blood feud. Or, when these things happened, they happened outside the pale of respectability. Instead, men and women went about their daily lives behaving quite reasonably with one another, and came to expect others to behave reasonably with them.

The goal of liberal education in the modern West has been to create people who would behave as rational actors. Each child would be raised to see himself as a distinct and unique individual.

He would be taught that he had certain fundamental human rights as an individual: He has the right to make up his mind for himself, to pursue his own vision of the good life independently, to exercise free speech. He was taught that he had an individual conscience, and that it was entirely up to him what religion he should follow or what political agenda he should support. Finally, he was taught that it was permissible for each person to pursue his or her enlightened self-interest, since ultimately such a policy would benefit both the individuals in question and the greater society of which they were members. If conflicts arose between two individuals who were both seeking their enlightened self-interest, there were reasonable procedures by which such conflicts could be peacefully settled.

The modern liberal West succeeded in creating popular cultures in which, by and large, people actually behaved like rational actors. Yet this very success made these actors forget that they were the products of a specific tradition of upbringing and education, deliberately aimed at creating people who would behave like themselves. This forgetfulness ended in seducing the West into believing that men are born rational actors—that it is "natural" for individuals to behave like rational actors. No illusion could be further from the truth.

Throughout most of human history, men have not behaved like rational actors but like tribal actors; and in many cultures of the world today, they continue to behave that way. They have no choice. When everyone around you is a member of a tribe, you must either belong to a tribe or be an outcast. Whereas the rational actor asks himself, "What is best for me," the tribal actor must ask himself, "What is best for us?" What matters for the tribal actor is not the pursuit of his enlightened self-interest but rather the success of his tribe. The rational actor is free to go his own separate way: He can invent his own religion; he can make what John Stuart Mill called "experiments in living"; he can dress himself as eccentrically as he wishes to, eat only the food of an exotic culture, and mock and ridicule the traditions and customs of his own culture. The tribal actor can do none of these things. Yet what limits his freedom is not so much the pressure of the tribal mind applied externally, but rather the fact that the tribal actor thinks with the tribal mind, and so cannot even imagine doing things differently from the way they are done by his tribe. For the tribal actor, departing from the ways of the tribe is simply unthinkable: He must remain true to his tribe through thick and thin.

The rational actor has the luxury of appealing to his conscience in order to condemn the behavior of his own community. During the Boer War, there were many in England who thought the English were acting unjustly toward the Afrikaners, and who were particularly outraged by Lord Kitchener's policy of interning Boer women and children in disease-infested "concentration camps" (the Nazi borrowed their word from the English phrase). The tribal actor, on the other hand, cannot take a moral stance outside the perspective of his tribe. For the tribal actor, the highest ethical idea is: "My tribe, right or wrong." The mere idea that his tribe could be wrong is unthinkable for the tribal actor, since he defines as right whatever the tribe deems right, and wrong as whatever the tribe deems wrong.

It has always been tempting for rational actors to look upon themselves, with smug superiority, as representing a higher stage of human development than that reached by tribal actors. For the rational actor, ethnocentric tribalism is primitive and backward; the culture created by rational actors is sophisticated and modern. The rational actor is not only on a higher stage of moral progress but a different kind of human being from the tribal actor—he has superseded the stage of tribalism, and he lives the life of a rational and autonomous agent. He has escaped the prison of the tribal mind and has learned how to think for himself, calculate his own advances, and pursue his own goals and objectives.

What this narcissistic self-glorification overlooks is that rational actors are the product of a serendipitous escape from the jungle— the rational actor can behave as he does only because he is confident that the other people he deals with will refrain from using tactics suitable to the jungle. For example, a man can build a home for himself, confident that he will not be driven from it by a marauding gang of thugs. He knows that to defend his home he need not learn how to fight off brutal killers—he need only call the police, and they will defend his home for him.

Because the rational actor does not need to learn how to survive in the jungle, he tends to forget the laws that rule it. He regards those who operate by the law of the jungle as uncivilized barbarians. The rational actor may actually be puzzled why anyone could possibly behave the way that human beings have always behaved. But this incomprehension is simply a reflection of the fact that the rational actor has only known a society in which the law of the jungle has ceased to regulate human conduct.

Yet what happens to the rational actor when the reasonable world that he has always known begins to unravel, and the world around him increasingly takes on the aspects of the long forgotten jungle? Or worse, what happens to him when he has not simply forgotten the jungle but has convinced himself that the jungle has been abolished for good, never to return? Subject to this delusion, how will the rational actor react to ominous signs of the impending return of the jungle?

At first he will try to minimize the threat. He will try to explain it away, or simply deny it. Or he might try to appeal to those tried-and-true techniques that work so well to keep a society of rational actors from conflict and turmoil. He will seek negotiations, peace talks, compromise. He will use the carrot and the stick; he may in fact exhaust all the channels by which rational actors are accustomed to thrashing out their own differences.

What the rational actor will almost certainly fail to grasp is that with the return of the jungle, he himself will become increasingly out of touch with the new realities that the jungle's return inevitably brings. To begin with, he will find a world in which, once again, tribal actors will take center stage while rational actors are pushed into the sidelines. The rational actor, after all, wishes to stand above the fray. He wants to be Adam Smith's disinterested spectator, able to look impartially on both sides of the conflict. He would like to be able to apportion blame and moral censure even-handedly. He refuses to commit himself to either side, in order to preserve his own moral autonomy. He resists all efforts of partisans to enlist him to their cause. He wishes to act as a referee or umpire, as a rational and autonomous agent, instead of losing his capacity for individual judgment beneath the irresistible pressure of the tribal mind.

Yet how can the rational actor keep his aloofness when all around him he sees people increasingly dividing themselves into warring tribes? What becomes the point of his lonely moral isolation in a world in which virtually everyone else has become passionately committed to his own side, and sees anyone lacking this passionate tribal commitment as a traitor, a coward, or an enemy?

That, it must be remembered, is the first consequence of the return of the jungle—the reawakening of the tribal mind, even in people who had been raised to behave like rational actors. If there is a tribe that hates me because they see me as a member of an enemy tribe, then my only hope of security lies in standing firmly with my own tribe. As the old adage goes, there is safety in numbers. What good would it do for me to assure those who hate my tribal identity that I am not really a member of my tribe, but a rational and independent actor, capable of moral autonomy? The law of the jungle is brutal on this point: If you're not with us you're against us. If you are not a member of our tribe, you are one of them—an enemy, and Us versus Them is the essence of the tribal mind. It is also the source of its immense power.

This brings us to something of a paradox. The rational actor who insists on staying a rational actor when his world has reverted to the ways of the jungle is not, in fact, acting rationally. Rationality, at this point, requires group solidarity. It involves the surrender of moral autonomy and the fanatical embrace of the tribe. Furthermore, it involves the discarding of the normal rules of engagement that work well in a community composed primarily of rational actors.

Today the political and intellectual leadership of the West is composed of men and women who are rational actors accustomed to dealing only with other rational actors. Yet the world that confronts them at the beginning of the new millennium is more and more becoming a world in which the law of the jungle rules human affairs. But who among our leaders even remembers what the law of the jungle is about? None of them has risen to power by virtue of brute force or even a bloodless coup d'état. Each of them obtained his or her position of power and influence by following the normal channels by which people rise to the top in a liberal society: they got appointed or elected; they earned degrees and credentials; they worked their way up the corporate ladder; or they learned how to win the confidence and trust of the dominant political parties. In short, they played by the rules.

The first law of the jungle, however, states that in the struggle for survival and supremacy, there are no rules. Anything that achieves victory is automatically self-justifying. Methods that are looked upon by rational actors as barbarous, savage, or bestial are all deemed acceptable if they obtain their objective. This objective, moreover, will not be the good of the individual but the advancement and dominance of one's own tribe. For the second law of the jungle says that loners are losers. If you lack a tribe to back and support you, you will perish. To survive in a dog-eat-dog world you must run in packs—and the tribe is the pack. Taken together, the first two laws of the jungle yield the third law: You must unconditionally support your own tribe or pack, and you must be prepared to act with utter ruthlessness toward those who belong to other tribes or packs. You must see members of the enemy tribe not as individuals or as fellow humans; you must see them as your existential enemy. That is all you need to know about them in order to be willing to kill them, torture them, or mutilate their corpses. Where the laws of the jungle rule, the very idea of humanity is forgotten.

Those who follow the laws of the jungle will regard as good and virtuous precisely those human qualities that are shunned and proscribed by the cultures of reason created by rational actors. Fanatical devotion and commitment to your tribe and pack, accompanied by a fanatical intolerance and hatred of your enemy, are considered sterling virtues. Likewise, the virtues of the rational actor, such as the avoidance of violence, the willingness to compromise, tolerance of other tribes and their traditions, are looked upon as signs of cowardice, imbecility, or a traitorous lack of loyalty to one's tribe. Thus it is virtually impossible for those who follow the laws of the jungle to find a common ground with those whose highest ethical aim is to abolish these very laws and replace them with cultures of reason. What is day to one is night to the other; what is good to one is evil for the other. The fanaticism abhorred by the rational actor becomes the collective bond that keeps the tribal mind together. Rational actors teach and train their children to hate fanaticism, and to behave by the canons of reason; tribal actors teach and train their children to re-gard fanaticism as the highest duty they have as members of their tribe. Rational actors pass on a culture of reason; tribal actors pass on their culture of fanaticism. To us, it is obvious that they are wrong, and we are right. To them, it is just as obvious that they are right, and we are wrong.

This book will not try to answer the question, Who is really right? Instead it will examine what are the strengths and weak-nesses of both the rational actor and the tribal actor. It will ask, If we are facing a return of the jungle, who, in the long run, will win: the rational actor, and his culture of reason; or the tribal ac-tor, with his culture of fanaticism? This is not a moral question—it is simply a question of who will prevail. Thus it is important from the outset to realize that the terms I use will be applied without any hint of censure or praise.

A culture of reason, for example, is not necessarily superior: It is defined simply as a culture in which virtually all the actors are rational actors. Nor is a rational actor necessarily superior, morally or otherwise—he is simply a different kind of actor from the tribal actor.

A rational actor is merely concerned with achieving his own in-dividual objectives and aims, and each will calculate the best method by which he may obtain what he wants. He will make ra-tional choices after deliberation and debate; but these choices will be his own choices. Together with other rational actors, he may devise systems for collective actions taken on the part of large numbers of individuals, but the basis for this collective action will always be voluntary and contractual.

Rational actors, for example, will enter into business ventures together. Each, of course, wants the corporation to succeed; but ultimately, the work the individual puts into the corporation is for the sake of the individual himself, and not the good of the corporation. In America, for example, a man who works for corporation A one day may be working for its rival corporation B a week later. In short, in a culture of reason, the basis of cooperation relies on a social contract: all the individuals have voluntarily agreed to a joint venture, and none is forced or coerced into any action; each is free to choose his own line of conduct for himself, provided he does not violate any of the universal ground rules that have been established by means of the social contract.

The fact that an individual is a rational actor does not necessarily mean that we ourselves would approve of his course of action. A rational actor may choose to do things we find abhorrent. A business executive might decide to concrete over a beautiful forest and build a hideous shopping center. We may not like what he has done—but we must still admit that he is behaving as a rational actor, as we are defining the term.

On the other hand, suppose there is a quiet poet who very much loves the beautiful woods that are to be concreted over. Outraged by the thought of seeing the woods destroyed, he decides that he will break the law in order to register his personal and vehement objections to the project. Indeed, let us imagine that he even throws himself in front of the bulldozer that is about to clear the forest he loves. In doing so, is the poet acting as a rational actor? Or is he behaving like a fanatic? Do we denounce him, or do we admire him?

The answer to this question is entirely up to us—the point of my example is simply to demonstrate that a rational actor may do many things that we loathe and despise, while a fanatic may do things that we admire and approve of, even if we would not do them ourselves.

When John Brown tried to foment an insurrection against the government of the United States in the hope of destroying the institution of slavery, he was not playing the role of a rational actor.

Henry David Thoreau, who admired John Brown, would never have said that Brown was behaving as a rational actor in trying to overthrow the Federal government. Thoreau was perfectly aware that Brown was a zealot, but he regarded his act of fanaticism as noble and inspiring.

So it is possible to acknowledge that someone is a fanatic and still find him admirable. It is also possible to acknowledge that someone is a rational actor, and still abhor both him and his conduct.

This is an essential point before we continue. Throughout this book, the term *fanatic* is not used as a term of moral reprobation or condemnation, nor is *rational actor* a term of praise or approval. Both are used simply to designate certain kinds of actors and their conduct. The fanatic is someone willing to make a sacrifice of his own self-interest for something outside himself. He is willing to die for his tribe or his pack or his cause. The rational actor is someone whose conduct is guided solely by his own enlightened self-interest, which, because it is enlightened, is willing to accept the rule of law. However, he is unwilling to die for anything, since death can never be in his self-interest, enlighten it however you please. The fanatic may be a saint or a terrorist, a revolutionary or a lone madman, while the rational actor may be a kind-hearted accountant, a devious business tycoon, a great scientist, a penny-wise housewife, or an officious government bureaucrat.

Now, of course, there are people who are mainly rational actors who are still willing to die for their country or for a cause. In this willingness, however, they are not acting as rational actors but as tribal actors. Indeed, an essential point of this book is that, in a crisis in which the law of the jungle returns to the fore, rational actors may suddenly begin to act like tribal actors. Often the danger is that they do not make this transition quite suddenly enough. Yet as the crisis deepens, those who refuse to stop playing the role of the rational actor find themselves increasingly friendless in a world full of enemies, until the day comes that they too must choose sides and embrace the tribal ethos of Us versus Them.

Both the tribal mind and fanaticism are rational adaptations to a world ruled by the law of the jungle—rational in the sense that they increase the odds of surviving. On the other hand, the rational actor doesn't have a chance of survival in the jungle. He who has neither tribe nor pack to defend him will perish. That is why the rational actor must be horrified at the very thought of a return to the law of the jungle—in order to exist at all, the rational actor must live in an environment in which the rule of law has replaced the law of the jungle. Yet in the modern liberal West, the rule of law has been so successful in pushing back the jungle that many in the West have forgotten that we are the exceptions, not the rule.

In short, today there are two great threats facing the survival of the modern liberal West. The first is its exaggerated confidence in the power of reason; the second is its profound underestimation of the forces of fanaticism.

Part One

I

FANATICISM AND THE MYTH
OF MODERNITY

N ot quite two centuries ago, when the English scholar of Arabic E. W. Lane first came to Egypt, he predicted that contact with European civilization "will, probably, in the course of time, materially diminish the [Muslim] feeling of fanatical intolerance." Yet in the final edition of his book, *Modern Egyptians*, Lane was forced to add in a melancholy footnote that his original "prediction has not yet been fulfilled; on the contrary, European innovations in the dress and domestic manners and customs of the grandees, and of persons in the employ of the government, have enormously increased the fanaticism of those who belong to the religious and learned profession, and generally speaking, of the bulk of the population." In short, contact with Western culture had not only failed to modernize the bulk of the Muslim population, it had actually made them more fanatically intolerant of Western ways than they had been before.

Lane's disappointment is representative of those who have assumed that all cultures over time would naturally begin to absorb the obviously "superior" values of the West—tolerance, liberalism, reason. For Lane, it was an article of faith that if a "backward" people could be given a choice, they would reject their primitive cultural traditions in order to rush headlong to embrace our obviously superior ones. How could people prefer fanatical intolerance over the blessings of toleration, the ways of the dusty past over the future, their silly and absurd superstitions to the light of reason?

Since the European Enlightenment it has become an article of faith among progressive Westerners that religious and cultural fanaticism, as exemplified by the Egyptians of Lane's time, would one day become the relic of the long dead past, never to return. Yet today, as in Lane's time, Muslim contact with the modern West has not led to the abandonment of fanaticism, but, on the contrary, to an intensification and revitalization of it. But strangely enough, few have been prepared to recognize this fact, much less think through its consequences. Instead, the West has responded to the return of fanaticism in one of two ways: first, by denial, and second, by moral condemnation.

It is time to take a different approach. Islamic fanaticism must be seen for what it is: a formidable weapon in the struggle for cultural survival. First, it has served as a powerful defense mechanism that has successfully thwarted all attempts by rival cultures to conquer, dominate, or even influence Islam. Second, it has given Islam the capacity to expand, not merely through the conquest of territory but through the conquest of hearts and minds. Unlike the growth of many ephemeral empires, based exclusively on force of arms, the expansion of Islam has, with few exceptions, proven permanent, effecting not merely a change in political regimes but a change in the entire mode of life of the people who have fallen under its sway. Wherever Islam has spread, there has occurred a total and revolutionary transformation in the culture of those conquered or converted—a transformation so thorough that it becomes difficult even to imagine a time when lands like Egypt or Iran were not Muslim. The secret of Islam's power to transform other cultures, and to create huge zones of complete cultural autarky, is and will always be the very fanaticism that Lane and others found so troubling in Muslim societies. In short, Muslim fanaticism should not be seen as a relic of the past to be set aside in the inevitable progress toward modernization, but as a potent weapon in the struggle for cultural survival and supremacy—as good a weapon now as it was in the distant past.

In the modern West, we have come to judge the success of a culture by purely utilitarian and materialistic standards. We believe that these are obviously the standards by which any rational actor should judge such things. To evaluate a culture, it is enough to provide an inventory of the economic goods it can produce; and by this standard it is obvious that the modern West has triumphed over all its rivals. Liberal democracy, combined with capitalism, has produced a level of wealth that was simply unimaginable only a few centuries ago. The secret of this success has been open and liberal societies in which rational actors were allowed to pursue their enlightened self-interest, free to make their own choices, to determine their own lifestyles, to innovate and to experiment.

What we Westerners fail to see is that our standard for measuring the success of a culture is itself a product of our culture. It is self-serving, flattering, and reassuring—so much so that many of us find it difficult to imagine that there could be some other standard by which to evaluate a culture's success. The bumper-sticker slogan, He who dies with the most toys wins, captures all too well the attitude of the West: The culture that creates the most toys must obviously be superior to one that provides fewer toys. Similarly, a culture that lets people choose their own toys, and to play with them as they wish, is clearly superior to a culture that prohibits such freedom. In the modern West, our whole idea of freedom is the inalienable right to buy what we want and do as we please. It is the freedom of a carpe diem ethos that tells us to seize the day and live for our own pleasure, without a thought for future generations. After all, if we can free ourselves from our parents' traditions, shouldn't our children have the right to free themselves from ours?

Today, in the West, we often take great pride in the extent to which we, as individuals, have liberated ourselves from the cultural traditions of our ancestors. We rejoice in having open minds, ready to discard antiquated ideals and hoary traditions. We teach our children to have open minds too. To us, fanaticism has become a dirty word; intolerance a sin. Everyone should be free to live as he or she wishes—and it is in terms of this freedom that we judge whether a culture is modern and progressive or backward and benighted.

Yet suppose we were to judge our culture by a different standard. Suppose we were to measure the success of a culture by its capacity to preserve its traditions over long periods of time; to keep its cultural identity intact; to resist the encroachment of foreign ways and values? Or, to put this more bluntly, suppose we evaluate the success of a cultural tradition by its ability to beat out and dominate other cultural traditions in the struggle for survival and supremacy. How, then, would we judge the relative success of Islam and the West?

When we compare the modern Western ethos of carpe diem with the fanatical loyalty to tradition found in Muslim culture, we have to ask the question: Should our basis of comparison be the present moment, the recent past, or what the French historian Fernand Braudel called *la longue durée*—the very *long* long run?

The English economist John Maynard Keynes, one of the most brilliant spokesmen for the ethos of modern liberalism, once remarked that in the long run, we are all dead. But those who are fanatically committed to holding on to the tradition of their ancestors have never shared this attitude. Yes, in the long run, I as an individual will be dead—but who cares about that? That is no big deal. What matters is whether my people, my tribe, will be alive. What matters is whether they will honor the same traditions that I honor now, obey the same laws, and observe the same customs.

In a showdown between a tribal tradition that is fanatically adhered to versus a tradition that is adhered to only through the utilitarian calculations of self-interest, who will ultimately win? If the West is content with Keynes's carpe diem approach to life, preoccupied only with us and our own pleasures, whims, and fancies, what chance of survival does it have over the long run, in the face of a culture that is still capable of drawing from its adherents the fanatical determination to keep their ancestral tradition alive, not just for the present moment but for untold generations to come? As one of the Chechen terrorists said during the siege of the theater in Moscow: "We will win in the end, because we are willing to die—and you are not."

The Chechen who made this remark hit on the Achilles' heel of the modern West's ethos. What is there that *we* are willing to die for? Western liberalism holds that men, as rational actors, should be guided by their enlightened self-interest; but how can it be in anyone's self-interest to sacrifice his or her own life? In contrast, the great strength of fanaticism is that it demands that the individual be prepared to make precisely this ultimate sacrifice: to give up his own life for the sake of something he regards as infinitely more important, his comrades, his country, his religion, his cultural traditions—in short, his tribe.

Instead of facing up to the challenge that fanaticism poses to the long-term survival of our liberal carpe diem ethos, the modern West has developed a self-protective myth—the myth of modernity. Because we are modern, we have convinced ourselves that modernity is the ultimate goal toward which all mankind is moving. Modernity is to mankind what maturity is to the individual, an inevitable stage that will in the course of time be reached, despite the tumult of the teenage years. Thus when confronted by the fanatical commitment of a Chechen terrorist, we console ourselves with the delusion that it is merely a passing phase in the Chechens' inevitable development. In our eagerness to delude ourselves, we have even devised the astonishing argument that such outbursts of fanaticism are caused by the lack of modernity. Yet for Muslim fanatics our modernity is not seen as inevitable progress over time; it is an alien and threatening culture that must be ruthlessly resisted and vanquished if they are to preserve their cultural identity. Modernity, for us, is the cure for Islamic "backwardness"; for many Muslims, modernity is the disease to be wiped out.

The myth of modernity is the product of the Enlightenment, when, for the first time, men came to believe that the law of the jungle could be permanently abolished. Human beings, instead of resorting to violent conflict to settle their differences, would begin to govern all their affairs by the light of reason alone. Today, this myth has become the conventional wisdom of the West's political and intellectual leadership. Few scholars, for example, have spoken so honestly and presciently about the fanaticism of radical Islam as Daniel Pipes; and yet even Pipes has spoken confidently of the "inevitable modernization" of Muslim societies. But is the modernization of Islam really inevitable, which is simply another way of asking an even more significant question, indeed, the central question of this book: Is the triumph of liberal Western values inevitable?

This book will argue that the triumph of Western liberalism is by no means inevitable, and that it is an immensely dangerous illusion to believe that it is. There is no reason why reason should prevail; no reason why fanaticism should disappear. Yet dispelling this dangerous, though comforting, illusion is no easy task. It will require a serious rethinking of many concepts that we in the modern liberal West have come to take for granted, and it will demand a searching reappraisal of some of our most cherished beliefs and convictions.

The approach this book will take is that there is no guarantee of inevitable progress because the law of the jungle can never be abolished, though it can be, and has been, ameliorated by various cultural traditions including our own. There can be no hope of an end of history or of a golden age in which men will no longer be driven to conflict and struggle. Furthermore, there can be no guarantee that these struggles will be merely inconclusive "clashes" between civilizations. On the contrary, there is every reason to assume that future struggles will end in the triumph of one civilization and the demise of another. The first Arab conquerors did not clash with the Sassanian Empire—they absorbed and transformed it. The Ottomans did not clash with the Byzantine Empire—they conquered it and remade it in their own image. The Spanish did not clash with the Aztec civilization—they annihilated it. The Anglo-Saxons in North America did not clash with the native American cultures—they wiped them out.

The myth of modernity asserts that life-and-death struggles between cultures and civilizations are a thing of the past. But this myth, as I shall argue, is the product of wishful thinking on the part of those people for whom the very thought of such life-and-death struggle is too disturbing to their own complacency to be seriously entertained.

Who are these people who do not want to have their complacency disturbed? They are us. We in the modern West simply want to be left in peace, to enjoy our carpe diem ethos, to follow our bliss, to amass our toys, to do as we wish. That is why we are so profoundly reluctant to acknowledge that there are violent forces that feel bitter dissatisfaction at what we in the West prefer to see as the end of history. Such reluctance comes naturally to those who, in the last life-and-death struggle, happened to come out on top, and who for that very reason are eager to call an end to any further struggles.

Our profound reluctance to face the possibility of future life-and-death struggles is completely understandable. Yet when this reluctance takes the form of denial and wishful thinking, when it refuses to face threats realistically and soberly, when it breeds fantasy and mirages and utopian delusions, then it can become a prescription for suicide.

Other civilizations have found themselves in this situation and have perished from their comforting illusions. Today, however, what is at stake in the West is not simply the survival of our own cultural traditions but the survival of a tradition that has distinguished itself from all the other cultural traditions known to our species. The modern liberal West has produced cultures in which rational actors have replaced the tribal actors that have constituted the bulk of the population in virtually every previous civilization we know of. In the modern liberal West, we have been taught to think for ourselves, to be guided by our own conscience, to follow our own star. We have been chided for relying on the tribal mind, taught to think that all forms of the tribal mind are bad. Ethnocentricity is a sin, open-mindedness a virtue.

In the West today, instead of grasping that the creation of a society of rational actors was the work of a tradition, we have come to think that all men are born rational actors. To us, the rational actor is not the result of a well-nigh miraculous social construction that requires what Norbert Elias has called "the civilizing process." On the contrary, the rational actor is what we are by nature. Furthermore, because nature creates us all as rational actors, there is no need to instill the ethical code of the rational actor in future generations. Our children come into the world already civilized, prepared by nature to take their role as rational actors in a culture of reason. There is no need to impose traditions on our children—let them think for themselves, and all will be well. In short, the myth that reason is innate permits us in the liberal West not to trouble about passing down our unique tradition of reason, thereby allowing us to indulge in the pleasures of a carpe diem society.

A carpe diem society is entirely organized around the principle of maximizing the happiness and pleasure of each individual—a society that puts the individual's pursuit of happiness above all other obligations to the community, the wider world, or to the future of the individual's own society. The hallmark of a carpe diem society is its complete lack of interest in its own historical and cultural foundation, and its relative indifference to the future: The past is ancient history, and the future will take care of itself.

A carpe diem society has emerged in the liberal West today; and like all sophisticated societies, it has produced a self-serving ideology to convince itself of its own rightness. Curiously, this ideology is shared across our so-called political spectrum. Its basic tenet is that feeling good about yourself is the highest aim in life. Born-again Christians don't worry about original sin; they're saved, and they love Jesus because he makes them feel good about themselves. Liberal educators teach children that the highest value is self-esteem: thinking that you're okay just the way you are. Many leftists today fashion their politics on the basis of what makes them feel good about themselves—they adopt causes that make them feel virtuous, enlightened, and superior, engaging in what Marx correctly derided as "utopian socialism." Libertarians argue that the highest good is to follow your bliss, as Joseph Campbell put it. In many ways, the maxim of all carpe diem societies is best expressed by the popular song, "Don't worry. Be happy."

The ideology of a carpe diem society will stress the individual over the community, rights over duties, the present over the future, feeling good about yourself over trying to improve. It will advocate a laissez faire approach to everything, from economics to parenting, and it will do this in good conscience because the foundation of the ideology of carpe diem is that we human beings don't have to worry about our fate—God, or Nature, or the Invisible Hand, or our natural faculty of Reason will take care of everything for us. Steven Pinker, for example, has argued in *The Language Instinct* that adults do not even need to worry about teaching language to their children—the children will do that for themselves.

The modern West's carpe diem society is the historical offspring of the specific cultures that produced the first generation of rational actors. Our contemporary carpe diem society could only have emerged from a background of reasonable behavior, rule-governed conduct, material abundance, the triumph of the rule of law over brute force, and the supremacy of the individual conscience, among other factors. Like the heirs of men and women who worked very hard to create wealth, we would not be in the comfortable position we are in today unless our parents had been raised in a world that was deeply suspicious of the carpe diem ethos—a world in which the future was more important than the present, the family more important than the individual, and hard work more ennobling than the toys one could buy with it. Yet our carpe diem ethos, though the product of our inherited culture of reason, now poses a grave danger to the culture from which it emerged—indeed, it puts at risk the very tradition of reason that has ennobled the West and that alone gives it a claim to superiority over other cultures, and not our wealth or our military power.

In short, the liberal West may be more threatened today by its own ethos than it is by the very different threat emanating from a culture like Islam, in which individuals, instead of following their own bliss, are willing to die—and, alas, kill—in order to impose their cultural traditions on those who have lost all sense of the precious value of their own.

2

The Denial of Fanaticism

Let us begin with the question: Why have we in the modern liberal West insisted on grossly underestimating the sheer *power* of Islamic fanaticism, i.e., the capacity it has shown to seize the historical momentum and take center stage? We can put this question in an even more emphatic form: Why have so many in the West refused even to recognize the mere existence of Muslim fanaticism?

Let us consider a few cases.

Not long after 9/11, the Bush administration made a decision to rechristen Palestinian suicide-bombers Palestinian *homicide-bombers*. Of course, suicide-bombers, when they kill innocent people, are committing homicide, and they obviously are intending to do so. Yet by suppressing the fact that such individuals are also giving up their own lives in the process, the Bush administration was deliberately downplaying what is most striking about such acts of violence, namely the fanatical devotion of those who were willing to experience a terrible death for the greater glory of the cause to which they have given themselves heart and soul.

That is what makes a fanatic a fanatic—the fanatic is willing to sacrifice himself heroically in the pursuit of an ideal: a personal heroism that we must recognize even if we ourselves have no sympathy for the ideal being pursued, and even if we are convinced that the act itself is, by our standards, purely irrational.

The same refusal to deny fanatics the glory of their fanaticism was displayed in President Bush's dismissal of the 9/11 hijackers as "faceless cowards." Faceless they may have been, at least after crashing jumbo jets into the Twin Towers and the Pentagon, but by what stretch of the most flexible imagination could the men who perpetrated these deeds be dubbed cowards? Anyone who is unafraid to die a horrible death in the pursuit of his objectives cannot be called a coward, no matter how much we may condemn the act.

Bush was not alone in being hesitant to use the word *fanatic* to describe the 9/11 terrorists. The same reluctance was evident on the other end of the political spectrum. The dean of postmodernism, Stanley Fish, in an article in *Harper's*, expressed a willingness to recognize the deep and genuine conviction that motivates radical Islam—and in this, Fish's position is far more realistic than those who refuse to credit the terrorists with such qualities as honesty, courage, and passionate conviction. Yet curiously, Fish is disturbed when the terrorists are called fanatics.

Despite his postmodernist critique of liberalism, Fish is still too much of a liberal at heart to see in the term *fanatic* anything other than an insult: What liberal (or conservative) wants to be called a fanatic, one of the most derogatory terms in the liberal lexicon of invective? Yet if Fish were true to his own principles, he would recognize that in the eyes of those who are supremely convinced of the absolute rightness of their own belief, the term *fanatic* contains nothing whatsoever invidious. In short, Fish's lack of consistent postmodernism is betrayed by his squeamishness in using the word *fanatic* to apply to those for whom fanatical devotion is the supreme virtue. One might argue that both Bush and Fish were showing sensitivity to Muslim feelings by refraining from using the "F" word. Diplomacy and good manners often require us to choose our words with care. Rich Lowery, in an essay in *National Review*, has argued, in essence, that our avoidance of recognizing Muslim fanaticism serves as a "polite fiction." But whose sensitivities are we trying spare? Ours or theirs?

The problem with much of the Western response to Islamic fanaticism is that our refusal to use the word *fanaticism* appears to be based on our reluctance to recognize the fact of fanaticism. We avoid the word in order to avoid having to think about the thing, thereby leaving the impression that our resistance to acknowledging fanaticism arises less from our sensitivity to Muslim feelings than from our wish to evade the momentous challenge posed by fanaticism itself.

For example, immediately after 9/11, indeed in the very first hours after the horrendous event, a leading advisor to the president, Paul Wolfowitz, dismissed the very idea that 9/11 could have been pulled off by "mere" fanatics. Only a reasonably sophisticated state like Iraq, he said, could have conceived and executed such a stupendous feat. Thus 9/11 had to be the work of Saddam Hussein. The attack revealed nothing about the attitude of ordinary Muslims toward the United States—a position that the Bush administration continued to maintain despite the undisguised jubilation that broke out spontaneously throughout the Muslim world on hearing of the collapse of the mighty Twin Towers.

As a result of this misconception, the Bush administration began to pursue the illusion that fanatical hatred of the United States and of Israel was not a fixed mindset of great multitudes in the Muslim world. Only such a profound misunderstanding could explain the ill-fated American project to get at the "root causes" of terrorism by bringing democracy to the Middle East. If the majority of the people in another culture passionately hate us, enough to celebrate 9/11 as if it were an American Fourth of July, what do we gain by handing them the reins of government?

As the Palestinian elections in 2006 amply proved, not much. In this case, free and fair elections in Gaza produced a landslide victory for Hamas, regarded by the United States and European nations as a terrorist organization. Many commentators in the West attempted to explain the victory of Hamas as a rejection of the rank corruption of its competitor, Fatah; few were willing to contemplate that Hamas might have won simply because it was the party with the most fanatically intransigent attitude toward Israel. The position of Hamas was that it would never accept the state of Israel—not now, nor in the future.

The dream of free and fair elections in Palestine was not just President Bush's idea; it was the utopian dream of all American policy makers who have refused to acknowledge the glaring fact that the Palestinians will never recognize an Israeli state, just as surely as the Israelis will never nullify their own existence as a Jewish state by permitting the return of the Palestinians. Yet how can we deal realistically with Israel or the Palestinians if we refuse to acknowledge their intransigence on those points that are, to them, matters of life and death?

In understanding the collective psychology of a people, one of the first characteristics to look at is their stubbornness under pressure. In a fight to the finish, how quickly are they apt to yield, and under what kinds of pressure? If an enemy knows that its foe is stubborn and ferociously resists surrender, then he must handle him quite differently from the way he would deal with those who can be counted on to fold under duress. Whenever the law of the jungle becomes the final arbiter of any conflict, those who are the most stubborn inevitably have the advantage over those who are more reasonable.

For example, late in the Second World War, Joseph Goebbels was disturbed by a joke that was sweeping through the German Reich, and which he feared would have a terrible effect on German fighting morale if it were allowed to spread. It was bad enough that the English were carrying out bombing raids all over Germany, virtually without interference from the once feared Luftwaffe; bad enough that the war had been dragging on for over three years—two years past anyone's worst expectation at the beginning. But then came this silly terrible witticism to undermine the German war resolve. It went like this: "The English are even more stubborn than we Germans are." The point of the joke was that the Germans, notorious for their stubbornness, had met their match.

What disturbed Goebbels about this remark was his own fear that the joke expressed the truth. He was terrified that the English *were* more stubborn, i.e. fanatical, than the Germans. He had seen how the English would not give up even under the most desperate conditions—conditions under which any reasonable person would seek terms. He was also distressed by the thought that the Soviets might be even more stubborn than the Germans or the English. As he repeatedly records in his diary for this period, the Russians simply kept on coming, "we don't know where from."

Goebbels realized that in war, which by definition is a return to the law of the jungle, it is often the sheer stubbornness of the warriors that ultimately matters. He also knew that in a total war, which by definition is a complete plunge into the jungle, the stubbornness of the people themselves takes on immense importance. For Goebbels, to call someone a fanatic was not to insult him but to praise him. Fanaticism was the highest goal a man could aspire to in this life. In his dairies Goebbels even shows a grudging admiration for the fanaticism of the Soviet soldiers who were pushing back his own troops. Despite being a superbly educated and brilliant intellectual, Goebbels utterly wallowed in fanaticism, drank it deeply, and even consented to the murder of his own children as one last proof of his fanatical loyalty to the man who had led his country to stupendous victories followed by the most abject and degrading disasters. In his last testament, Goebbels wrote that for the first time in his life he was disobeying a direct order of his führer. Instead of fleeing Berlin with his wife and children, as Hitler had instructed, Goebbels wished to die with his tribal leader, and with his entire family.

In this Goebbels was acting as other fanatics have done throughout history. Consider, for example, the ancient tribe called the Taochi. We know about these otherwise obscure people because the Greek historian Xenophon left an eyewitness account of them in his history of the ill-fated Persian expedition. The stranded Greek mercenary force, the famous Ten Thousand, came across the Taochi in their mountain fastness midway in their own journey back from the heart of Persia to their Greek homelands. According to Xenophon, "the Taochi lived behind strong fortifications inside which they had all their provisions stored"—provisions which the Greek mercenaries desperately wanted to get their hands on. These fortifications had been erected on top of precipitous ground, making any attack by the Greeks difficult. In addition, the Taochi, when they saw the Greek warriors trying to struggle up the steep cliffs, adroitly rolled down large boulders that crushed the limbs and ribs of their attackers. Eventually, however, the quick-witted Greeks figured out a ruse by which they could ascend to the summit and enter into the Taochi's fortification. "Once they were inside," Xenophon tells us, "no more stones were thrown from above."

What happened next, however, comes as a shock to Xenophon. "Then," he writes, "it was certainly a terrible sight. The women threw their children down from the rocks and then threw themselves after them, and the men did the same. When this was going on Aeneas of Strymphalus, a captain, saw one of them, who was wearing a fine garment, running to throw himself down, and he caught hold of him in order to stop him; but the man dragged him with him and they both went hurtling down over the rocks and were killed. Consequently, very few prisoners were taken. . . ."

These prisoners were, of course, led off to the nearest city to be sold as slaves—that was one of the methods by which the Greek mercenaries were able to survive their long march home. No doubt the Taochi were perfectly aware that this would be their fate and the fate of their children; no doubt it was to prevent their enslavement that the women were willing to hurl their own children to their deaths.

The Greeks hated the very thought of being enslaved, and yet when a Greek city was conquered, their women did not kill their children or themselves. That is why Xenophon describes the scene as a terrible one—it displayed a collective behavior on the part of the Taochi that he was unable to understand. Earlier on their march, the Greeks had come across many other tribes that they had easily conquered and who did not react the way the Taochi did. On the contrary, some of the prisoners taken, both females and boys, had become quite attached to the Greeks who had seized them. So what was it about the Taochi that made them respond as they did? Why did they, in their moment of crisis, choose death over slavery, not only for themselves but for their children?

The Greeks had no interest in killing the Taochi—they wanted simply to steal their food, to take them as prisoners, and to sell them as slaves. The fate that awaited the Taochi was the same that awaited many other tribes and peoples across the globe—yet it was a fate that virtually the entire Taochi community rejected with scorn.

The conduct of the Taochi was by no means unique in history. During the Jewish rebellion against Roman domination that occurred around A.D. 70, there were similar instances of mass suicide. The Jewish historian Josephus, who had himself played a role in the early part of the rebellion, provides an eyewitness account of the decision of the trapped Zealots to kill their families, and then to take turns killing each other. Masada, their last refuge, derives its fame from the same grim determination of the Jewish rebels who refused to surrender to the Romans, and who preferred, like the Taochi, the path of collective self-annihilation.

During the Second World War, the American troops fighting in the Pacific encountered the same fanatical resolve on the part of Japanese soldiers not to surrender under any circumstances, and to accept the most terrible death rather than yield. To the Americans, a stubborn people themselves, there was something uncanny and terrifying about the suicidal fanaticism of the Japanese soldiers. Yet the Japanese warrior tradition of the samurai had developed suicide into an art. The ritual of seppuku, vulgarly known as hara-kiri, or belly slitting, had been devised as a way of avoiding the humiliation of surrendering to an enemy, but it was also designed to serve another purpose. Because it was well known that a warrior taken alive would be subjected to the most gruesome tortures, there was the danger that ordinary suicide might appear to be the coward's way out. How much easier simply to slit your wrists than endure days of agony at the hands of a triumphant and merciless enemy. Therefore, the samurai warrior could not slit his wrists, the way Roman Stoics did; instead, he had to perform the agonizing ritual of seppuku. He must thrust a knife into his stomach, and then cut all the way around his abdomen, disemboweling himself with his own hands. Only then could his second chop off his head with his sword.

The point of this exercise was not just to show that the samurai warrior was unafraid of death, but that he was unafraid of the most terrible death imaginable.

Native American Indians also enjoyed torturing their captured enemies; but in this case, among the most ferocious warriors, a different policy was evolved to show one's indifference even to the most hideous torment. In the midst of his agony, the valiant warrior would taunt his torturers for their ineptitude and lack of inventiveness. His attitude could be best expressed by the withering phrase that springs so naturally to the lips of tough guys confronting the blows of an adversary: "Is that the best you got?"

To those of us who have been raised in the modern liberal West, the fanatic's willingness—even eagerness—to embrace the most violent and horrible forms of death is profoundly disturbing. We have been taught to think that people are like us, and that their behavior will be motivated by the same kinds of considerations that motive us. We expect them to behave like rational actors— the way we behave. For us, to understand other people involves getting inside their heads and seeing the world as they see it— something that is relatively easy for us to do when we are dealing with people who are basically motivated by the same things as we are. But our ability to understand other people has a limit.

For example, in the early 1960s, Americans were horrified by images coming across their TV screens from South Vietnam. One after another, a series of Buddhist monks doused themselves with gasoline, then, as their bodies were being burned, they continued to sit quietly, in the famous Buddha pose, until they were turned into ashes. Not a single one of them tried to put out the flames that were engulfing him. Watching these scenes, Americans felt a profound shock. We simply could not get into the minds of the monks who could do something like that—and almost immediately our cultural defense mechanism kicked in and provided us with a convenient answer: They don't respect human life. This had served us well in our attempts to decipher the motivation of the Japanese kamikaze pilots, and it has served us in "explaining" all other examples of the fanatic's willingness to sacrifice his life for something else of greater value to him.

Just as we could not get into the minds of the Buddhist monks, so too we cannot fathom the motivation of a teenage Palestinian boy, whose life is all before him, when he rigs himself with amateur explosives in order to blow himself to smithereens for his cause. We cannot grasp what would make nineteen young men drive jumbo jets into skyscrapers instead of doing what most other young men of their age might be doing on a beautiful September morning in New York.

At the extreme limits of our interpersonal understanding lies the uncanny, the creepy, the eerie; and it is only natural that we become viscerally agitated when we reach these limits. "I am a human being; therefore I count nothing human as alien to me" is a line from the Roman comic writer Terence, which Montaigne had inscribed on one of the beams in his study. Yet in the case of the Buddhist monks and the suicide bombers, we are dealing with the Radical Other, that is, human beings who challenge our basic model of humanity. I am a human being—but what is the Radical Other?

The Radical Other always prompts a strong visceral reaction. Such people are incomprehensibly alien to us. They do not conform to our expectation of normal human behavior; indeed, they shatter all such expectations. They fill us with panic and anxiety because we, as rational actors, cannot fit them into the conventional model of human action that we have acquired from the culture around us. To relieve this panic and anxiety we must either ignore them or else force them to fit into a category of human action with which we do feel comfortable—all in an effort to make their uncanniness less threatening to our comforting vision of the world.

Yet it is precisely this uncanny quality that gives the fanatic his power. Consider the origin of the English phrase: to go berserk. In the Ynglinga saga, the Icelandic chieftain and historian Snorri Sturlusson (1178–1241) used this word to describe the uncanny behavior of certain groups of Norse warriors who "went without hauberks and raged like dogs or wolves. They bit their shields and were strong like bears or bulls. They killed men, but neither fire nor iron hurt them. This is called berserksgangr." The modern historian Michael P. Speidel has argued that there are two qualities that define berserk or "mad warriors." First, they "scorned armor, willfully foregoing body armor," and often fought in the nude. Second, they "raged uncontrollably in a trance of fury." Furthermore, Speidel has provided evidence showing that there was nothing uniquely Norse about the berserk tradition, and that "mad warriors" can be found as early as the end of the Bronze Age, throughout Indo-European history, as well as in fighting styles of the Aztec quachics and India's amoks. The persistence and diffusion of berserk warfare demonstrates the power of the fanatic to engender fear in their opponents precisely through their weird and uncanny behavior. To insist on fighting without armor, or in the nude—what could be more bizarre than that?

This violent departure from the general expectations of how we think human beings behave is a source of profound visceral shock. It stuns us, and leaves us not quite sure how to react or to respond. If the fanatic refuses to behave in ways that we, as rational actors, can understand or predict, then we cannot hope to deal with him in the same way that we deal with those whose behavior is motivated by the kinds of things that motivate us and the other people we know. Our inability to deal with the fanatic leaves us with a disturbing sense of loss of control. None of the usual techniques work: He cannot be bribed, or coerced, or even appeased. Because he is not a rational actor in our sense of the word, we cannot respond to him as rational actors—and this leaves us clueless as to what methods we should use in dealing with him.

In summary, a number of factors explain the West's reluctance to recognize the existence of Muslim fanaticism. Unlike Joseph Goebbels, most liberal Westerners have been taught that fanaticism is a bad thing, and not a quality worthy of commendation and praise. Hence for most of us, to call a man a fanatic is to insult him. Yet this attitude, though often justified by an appeal to the fashionable principle of multicultural sensitivity, results in a radically ethnocentric interpretation of the cultural Other. Because we refuse to attribute to the cultural Other traits and characteristics that we in the modern liberal West find deplorable, we inevitably end by constructing an illusionary Other who has been stripped of his unique character and has become merely a sanitized copy of ourselves—a mirror image of the Western rational actor that differs only in cultural details like style of clothing and cuisine. By refusing to recognize that the cultural Other may passionately hold convictions that profoundly challenge our own, we create the illusion that our own convictions are universal and obvious to everyone. By ascribing to the cultural Other the same motives that motivate us, we delude ourselves into believing that we are all motivated by the same desires and goals. "We all want the same things!" is the alleged self-evident truth that has guided American policy toward the Middle East. George W. Bush and the neoconservatives did not invent this slogan: It is a fundamental principle of the myth of modernity that has guided American policy for several generations.

But *do* we all want the same things?

This question squarely confronts us with what is most disturbing about fanaticism. The fanatic screams in our ear: "I do not want what you want. I reject all that you accept. I want a different world from the one that makes you happy, and I will not rest content until I have it." The fanatic by his shock tactics reveals to those who like the world more or less as it is that there are people who do not share this sentiment; that there are other people who are filled with bitter and violent resentment toward the order and stability that we in the West have come to take for granted, and who wish to overturn our world and to destroy everything that we find of value in it. Yet this is precisely the aim of the fanatic— a fact that explains why we in the modern liberal West are so reluctant to take the challenge of fanaticism seriously. To recognize fanaticism would require us to recognize how fragile our world is, and how profound is the challenge to the politics of the rational actor that is posed by the politics, or more correctly the antipolitics, of the fanatical tribal actor.

3

FANATICISM AND RESENTMENT

I n addition to outright denial, there is a more subtle way of
dealing with the challenge fanaticism poses; and that is simply to minimize its significance. Yes, of course, there are fanatics;
and there will always be fanatics. Consider the cults centered on
Jim Jones, or David Koresh, or the Heaven's Gate castrati—all
these made headlines, to be sure, but they did not make history.
Even Timothy McVeigh's bombing of the Federal Building in
Oklahoma will be remembered simply as one of the many bloody
and senseless footnotes in history books. But did McVeigh change
the world by his act of fanaticism? No—and the same thing ap-
plies to other lone nuts and fringe cults. In the bigger picture,
they shrink to historical irrelevance.

Yet looking back over history, it is easy to find fanatics who did
not shrink into such irrelevance but, on the contrary, played a
critical role in the shaping of events. John Brown's raid on the
Federal Arsenal at Harper's Ferry had a crucial impact on the out-
break of the American Civil War. The various fanatics who hijacked the French Revolution provide another example, while the

Protestant Reformation would have been a very different event had it not been for those zealots who ravaged cathedrals and smashed priceless objects of art that they saw as shameless examples of idolatry. The fanaticism of the Jesuit Order was responsible for winning back Poland for the Roman Catholic Church, and for stemming the rising tide of Protestantism in Europe. Similarly, it is impossible to explain the great wave of Arab conquests in the seventh century A.D. without taking into account the fanatical zeal of the holy warriors who fought to spread Islam. In the twentieth century, what could a historian make of the triumph of Bolshevism in Russia without taking into consideration the fanaticism of those who were convinced that they were fighting on "the right side of history"? What sense could one make of the rise of the Nazi party if one refused to acknowledge the cultivation of fanatical loyalty among its members?

The list of examples could be continued for many pages, but these are enough to demonstrate that fanatics and their fanaticism have played a decisive role in history—fanaticism, realistically considered, does not merely provide color and incident to history but has made history, over and over again. Fanatics possess the power to seize the historical momentum—to make those who are defending the status quo react to them, or else succumb. In order for fanaticism to get the upper hand in a culture or a society, the fanatics need not be the majority—all that is necessary is for the majority to stand aside and let the fanatics take charge.

Yet despite the overwhelming impact of fanaticism on history, there is a baffling reluctance in the West today even to consider the possibility that fanatics and fanaticism may continue to play a decisive role in shaping the human future. If there is one thing that unites contemporary thinkers in the West today, it is the curious notion that fanaticism has played itself out as a historical force and that man's future will be largely unaffected by the fanatics' agenda. In short, our current paradigms of history are unanimous in their neglect of the power of fanaticism to make and alter the course of history.

Fanaticism, for us, has become a mere epiphenomenon, not a thing in itself but a symptom of an underlying "deeper" cause such as poverty or a lack of democracy. Fanatics may have toppled empires in the past, overthrown monarchies, and altered the religious faith of entire peoples, but we can no longer expect them to unleash such upheavals today. Our pleasant status quo in the West is not fated, like so many of its predecessors, to be rendered the status quo ante at the hands of fanatics bent on creating their own world order. If we are not at the end of history, we hope to be getting close—and what place could fanaticism possibly have at the end of history, when everyone will be satisfied with a world order that is so just and equitable that no one could wish to see another in its place? Our status quo will last forever—which is why we need not worry overmuch about tomorrow.

But fanaticism is not dead, because by the nature of the human condition, it cannot die.

The Arab philosopher of history Ibn-Khaldun argued that humankind could never achieve a final and definitive state of harmonious coexistence: The inherent human desire for revenge would keep people perpetually in conflict. Those who won the last battle may think the losers have been subdued, but the losers will always thirst for vengeance, animated by an intense resentment against the status quo established by the winners—and it is this resentment that is the "root cause" of fanaticism. Fanaticism will always be the weapon of choice for those who refuse to accept the status quo as determined by the winners of the previous struggle for supremacy. Meanwhile the winners, immediately after their hard fought victory, will inevitably delude themselves that this last struggle was the final conflict, a war to end all wars, indeed, the end of history itself.

On the other hand, the losers will not be so eager to declare the winner's settlement of the world final and definitive—and why should they? Why should they have any interest in supporting the settlement imposed by the winners? It might be in their immediate self-interest to pretend to accept the new world order; but they will naturally feel resentment at an order imposed by someone else, often at their expense. To those who sit outside the victory circle, the winner's decision to call an end to history just at the moment of their accidental achievement of hegemony seems self-serving and opportunistic, like a boy who, having scrambled to the top of the hill in a game of king of the mountain, decides forthwith that the game is over, and all who continue to challenge him are criminals and rebels.

The resentment of those left outside the winner's circle means that many of them will look on a return to anarchy as preferable to the maintenance of an order that they resent, since only by overturning the established order can a new and radically different order emerge—*their* order, not the order imposed upon them by their enemies. The defenders of the status quo, on the other hand, are at first keenly aware that their order—which they have sacrificed so much to achieve—must be preserved at any cost, and they will naturally struggle to keep anarchy at bay. Yet at some point, if the forces of resentment are able to disrupt the established order, those defending this order will be faced with a grim choice: Either they let themselves be overwhelmed by the forces of resentment, or else they are compelled to accept that they are faced with a new struggle for survival and supremacy, in which case the dream of the end of history must be rejected, and the law of brute force will again prevail. The recent status quo will be swept away, and mere anarchy will be loosed upon the world.

The profound reluctance of an established order to recognize that its future is being threatened explains why its supporters so often delude themselves into thinking that they can preserve the old order without reverting back to the law of the jungle. Out of this perfectly understandable reluctance comes a phenomenon akin to the psychological mechanism of denial, though in this case it is a collective denial. The form this denial takes is the refusal to take seriously the depth and strength of the forces of resentment. Instead of acknowledging the fanatic's fierce determination to overthrow the established order, defenders of this order will systematically minimize and explain away the threat, but by their very denial they unwittingly render the established order more vulnerable to the forces that are only interested in overthrowing it.

Consider the end of the First World War. The victors in this brutal struggle immediately set to work making sure that there would be no more such struggles. Their desire to create a world order in which such a catastrophe could not occur again was both admirable and entirely understandable. As Woodrow Wilson put it, the Great War had been fought as a war to end all wars. No one wanted another war that cost the lives of millions upon millions of men. Yet the world order devised by the winners left the losers with a profound resentment against the terms imposed on them. The new maps drawn under the Treaty of Versailles—meant to be permanent—divided and cut up the old German Reich. Resentment among the Germans at what they perceived as an unjust order began during the Peace Conference and continued to smolder under the Weimar Republic. Nor was this resentment limited only to fringe elements of German society. The liberal and eminently rational sociologist Max Weber, for example, said that he would willingly shoot the first Pole who tried to take control of the German city of Danzig, which, according to the Treaty of Versailles, had been rendered non-German.

The fruits of this deep and visceral resentment were eventually gathered up by the Nazi party under the spellbinding leadership of Adolf Hitler. For the Nazis, fanaticism was not a term of abuse but an ethos they rapturously embraced and which they tried, with no small success, to instill in the German people.

The history of the attempts of the victors of the Great War to minimize and explain away the phenomenon of Nazi fanaticism is well known—it resulted in the policy known as appeasement. Today this policy, adopted by both England and France, is unfairly looked upon as the rankest of historical follies. To us, with our retrospective knowledge of the failure of appeasement, it seems obvious that the Nazi threat should have been nipped in the bud at the very first violation of the terms of the Treaty of Versailles, namely, Hitler's daring decision to march a relatively small number of German troops into the demilitarized Rhineland in 1935. Yet our retrospective condemnation of France and England's inaction overlooks their deep reluctance to acknowledge that, a mere fifteen years after the end of the war to end all wars, there could be another great European war and a return to the brutal law of the jungle from which they had hoped to escape once and for all. The principles of liberal internationalism, enshrined by the League of Nations, had given hope that such a war could never come again.

To us, because we see the Second World War as inevitable, it is natural to argue that France and England should have also seen such a cataclysm as inevitable, in which case it would have been far better to strike at the reviving Germany while it was still relatively weak. Yet such vision would have required the complete abandonment of the dream of perpetual peace that had beguiled the victors at the end of the First World War; it would have demanded an admission that the Great War had simply been another episode in the endless human struggle for survival and supremacy, with no claims to any definitive settlement—in which case the millions of men who died in trenches would have died just as pointlessly and meaninglessly as the victims of mankind's previous outbursts of carnage.

To take the position, in the 1930s, that war was still endemic to the human condition, and that there would be further conflicts and struggles, was to reject the optimistic myth that had been bequeathed to Western civilization by the Enlightenment—the myth that mankind could one day rise permanently above the law of the jungle that governed all animal existence on the planet.

What we today call the policy of appeasement was in fact the refusal on the part of the civilized leaders of France and England to abandon the politics of reason. They were sincerely convinced that by reasoning with Hitler, by making compromises with him, they could avoid the horrors of reversion to the law of the jungle. Hitler, knowing that his opponents were loathe to abandon the politics of reason, was able to use the politics of fanaticism to force his more reasonable adversaries to make concessions in their fervent desire to keep the peace, and to avoid another great European conflagration.

Though he deftly played on his adversaries' fear of another Great War, Hitler did not himself contemplate launching another world catastrophe, whose horrors he knew from firsthand experience in trench warfare in the killing fields of Flanders. That, after all, was the whole point of Blitzkrieg—Hitler's wars were not to be won by sheer carnage but by machinelike efficiency that would destroy his enemy's armies within a matter of weeks rather than years. While our history books tell us that Hitler started the Second World War on September 1, 1939, this is not at all what Hitler thought he was doing. It is striking to read an entry in Goebbels's diary for the year 1943 in which he remarks that "it appears like our war is turning into a genuine World War." Hitler's ambition had not been to cause a second Great War; his Blitzkriegs had been designed to create what Hitler called "A New World Order," one that would reverse the position of winners and losers in the old world order that he despised.

It is reassuring to us to dismiss men like Chamberlain as simpletons and fools rather than to see them as men dedicated to the politics of reason. No one wanted another Great War, not even Hitler. Surely reasonable men could avert such a disaster, but disaster came, and the politics of reason could not stop it.

Because we in the West have been brought up to cherish and espouse the politics of reason, it is terrifying for us to realize how easily reason can commit suicide the moment it fails to remember that there are limits to what reason alone can achieve. Reason can make a clearing in the jungle, but it can never hope to abolish the jungle. Reason can make less horrible the struggle for survival and supremacy but cannot eliminate that struggle. Reason can help create an order out of chaos, but reason deludes itself if it imagines that it can construct an eternal order that will satisfy everyone and leave no deep resentments to smolder for awhile before bursting into flame. Reason can persuade reasonable men to accept an order of which they are the beneficiaries, but reason can do nothing to convince those left out in the cold that they should accept the order that has left them there. Reason can work wonders with those who accept the basic rules of order at the bottom of any stable society or civilization, but reason is helpless to dissuade fanatics from seeking to break those rules in the hope of overturning an order of which they are profoundly resentful and to which they are bitterly opposed.

The great weakness of America's post-9/11 policy was its refusal to grasp the fierce resentment of the Muslim world against the status quo represented by the Pax Americana. The question is not, Should they in fact feel such resentment but simply, Do they feel it? The answer is a resounding yes—a fact that should have been brutally clear to our leaders in the wake of the Muslim glamorization of Osama bin Laden and the 9/11 hijackers.

Furthermore, it is not the Muslim world alone that is animated by this deep resentment of the Pax Americana; increasingly since 9/11, other nations across the globe have come to share it. In South America, there are now rumblings of a revival of socialism by populist leaders whose most appealing theme is virulent anti-Americanism. In Russia, the big loser in the West's last "total victory," there are growing signs of a deep resentment against the American world hegemony that resulted from the collapse of the last ancien regime, the USSR. North Korea, in its development of nuclear weapons and long-range missiles, is also expressing its resentment at a new world order from which it feels left out. Likewise Iran, under its own populist leader, is displaying the same restiveness: Why should the Iranians be excluded from the world's nuclear club—indeed, why should any nation be excluded? If the possession of nuclear weapons gives a nation entry into the privileged positions of power players on the world stage, who has the right to forbid it to make such a bid for power? And in the name of what?

There is only one justification for keeping other nations from entering the club, and that is the desire to preserve the status quo. But here we return to our basic argument. Why should those who are not beneficiaries of the status quo accept it, let alone defend it? If so many other nations and populations do not feel a commitment to the maintenance of the status quo, and if, even worse, they feel deep resentment at its unequal distribution of wealth and power, then what can motivate them to support and defend the status quo—especially if they have their very own ideas about what the world order ought to look like?

This brings us back to the myth of modernity. One of its essential tenets is that with the inevitable modernization of Muslim societies, along with the rest of the world, there will no longer be any grounds for resentment at the status quo. On this view, it is the gap between the West and the rest that is the sole source of resentment; and if we can close this gap, there will no longer be any cause for others to feel resentment toward the status quo achieved by Western power and influence. Instead, everyone will have a stake in preserving it—and with the disappearance of the last pocket of resentment, there will be no more violent upheavals and conflicts. With the end of resentment will come the end of history.

4

THE END OF HISTORY?

In the late 1960s, Senator J. William Fulbright wrote in his book *The Arrogance of Power*: "The West has won two 'total victories' in this century and it has barely survived them. America, especially, fought the two world wars in the spirit of a righteous crusade. We acted as if we had come to the end of history, as if we had only to destroy our enemies and then the world would enter a golden age of peace and human happiness. . . . But to our shock and dismay we found after 1945 that history had not come to an end."

A generation after Fulbright wrote these words, the unexpected collapse of the Soviet Union led a bright young scholar to write a book that would become not only a best-seller but would articulate the hopes and sentiments of many in the West. Once again, the West had won a "total victory," though one that did not require the vast bloodletting of the two world wars: The Cold War, to quote T. S. Eliot, ended not with a bang but with a whimper. Again came a declaration of the end of history, only this time, according to the young scholar, Francis Fukuyama, the world was definitely and without any question heading toward "a golden age of peace and human happiness" provided by that triumph of reason over brute force that goes by the name of liberal capitalist democracy—or what Westerners like to call modernity.

On the morning of September 11, 2001, Fukuyama's end of history thesis took a direct hit. It came in the form of nineteen young men who, driven by the fanaticism of radical Islam, hijacked and flew two jumbo jets into the Twin Towers of New York City, reducing them to a massive heap of rubble within a matter of hours. As soon as news of the event spread across the world, Muslims, men, old women, and children, danced with joy in the streets of their cities. Again, it seemed, fanaticism had hijacked history, and its force was again to be reckoned with as a decisive player on the world stage.

In a world governed by the law of the jungle, America would have responded to this attack with blind and immediate retaliation: *They* had killed thousands of *our* people, now *we* will kill hundreds of thousands of *theirs*—and it matters not at all which ones we kill, nor whether they were in any way responsible for the attack. This, after all, was how even the civilized English had responded to the German attacks on London—they fire-bombed Hamburg, killing sixty thousand men, women, and children over a few days, and later, and even more pointlessly, they would fire-bomb the city of Dresden, incinerating so vast a number of innocent civilians that no one even today is quite certain whether the number killed is closer to sixty thousand or a hundred and forty thousand.

This was not how the United States chose to respond to the terror attacks of 9/11. No responsible leaders cried out for revenge attacks on the Muslim world. None evoked the remorseless Us versus Them logic of the tribal vendetta. We were far too civilized to resort to such primitive behavior. On the contrary, the consensus of "enlightened" American opinion was that 9/11 was the act of desperate men, pushed over the edge by American imperialism, or by poverty, or by the lack of democracy in their homelands. All dismissed the possibility that the 9/11 attacks could be motivated by pure fanaticism—the terror attack was explained, or more correctly, explained away, by an appeal to a variety of "root causes." Get to these root causes, it was generally argued, and voila! terror attacks on the West would stop. Again, fanaticism was merely an epiphenomenon, a symptom. Deplorable, no doubt, but still fixable.

Thus began one of the most curious episodes in mankind's history—a nation that had been brutally and wantonly attacked bent over backward in order to find moral justifications for its attackers. If only the West had not been such imperialists; if only the hijackers had been raised in a democracy and had been able to participate in free and fair elections, then the nineteen young men would have lacked any motive to attack us. If only Islam could be modernized, then all this terrorist nonsense would stop. True, those who apologized for the terror attack by pointing to American imperialism were most often the political enemies of those who apologized for the terror attack by pointing to the lack of democracy in the Muslim world—and violent polemics were passed back and forth between them. But, in the final analysis, the difference between Noam Chomsky and Paul Wolfowitz was largely illusionary. Both agreed that you couldn't really blame the terrorists, since they were merely the victims of an evil system— for Chomsky, American imperialism, for Wolfowitz, the corrupt and despotic regimes of the Middle East. Both agreed that if you could only topple the existing iniquitous system, terrorism would disappear. Thus both were revolutionaries, eager to overthrow the status quo—the only difference was the status quo that they wished to overthrow.

Miraculously, incredibly, in the aftermath of 9/11, the end of history myth was once more resurrected. Once more American power, economic and military, would be used "in the spirit of a righteous crusade" to bring democracy and freedom to the Middle East, though, as President Bush quickly learned, it was a mistake to use the tainted word *crusade* to describe this latest attempt to usher in a new "golden age of peace and human happiness." The word *crusade* unpleasantly reminded Muslims of the Christian crusaders—those Western fanatics who set out to win back for Christianity the lands that earlier Muslim fanatics had conquered, and whose wanton butchery often rivaled the worst excesses of the original Arab holy warriors.

So instead of *crusade*, the metaphor used by the Bush administration to express the righteousness of its mission was drawn from early wars: American force was not being used to impose our Western ways on the Muslim world but to "liberate" Muslims from evil regimes. Once the oppressors had been toppled, then Muslims would be free to choose what kind of government they wanted—and how could they fail to want one like ours?

The Bush administration derived the liberation metaphor from the Second World War, when the Allies liberated Europe from the Nazis. Yet the first time the idea of liberation had been used to justify a war was during the French Revolution, when the French National Convention decided that it was not enough for them to overthrow the ancien regime in their own nation—it was their duty to liberate the entire human race from religious superstition, monarchical tyranny, and all other forms of despotism. Thus on November 19, 1792, shortly after the National Convention had abolished the Bourbon monarchy in France, it issued a proclamation that offered French military assistance to all peoples who wished to throw off their own governments.

The remarkable fact that a Republican administration had adopted the liberationist ideals of the French Revolution and set about on a mission to bring about the end of history put the Left in a quandary. It is essential for the Left to be to the left of the Right, but when the Right is already so far to the left, what options are left to the Left?

Those on the Left, unable to attack the revolutionary fervor of the Bush administration on ideological grounds, were forced into attacking it for a variety of other reasons. Both before and after the invasion, many critics on the Left argued that Bush's lofty rhetoric about the march of freedom was simply a cover for American imperialism or, worse, merely a pretext to justify Halliburton's sinister designs on the oil wealth of Iraq. As Iraq sank into violence and chaos, however, it became increasingly implausible to explain the mounting cost of occupying Iraq in terms of greedy oil interests. No doubt, there are many unsavory types who have been able to profit from the Iraqi war, just as there were despicable businessmen who, during the American Civil War, made their fortunes by selling defective guns at outrageous prices to Lincoln's government; but no one ever accused Lincoln of initiating the war in order to permit such men to make a killing. Can anyone seriously believe that Bush began the Iraq war to make his rich cronies a bit richer?

As the Iraqi war dragged on futilely, attempts to explain it in terms of rational economic self-interest became less attractive. It was at this point that many on the Left began to see the Iraqi war as the result of the president's cozy intimacy with a Heavenly Father who evinced a disturbing zeal to meddle in the geopolitical affairs of his creatures. These critics tended to interpret Bush as a religious fanatic, spurred on by his "born-again" Christian fundamentalist faith: Yes, Bush *was* sincere when he spoke of America's mission to the Middle East, but his sincerity was that of a dangerously deluded Christian zealot. This criticism of Bush, however, overlooked two important considerations. First, it is not rare for American presidents to invoke the aid of the deity during times of crisis, yet, to use the example of Lincoln once again, no one has ever argued that the Civil War was caused by Lincoln's religious fanaticism. Second, and more importantly, the criticism that Bush is a fundamentalist Christian fanatic disregards the fact that Bush's vision of a transformed Middle East has had a wholly secular character from the very beginning. The invasion of Iraq was not undertaken to win souls to Christianity, but to win them to liberal *and* secular democracy. The culture that Bush wished to see spring up first in Iraq, and then throughout the Middle East, was precisely the kind of culture that most of Bush's liberal critics would also have been happy to see in these regions: a culture in which there was genuine freedom of religion, in which the rights of women were respected, in which everyone could put aside their ethnic, sectarian, and tribal divisions in order to work for the common welfare.

Those who have chosen to deride Bush as a warmonger or to caricature him as a religious fanatic are concealing from themselves the tragic lesson of America's catastrophe in Iraq. The administration's fundamental error lay in thinking that culture didn't matter, and that the values of the modern liberal West are those desired by all men and women, regardless of their religious and ethnic traditions, their history, and their material conditions. Yet this error did not begin with the Bush administration; it is the legacy of American idealism at its exasperating best. Shortly after being nominated for the presidency in 1860, Abraham Lincoln declared his conviction that the principles enshrined in the American Declaration of Independence were not just meant for Americans, but for all people everywhere—a sentiment that President

Bush has repeatedly espoused. The difference between Lincoln and Bush lies not in the relative sincerity of their convictions, but in the fact that President Bush, unlike Lincoln, could back his visionary idealism with the colossal military and economic might of the United States, and at a historical moment in which America had no rivals. Yet this immensity of power does not make Bush's idealism a bit less visionary than Lincoln's—tragically, it only serves to make it more dangerous.

Here we come to the cruel reality behind America's involvement with Iraq ever since the first Gulf War. Our current disaster in Iraq is not the product of evil designs made by wicked men or deluded fanatics; it is the dream turned nightmare of those liberal idealists who worked so courageously to eliminate the brutal struggle for survival from international affairs. To see this, let us glance back at the "lessons" that we are supposed to have learned from the terrible experience of the Second World War.

After 1945, the conventional wisdom among liberals was that the horrors of the Second World War could have been avoided if only the United States had joined the League of Nations, the international peacekeeping body that was created in the wake of the First World War. Though the League of Nations is often associated with President Woodrow Wilson, the drive to create such a league had long been the pet project of those who believed that the world had reached a point where war no longer made any sense, economically or politically. By establishing a concert of nations who were prepared to cooperate together to keep the peace, all differences between nations could be resolved by negotiation and arbitration, rather than being decided by bloodshed and gunfire. Those who ascribed to this optimistic viewpoint were liberal internationalists—men and women who believed that the entire world could one day be governed by the same rational and nonviolent principles that were observed in the great liberal societies like England, France, or the United States.

Unfortunately, the League of Nations completely failed in its original purpose. Only twenty years after it was founded, the Second World War broke out. How had this disaster come about, despite the best intentions of so many peace-loving men and women? Was the liberal internationalist's vision of world peace simply unrealistic? Or did the failure of the League have another cause? To this question, conventional wisdom had a ready answer: The failure of the League was not due to a defect in its original ideals; it was due to the fact the United States had refused to join, despite Wilson's passionate advocacy of it. If only America had joined, all would have been well, for, in that case, there would have been a great power prepared to use its economic and military clout to prevent acts of aggression, such as Italy's invasion of Ethiopia or the Japanese attack on China.

After the Second World War, with the creation of the United Nations, new hope filled the breasts of the liberal internationalists. This time there was an international peacekeeping body that America was prepared to back to the hilt. The only problem was the existence of the USSR, whose veto power in the UN Security Council became a new roadblock to the realization of the idealistic vision of the liberal internationalists. But with the collapse of the Soviet empire, even this last obstacle was removed. Thus, when Saddam Hussein invaded the oil-rich nation of Kuwait, the glorious dream of the liberal internationalist was finally realized. An act of overt aggression, such as Italy's invasion of Ethiopia, could now be stopped in its tracks. Even more astonishing, such an invasion could be rolled back and wholly nullified, thanks to American military power and America's willingness to use it to secure what the first President Bush called "the New World Order."

Oddly enough, there were many who called themselves liberals who did not see the first Gulf War as the consummation of the dream of liberal internationalism. They complained that this war was all about oil, overlooking the obvious fact that it was by no means unusual for acts of international aggression to be all about something rather grubby and materialistic. When the Japanese attacked the Dutch West Indies at the beginning of the Second World War, that invasion, too, was all about oil. The Japanese needed oil, and that was the closest place they could get it. Was it wrong to try to drive the Japanese back? The whole point of liberal internationalism, after all, was to put in place an effective system to punish and penalize those nations who might be tempted to go to war in order to grab something grubby and materialistic that happened to belong to someone else. Therefore, for liberals to argue that it was wrong for the USA and the UN to go to war over "oil" in Kuwait was to abandon the most basic principles of liberal internationalism, which was to stop any act of aggression made by any nation for any reason whatsoever. Yet this first attempt to fulfill the dream of liberal internationalism fell considerably short. True, it put a halt to Saddam Hussein's aggression; but it left him in power.

Here again, the liberal internationalist could invoke memories of the failure to prevent the Second World War; they could recite the lessons taught by the policy of appeasement. Hitler could have been stopped from committing his acts of aggression if the French and the English had insisted forcefully that Nazi Germany adhere strictly to the letter of the Treaty of Versailles. Goebbels, who was certainly no fan of Churchill, once remarked that the Nazi regime would never have gotten off the ground if the pugnacious Churchill had been prime minister during its rise to a world power: Churchill would have nipped the Nazis in the bud. Would it not have been far better for the future of mankind if Churchill had brought about a relatively bloodless "regime change" in Berlin circa 1934, even if the casus belli for this action was a mere technical violation of the Treaty of Versailles?

President George W. Bush unwisely sought to justify his regime change in Iraq by claiming that Saddam Hussein possessed weapons of mass destruction. But Bush could have found a perfectly valid casus belli in Saddam Hussein's failure to abide by the conditions imposed on him in the aftermath of the first Gulf War. True, this might not have been enough to persuade Americans, or the world in general, that military force should be used to remove Saddam Hussein, but Churchill would have faced even greater opposition if he had gone to war with Nazi Germany over a technical violation of the Treaty of Versailles in 1934, or even a rather major violation of it, like Hitler's march into the demilitarized Rhineland in 1935. Had Churchill launched a preemptive strike against the Nazi regime before it became a world power, who would have gone down as the warmonger, Hitler or Churchill?

The lessons garnered from the tragedy of the Second World War appeared to offer a powerful moral for those who sought to avert such disasters in the future. If liberal internationalism was to work at all, there had to be a mighty nation that would promptly and effectively act to bring down potential aggressors *before* it was too late to stop them. Unless international troublemakers were taken out early and decisively, they were bound to keep on pushing their luck, escalating their aggression after each ineffectual attempt at curbing their appetites for expansion. If one nation, like Iraq, could invade even the tiniest oil-rich state, or defy the mandates of the international community, then gradually, eventually a fearsome genie would be released from its bottle. Either the aggressor would keep on aggressing, or else others would follow its example and commence their own policy of aggression. In either scenario, brute force would again triumph over the principles at the heart of liberal internationalism, and the bloody lessons of the two world wars would have gone for naught.

This, once again, *appeared* to be the moral taught by the twentieth century; and it is in terms of this "lesson" that the American policy toward Iraq must be understood. In the world that came after the collapse of the USSR, America would not make the same mistakes that it made at the end of the First World War. It would not pursue a course of isolationism or refuse to concern itself with the fate of nations and people in remote parts of the globe. Instead, it would strive to bring about a world that would not only be safe for liberal democracy, but a world in which liberal democracy would triumph once and for all over the various forms of tyranny and despotism that has been the lot of the human race for the vast majority of its time on this planet. President Bush may be severely criticized for assigning himself a far too grandiose role in the shaping of human destiny, but he has tried to shape this destiny in accordance with the noble ideals that uplifted the minds of the Abbe St. Pierre, the Marquis de Condorcet, and Immanuel Kant. Those who wish to condemn Bush for his undue faith in America's capacity to transform the world should also be prepared to recognize that if he is deluded, he is as deluded as Lincoln was when he said that the principles of the Declaration of Independence were for the entire human race, or as Woodrow Wilson was when he believed that American power should be used to spread the blessings of democracy across the face of the globe.

Thus we are left with a number of bitter ironies.

First, the United States today is widely hated around the world for taking upon itself the responsibility that it was criticized for shirking in the aftermath of the First World War. Before the

Second World War, people longed for a great and relatively benign power to check aggression among nations; today the existence of such a power is deeply resented, even by those who gained the most advantage from its protection.

Second, the pursuit of the ideal of liberal internationalism has not made the world more liberal or more peaceful—in our determination not to repeat the mistakes of the past "ravaged" century, we have made new mistakes that are threatening to return us to the very dog-eat-dog world we thought we had just escaped.

Third, President Bush, though attacked by liberals, shares the same delusions about the progress of mankind that have always been the hallmark of the liberal reading of history. He genuinely believes that the march of freedom is inevitable, and that it is the mission of the liberated West to help to liberate the rest of the world, so that all people may live by the principles embodied in the American Declaration of Independence.

Fourth, it is because President Bush is so genuinely sincere that America's most recent "righteous crusade" has proven so disastrous. A cynic would have pulled out long ago.

Liberals often refuse to acknowledge the sincerity of those they dislike, and there is a deep reason for this. If we have been brought up to think that we should all be able to get along, and to settle our differences by rational discussion, then those who insist on differing from us are undermining our faith in the capacity of reason to solve our problems. Instead of admitting that different people can have valid but different reasons, it is cognitively less stressful to assume that those who disagree with us have been led to their position by sinister self-serving motives. If they were not wicked, or deranged, or guided by a hidden agenda, then they would see eye to eye with us. That is why it comes naturally to liberals to prize the quality of sincerity, and to deny it to their enemies.

Yet, in truth, sincerity is a very treacherous virtue. It may be an admirable personal attribute, but it is no guarantee that the person who is sincere will not commit crimes and follies in pursuit of his sincerely held goals. The person who is sincere may in fact have a much harder time recognizing when he has made a mistake than the wily pragmatist. His intense belief in the rightness of his convictions will delude him into maintaining their rightness even when events appear to be demonstrating their wrongness. "Stay the course" is a motto that comes naturally to the sincere. Lacking the adaptability of elastic convictions, it becomes difficult, if not impossible, for the person who is sincere to change his course without convicting himself in his own mind of abandoning his principles—and that is the one thing that the sincere person cannot do.

The refusal of the sincere to abandon their principles may cause headaches for those who have to deal with them in everyday life. But when men of sincerity are placed in positions of great power, then the result is often catastrophic. Unable to change their course when it has become clearly untenable, they continue doggedly to pursue the same phantom vision, convinced that something will turn up, some miracle will happen, and history will vindicate their sincerity.

The realist must regard sincerity as a luxury, and especially the realist who must deal with the stubborn stuff of which we humans are made. He must learn to shift courses, often swiftly and even shiftily, in order to avoid the fate that awaits those who insist on staying the course when the course runs straight to disaster.

Fatal sincerity, linked with awesome military power, is now driving American foreign policy on the same course followed by the radicals of the French Revolution—and like their predecessors, the Bush administration is being lured on by the illusionary belief that there can be a definitive world order in which no one is unhappy, or resentful, or ready to do whatever it takes to destroy the status quo. The administration believes that free and fair elections, parliaments, and constitutions can create a universal Republic of all Humankind, in which all tyrants have been toppled and all despots overthrown.

In heeding Senator Fulbright's warning about the arrogance of American power, we must keep in mind that there are different ways in which this arrogance can manifest itself. The Left has routinely attacked the Bush administration for its alleged pursuit of empire. But the arrogance of power that has driven the great empire builders expressed itself in a diametrically opposite way than the arrogance of power of the Bush administration. The whole point of all historical empires was to extend their domain over those peoples that the holders of power could tax and exploit for the material benefit of the power holders themselves. The great Oriental empires, for example, were always in search of new sources of tribute and wealth. Hitler's dream of empire aimed at achieving the same objectives—his empire was to be created for the sake of Germany. From the point of view of these classical empire builders, American behavior in Iraq has been utterly senseless—indeed, downright counterproductive. The classical empire is designed to conquer, and not to liberate; its objective is to exploit its conquered subjects. But in Iraq, America has been spending billions of dollars and thousands of American lives in order to create an independent democratic society. The Bush administration could have imposed a puppet government in Iraq within weeks of the invasion; but, instead, they chose to leave it up to the Iraqis to select their own leaders. Furthermore, once this leadership was finally determined, vast American resources were spent to support the new Iraqi government.

Those who wish to blame George W. Bush alone for America's debacle in Iraq have no shortage of ammunition to use against him. But it is dangerous to think that "the mess" in Iraq is all due to the bumbling incompetence, or the lust for oil, or the deluded zealotry of a single individual. What failed in Iraq was not just the policy of George W. Bush; what failed there is liberal internationalism—an unhappy truth that has been hidden behind the misleading rhetoric of both Right and Left.

The liberal internationalists who hoped to create a New World Order in the aftermath of the Second World War believed that aggression should be stopped and dangerous regimes over-thrown; they held firmly to these principles because they believed that the failure to observe them had brought about the catastro-phe of the Second World War, with its staggering death toll of fifty million souls. Those who called themselves liberals during the cold war desperately wanted to keep brute force from govern-ing international affairs, but as realists they were perfectly aware that there were times when force was necessary in order to stop aggression and to eliminate the aggressors.

Today, on the other hand, many of those who call themselves liberals seem to hold that the way to achieve world peace is by vi-sualizing it with the aid of bumper stickers. For them, all violence is anathema and all wars are wrong—even wars fought to stop ag-gression or to remove ruthless dictators. They hold these views not because they favor either aggression or ruthless dictators, but because they believe that there must be some peaceful way to keep ruthless thugs from acting ruthlessly, despite the bitter les-sons not only of the twentieth century, but of every century be-fore. Hence they complain that Bush did not exhaust all his options before using force against Saddam Hussein; but what op-tions, realistically speaking, were left? We, together with the UN, had defeated Saddam's army in 1991; we had imposed harsh sanc-tions on his nation that seemed only to hurt his people; we had used persuasion and threats to try to force him into compliance with the United Nations' own mandates—but none of these methods proved successful.

There was, of course, always the option of doing nothing. We could have permitted Saddam to annex Kuwait; we might even have ignored further annexations of the various impotent oil-rich states in the gulf. Similarly, we could have just shrugged off Saddam's failure to abide by the terms imposed on him by the United Nations after the first Gulf War, just as France and England shrugged off the Nazis' failure to abide by the terms imposed on Germany after the First World War. We could have easily taken this route, and it is entirely possible that the world might now be better for it; but to have done so would have been a rejection of every lesson that we thought we had learned from the horrendous experiences of the twentieth century. It would have meant a complete repudiation of the ideals of liberal internationalism and a return to the very American isolationism that was alleged to have been one of the causes of the world's descent back into the rule of the jungle in the decades following the First World War.

Attack Bush and his administration as much as you wish, but it is imperative to recognize that in invading Iraq and overthrowing Saddam Hussein, the Bush administration was sincerely seeking to bring about what all liberal internationalists have sought to realize from the time of the Enlightenment: an end to the brutal struggle for existence in human affairs. That they failed so badly is a sobering reminder that this struggle will not be terminating any time in the near future, and that the end of history is as far from us today as it has ever been.

5

CLASH OR CRASH?

I n the wake of 9/11, when Fukuyama's end of history thesis
suffered a setback, many in the West turned to a rival paradigm that, like Fukuyama's, had been developed prior to 9/11.
Taking their cue from the title of Samuel Huntington's best-
seller, *The Clash of Civilizations*, they saw Islam and the West engaged in a struggle that some called World War Three. But this
model of conflict, like Fukuyama's, failed to take into consideration the phenomenon of fanaticism.

In a clash of civilizations model, each civilization represents an
achieved status quo; each is concerned with defending itself
against the aggression of other civilizations that also have an
achieved status quo. None of the civilizations has any interest in
overthrowing the status quo of its opponents; each is interested
only in winning advantages for its own side. Like players in a
game of poker, they wish to increase their holdings without anni-
hilating their fellow players.

For example, during the Franco-Prussian war, both sides had
limited strategic and political objectives. The Prussians, on their

victory, claimed certain pieces of French territory and demanded a huge indemnity from the French people—but that was the limit of their ambition. Prussia did not wish to "liberate" the French or remake them into good Prussians. Nor were the Prussians under the illusion that they had fought a war to end all wars. Instead they were playing the game by rules that had been defined by the German theorist Carl von Clausewitz—war was simply politics carried out by other means. It was not a righteous crusade or a mission, and certainly not an attempt to end either history or evil.

Huntington's paradigm was modeled on the kind of conflict that was typical of European nation-states. Each state pursued its self-interest, and in so doing, came into conflict with other states. Yet these conflicts did not involve any profound challenge to the overall status quo that had been achieved by the European system of nation-states. On the contrary, wars were more often fought to preserve the status quo, as in the Crimean War—indeed, this was the basis of the balance-of-power paradigm that governed so much of nineteenth-century foreign policy. It was undesirable to let any nation-state gain too much power, since this would disrupt the status quo; thus, wars were waged not to overturn the status quo but to bring it back into balance.

Huntington's thesis was that, in the period after the collapse of the Soviet Union, nation-states were no longer the entities that needed to be kept in balance in order to preserve the status quo—they had been replaced by what Huntington called civilizations. For example, the nations of the West no longer needed to resort to war to preserve the balance of power; the West now acted, in effect, as a single nation-state. Yet according to Huntington, the same simplifying principle was at work in other civilizations, so that new large units, like Islam or China, played the role assigned to nation-states in the old European system.

From this basic premise, all of Huntington's prescriptions for a stable and peaceful world order followed quite logically. Once again, a careful balancing of power was necessary, but the powers to be balanced were now giant conglomerations: the West, the Muslim world, Latin America, China, and so on. Hence Huntington's stinging criticism of what he saw as the West's overbearing and arrogant attitude toward the other great cultural units. The West, in his view, was at fault in not playing by the rules governing the balance of power; instead, it tended to assume that its own values were universal and tried to impose its ways on the other civilization, thereby disturbing the status quo. Thus Huntington's position is a modern adaptation of the wise and prudent conservatism that counseled each nation-state to keep from disturbing the balance of power by attempting to aggrandize itself at the expense of its rivals, and it served as a reminder to the West, and to the United States in particular, that if there was to be a stable and peaceful world order, the West and the United States had to curb their urge to dominate the other members of the new world order.

What Huntington's paradigm does not take into account is the possibility of conflicts in which new forces arise that are interested not simply in gaining tactical advantages over other players but seek to destroy the status quo itself; not to improve their position in the balance of power equation but to reject the whole concept of a balance of powers. In this case, it is like playing a game of poker during which one of the players takes out a gun and kills the winner of the last hand. Is it wise to explain patiently to the killer the rules of poker, in the hope that he will not commit the same error again?

In a world in which men are driven by fanaticism, Huntington's prudent counsel is no longer relevant—for it will have value only to those players whose self-interest lies in preserving the stability and order of the status quo. To those who wish to demolish the status quo such maxims of prudence will fall on deaf ears.

The fanatic is not interested in preserving the rules of the game that provide stability and order, since his objective is to destabilize and destroy this order. That is why, in a world increasingly turning to the politics of fanaticism, the clash of civilizations paradigm will fail to offer either insight or wisdom.

Those who pursue the politics of fanaticism envision a totally new world order, one that, unlike all previous attempts to achieve a world order, will be the final and definitive world order, one that is not doomed to pass away, decay, or collapse. Yet what is this vision of a permanent world order other than the mirage of the end of history? It is this lofty goal of an end to human conflict that permits the fanatic to justify his violation of the normal rules of the game. What violence cannot be excused on the basis that this act of violence will usher in an age in which violence no longer governs human affairs?

The clash of civilizations paradigm is no longer relevant. In the post-9/11 era several parties are each convinced they are pursuing the end of human conflict, the end of history. It is the clash of these different visions of the end of history that threatens to unravel the status quo that Huntington's paradigm takes for granted as a universal desideratum. It is precisely because different forces are pursuing different visions of an utopian future that the world crisis is one in which the politics of fanaticism is increasingly replacing the politics of reason, compromise, and rule-governed behavior.

Yet because each of the conflicting utopian visions is no more than an ideological mirage, the danger arises that a clash among them will lead to an escalating process of decivilization, as the fanatics fight it out to impose their utopian visions of the future on those who are understandably reluctant to accept it. This decivilizing process is the necessary result of the breakdown in the status quo. When Huntingtonian civilizations are no longer merely interested in readjusting their relative position within the framework of a stable world order but are determined to destroy this world order in the name of an utopian goal that is deemed superior to the old order, then the result is the complete abandonment of the rules of civilized behavior. With the rejection of the Huntingtonian maxims of political prudence, there are no longer rules of the game. The struggle between the competing utopian visions of the end of history inevitably turns into the brutal struggle for survival and supremacy that had only been temporarily overcome thanks to the now discarded and discredited status quo ante. Once things have descended to this point, the status quo becomes merely a dim memory, an ancien regime that is no longer obtainable and that, like Humpty Dumpty, can never be restored.

In short, the collapse of an established order sets off a decivilizing process in which the struggle for power increasingly reverts back to the law of the jungle. Today, this decivilizing process has already gained powerful momentum—and the question we face is, Can this lethal process be stopped? If so, what can stop it?

Here we come to the greatest challenge that is facing the liberal West: Can reason save us?

No, but an exaggerated confidence in the power of reason may well destroy us.

In the next chapter, we will examine how highly intelligent rational actors can become the enemies of civilization. This occurs whenever rational actors decide to remake the world on the assumption that all the people in it are rational actors like themselves, and that, because of this, societies can be started from scratch, just as the rational actors known as businessmen can create new corporate enterprises virtually out of thin air.

6

THE FANATICISM OF REASON

In the aftermath of 9/11, the West continued to hope that the politics of reason would prevail over fanaticism. In the previous chapters we argued that the West held so tenaciously to this hope because it had no other choice: Had the West accepted a blatant return to the law of the jungle, it would have been forced to discard the rules that had been the source of its stability, prosperity, and relative tranquility. In order to avoid a plunge into anarchy, the West has had to deny, minimize, or apologize for those who were seeking to destroy the status quo. Thus, a collective denial set in, one that has kept us from confronting the vulnerability of the West head on.

If there were people in the world who were willing to die as the hijackers died, and many more who were prepared to honor them as martyrs and heroes, then what more powerful evidence could there be of a massive resentment against what we in the West regarded as the final order of things, namely the inevitable triumph of Western values in the form of liberal capitalist democracies throughout the world? But where there is such fanatical resentment, how can the defenders of the status quo sincerely believe that their values are universal and bound to prevail? Such resentment is itself proof that the triumph of the West is in fact an illusion, subject, like all illusions, to be shattered by cruel reality. In order for the West to spare itself that greater shock, it became necessary, on both ends of the political spectrum, to deny the reemergence of fanaticism in the Muslim world. A similar self-deception was evident among those who counseled appeasement of the Nazi regime.

The United States under the Bush administration was not satisfied with merely entertaining illusions of appeasement. Rather than denying the reemergence of Muslim fanaticism, it proposed to eliminate the "root cause" of terrorism, which was, according to the neoconservatives, the evil status quo that existed in the Muslim world. The invasion of Iraq was meant to bring liberal democracy to that nation, setting in motion a process that would finally pull down the entire system of corrupt and illiberal government throughout the Islamic world. In short, the United States under a conservative president adopted precisely the same course as that of the radical Jacobins when they decided to topple the European status quo of their time: to bring down all the ancien regimes, annihilate all borders, erase all ideas of national self-interest, in order to establish a permanent and universal Republic of Mankind.

The great nineteenth-century French historian Albert Sorel referred to the French revolutionaries as representing "the fanaticism of reason," by which he meant a politics that, rather than using reason as an instrument for preserving order and stability, wishes to destroy all existing traditions root and branch, to raze the status quo and start all over again from scratch, using reason alone to reconstruct an entire social order. Sorel also pointed out that such an approach inevitably ends in violence and terror, since once the status quo has been annihilated, it proves impossible to reestablish legitimate authority on the basis of reason alone.

The fanaticism of reason comes from an exaggerated and hopelessly unrealistic overestimation of the power of reason alone to settle differences and to prevent conflict. Since 9/11 those who have displayed the most exaggerated faith in the power of reason have been those American neoconservatives who enthusiastically promoted the idea of a sweeping democratic revolution throughout the Middle East. Despite the label by which they are known, the very fact that the neoconservatives sought to topple ancien regimes and bring about a virtually global revolutionary movement puts them squarely in the same camp as all other modern revolutionaries who sought to destroy the old world and establish a new order on the basis of reason alone.

All modern revolutionary movements since the French Revolution have displayed the same unrealistic overconfidence in the power of pure reason. All revolutionary movements aim to liberate the people from their inherited traditions and create a new man. This new man would not see himself as the member of this or that tribe, sect, or pack—he would see himself as an autonomous ethical agent, capable of making choices and rationally setting objectives. In revolutionary France, for example, there were to be no more aristocrats, merchants, or peasants—there would only be citizens, all of whom would be rational actors. As rational actors they would, needless to say, eagerly cooperate—rationally—to create an ideal society governed by reason alone.

In fact, the fanaticism of reason has always produced the opposite effect. Instead of creating cultures of reason, the reliance on reason alone has invariably brought about a return of the law of the jungle, often in its most brutal and atrocious form. The neo-conservatives who thought that they could build a new Iraqi from scratch were following the same course that all other modern revolutionaries have followed: Destroy and dismantle the corrupt and wicked ancien regime, then rely on the liberated rational actors, i.e., the Iraqi citizens, to fashion for themselves the kind of government they want, using the same rational procedures employed by modern liberal democracies in the West: free and fair elections, a written constitution, an assembled parliament.

The good intentions and high ideals of the neoconservatives, when applied to the reality of Iraq, have brought about a stunning return of the law of the jungle, so savage and violent that hundreds of thousands of liberated Iraqis are now desperately fleeing their own country. Yet this is by no means the first time that the fanaticism of reason has ended in a completely unanticipated eruption of anarchy and terror—and in order to better understand the fatal consequences of this modern and purely secular form of fanaticism, let us consider two examples. First, the fate of the goddess of reason enshrined by the French Revolution; second, the attempt by Napoleon's brother, Joseph, to liberate Spain from despotism and the Inquisition.

On November 10, 1793, the revolutionary government in France decided to hold a Festival of Reason. The nineteenth-century historian of the Revolution Jules Michelet sets the scene: "In the exceedingly narrow choir of Notre-Dame," he tells us, a Temple of Philosophy was "erected on a mountain and decorated with pictures of the wise old fathers of the Revolution. On a nearby rock burned the torch of Truth. The magistrates sat at the feet of the columns; neither weapons nor soldiers were to be seen. Two rows of very young girls—dressed in white and garlanded with oak leaves . . . provided the only festive touch."

"And what would Reason itself look like?" Michelet asks. On November 7, the organizers of the Festival had considered putting up a statue of Reason, "but people objected: a permanent symbol might be reminiscent of the Virgin. . . . They favored an image less fixed, something animated and alive which changed with each holiday and did not give rise to superstition. The founding fathers of the new cult had no desire to debase it."

The architects of this new religion of Reason—reason with a capital "R"—did not want to reinstate the idolatry of the Roman Catholic Church. They did not want the simple masses falling back into the old vicious habits; after all, wasn't that the point of the religion of Reason in the first place? It was to be a replacement for the old religion in the hearts of the people, but one entirely stripped of all that was objectionable in the Christian faith. For example, the watchwords of the new religion were "moderation and indulgent justice"—and what heart can fail to thrill to such stirring ideals as these two? To further stir the emotions of the people, the fete's organizers commissioned the leading revolutionary and patriotic composer of his day, François-Joseph Gossec, to write a suitable chorus for the occasion based on the words of the poet Andre Chénier.

At the celebration in Paris, as in the other larger cities in France, Reason became a goddess. She was chosen from among "the young ladies from eminently respectable families who, willingly or not, undertook to embody Reason." In the festival at Notre Dame, "garbed in white under a cloak of azure blue, Reason emerges from the temple and takes her place on a seat of pure greenery. After the young girls intone her hymn, she crosses to the foot of the mountain, meanwhile bestowing the gentlest of smiles on the spectators. She re-enters the temple. There is further song . . . Everyone waits . . . And that's all."

Michelet's damning summary: "A ceremony chaste, sad, stale, and wearisome."

A bit over two months earlier, on September 5, 1793, a Jacobin delegation to the French Revolution Convention had proclaimed: "It is time that equality bore its scythe above all heads. It is time to horrify all the conspirators. So legislators, place Terror on the order of the day." In other words, the Festival of Reason was actually held during the period known subsequently as the Reign of Terror. One of its victims was the poet who had written the verse celebrating the Festival of Reason, Andre Chénier.

The French revolutionaries were convinced that Reason would finally triumph over the irrational, that this was indeed what their great revolution was all about. It was not an internal upheaval restricted to France, but the dawn of a new era. Witness, for example, the decision to begin renumbering the years: 1793 became the Year One in the Revolutionary Calendar, for this was the year when the goddess of Reason would begin her reign—a reign that would end by encompassing all of mankind, in every clime and corner of the globe, universally disseminating the blessings of reason, tolerance, and humanity to every race and sect and culture. From the Year One onward, men would cease to be ensnared by superstition and cant; they would overcome the prejudices that sinister men had instilled into them; they would tear down the altars of gods they had previously worshipped, and with a joyful countenance they would lift their eyes to the chaste and modest goddess of Reason—and she would solve all their problems with her gentle smile.

Because of Reason, human beings would henceforth march forward toward what the revolutionary French thinker Marie

Jean Caritat, Marquis de Condorcet called "the true perfection of mankind." Because of Reason, all men would become brothers. The priests could no longer deploy their demonic arts to bamboozle the masses. Tyrants and despots would quickly become vague historical memories. Individuals would begin to question traditional authority, to learn to think for themselves, and to govern their own lives as they saw fit. Because of Reason, all people could enjoy the liberty that was their primary natural right.

In the France of 1793, Reason was not only a god that failed, she was a goddess who cut her own throat. The fanaticism of reason that gripped the French revolutionaries convinced them that they could create a republic of reason out of thin air—or more correctly, out of hot air. The men who came up with the idea of celebrating the Festival of Reason were all quite intelligent men— rational actors in the most pronounced sense of this word. They were determined not only to think for themselves and control their own lives, but to build a society that would meet their ideals.

During the French Revolution, it was taken for granted that the goddess of Reason would provide the same wise counsel to all; yet when the revolutionaries appealed to Reason, they found themselves coming up with violently contrasting solutions to the same problem. Did the goddess of Reason want Louis XVI to be executed or spared? As Jules Michelet said, "Reason meant so many things to different men," and herein lay the problem. The goddess of Reason could not provide the consensus that the now-discarded conventions of the ancien regime had previously offered. Tradition usually has all the answers: you simply do what the people before you did. But when you throw away these traditions—even if they are pernicious ones—the result will be the same: People will not agree on new traditions, since everything is now simply an option to be considered and every rational actor is free to put forth their favorite. Anarchy and chaos will follow the overthrow of the ancien regime until the day arrives when people are so sickened by the law of the jungle that they joyfully hail the first strongman who offers to end it by establishing himself as dictator—as Napoleon did.

With the advent of Napoleon, the ideals of the French Revolution underwent a change. It was not enough merely to invite the people of other nations to liberate themselves from their ancien regimes with French help. The only way to get rid of these old regimes was to conquer them and dismantle their institutions. The people had to be forced to discard the traditions under which they had been raised, and which they themselves regarded as being both right and obvious. The bulk of the population, held back by superstition and prejudice, would have to be remolded and reeducated in order to become rational actors. Thus when Napoleon "liberated" Spain in 1808 from the corrupt and imbecilic Bourbon monarchy, he had no qualms about imposing the superior values of the French Revolution on the Spanish people. The rights of man and freedom of conscience were to replace Bourbon absolutism and the infamous Spanish Inquisition. Napoleon put his own brother, the humane and decent Joseph Bonaparte, on the vacated throne of Spain. With the best of intentions King José, as Joseph was dubbed, set about freeing the Spanish people from the old iniquitous system that had kept Spain living in the Dark Ages. He was aided in his efforts by many educated and enlightened Spaniards, who saw in the new king the answer to their prayers. Yet the Spanish people did not welcome the liberation from despotism and obscurantism that they had been offered by the French army. In one of the few genuinely populist rebellions in European history, they spontaneously rose up against the new order and demanded a return to the old. They wished to put the vile and despicable Ferdinand VII back on the Bourbon throne as an absolute monarch, and even clamored for a return of the Inquisition. They developed guerrilla warfare, attacked the French troops, and even secured one astonishing victory against them at the battle of Baylen on July 20, 1808.

The Spanish uprising that began in May of 1808 challenged the myth that all men yearned to become citizens of a universal republic founded on reason. Here was a country whose population by and large did *not* want to be liberated from their ancien regime, and the response of the enlightened liberator was identical to that of the French revolutionaries to the populist uprising in the Vendée that occurred in March, 1793—those who claimed to be liberating the human race resorted to lethal force in order to crush whoever resisted the blessing of liberation.

What makes the Spanish uprising of 1808 so instructive for our purposes is that it is virtually impossible for anyone in the West today to take sides in that conflict. If we choose to support the aspiration of the Spanish people to free themselves from the yoke of Napoleon, we must also be prepared to accept that they sought this liberation in order to bring back one of the most loathsome and vile tyrants who has ever sat on a throne, Ferdinand VII—whose character may be glimpsed in the portraits by Goya—as well as that epitome of fanatical intolerance, the Spanish Inquisition. And who today among liberals or conservatives is prepared to take the side of these sinister forces?

But the same question can be asked about the other side. On both ends of the political spectrum in the West today, elimination of absolute tyrants and fanatical grand inquisitors can only appear to us to be a positive step forward. Yet who among us would be comfortable forcing a people to accept such progress at the point of a gun? If a people says, "We are content with our traditions, and we wish to live by them," then who are we to compel them, by brute force, to abandon their illiberal reactionary ethos in order to adopt our liberal progressive values?

Throughout the entire political spectrum of the modern West, virtually everyone, from Noam Chomsky to Jerry Falwell, will look upon the elimination of political absolutism and the inquisition as progress—indeed, this conviction will be so deeply ingrained that it does not even seem like a conviction. It will appear to us as obvious—what other option is there? Yet virtually everyone will also agree that it is not right to use brute force in order to impose our values on a people who don't want them and are quite happy as they are. This, too, will not seem right to us. In the modern liberal West, we have all learned to have too much respect for the right of other people to abide by their own values and customs.

In the West today there is a vast consensus on these two critical issues. First, there is a general acceptance of the idea that the elimination of tyranny, despotism, and fanatical intolerance represents progress, and is much to be desired. Second, there is a general acceptance of the idea of respect for the traditions and cultures of others—at least, enough respect to prevent us from the high-handed approach taken by such liberators as the French revolutionaries and Napoleon. In short, there is virtual unanimity that progress is good, and that multicultural sensitivity is a desirable trait.

The term *multiculturalism* has become a political fighting word. For those who label themselves conservatives, the word stands for something bad, though it is not quite clear what; for liberals, the word stands for something good, though here again, what is not clear. Yet behind the fighting word there is an actual idea, and this idea is embraced by virtually all Westerners: There are different cultures in the world, and the best way to deal with them is on a live and let live basis. We have our ways, they have theirs. Therefore let us leave each other in peace.

Just as Huntington's paradigm has its roots in nineteenth-century balance-of-power diplomacy, the multiculturalist's "live and let live" attitude to other peoples and their cultures also stems from the nineteenth century—it is the liberalism of John Stuart Mill and of William Gladstone. Just as Mill argued that a decent society should accept, and even encourage, "experiments in living," so a decent world order should accept, and even encourage, experiments in culture. Just as the diversity of individuals promotes greater creativity in a society, so too does a diversity of culture. Therefore, just as pop guru Joseph Campbell once advised each of us "to follow our bliss," so each culture should be encouraged to follow its own traditions and customs.

Herein lies the critical difference between the liberationist ideals of the French revolutionaries and those of the American neoconservatives. Both were deeply convinced that the destruction of despotism, tyranny, and religious fanaticism was the path of genuine historical progress, and only after these sinister forces had been overthrown could mankind enter the "golden age of peace and human happiness." Yet while the French revolutionaries rejected the very idea of multiculturalism as incompatible with the coming universal republic of humankind under the guidance of enlightened reason, the American neoconservatives were compelled by the spirit of their times to adopt the ideals of multiculturalism as their own. American power would not be used in Afghanistan and Iraq in order to impose our values on people who adhered to a different tradition; instead, American power would be used to overthrow the corrupt status quo, after which it would be left to the Afghan and Iraqi peoples to govern themselves democratically through free and fair elections.

The hope of the neoconservatives was that, once the tyrants who ruled them had been removed, the people would become rational actors like themselves, and would freely choose to adopt the enlightened liberal values that had brought so much success to the leading nations of the West. The rationale for overthrowing the evil status quo in the Middle East was to get the region's people to accept their role within the world order established through the Pax Americana. In other words, it was hoped that, once they had been liberated, they would be willing to accept another status quo, that achieved by the West's series of "total victories" over the sinister forces that have caused so much havoc during the twentieth century—a status quo that would obviously be acceptable to all rational actors.

Fukuyama's original end of history thesis had supposed that the world was moving inevitably toward liberal capitalist democracies; the Pax Americana would triumph because all other nations would be drawn to imitate the model offered by the West. The vision of the end of history that dominated neoconservative thinking in the post-9/11 era, however, did not share Fukuyama's optimistic scenario of inevitable historical progress—a scenario derived ultimately from Karl Marx. Instead they believed that the West had to interfere actively in the Middle East to remove the final obstacles to the triumph of freedom and democracy throughout the region, hence the world. Get rid of the evil Muslim status quo, and the Muslim population would eagerly find their proper places in the unipolar American-dominated world order. The status quo of the Pax Americana, disturbed by the events of 9/11, would thereby be restored on a sound and permanent foundation—and the end of history would be at hand.

It is impossible not to sympathize with the neoconservatives who sincerely wished to bring progress to the Middle East, and equally hard to sympathize with the terrorist insurgency that has pushed Iraq into anarchy and civil war. On the other hand, it is difficult to suppress the feeling that, despite its obvious sincerity, the American mission in Iraq was a dismally conceived misadventure in utopian social engineering, doomed from the start because of the sheer lack of political realism among those who sought to use American power to bring about an apocalyptic end to evil.

This lack of political realism stemmed from the assumption that once Iraq had been liberated, the Iraqi people would immediately begin to behave like rational actors—very much like the American planners themselves. It did not even occur to them that the overthrow of Saddam Hussein would free the bulk of the population to begin behaving tribally. Instead of becoming Iraqi citizens, pure and simple, they redivided themselves into their hereditary tribes: Kurds, Shi'ites, and Sunnis. Furthermore, in the power vacuum left by the American failure to impose a strong central government at the outset, the resultant slide into anarchy brought about a return of the law of the jungle in which even those Iraqis who wished to behave like rational actors were forced into becoming tribal actors, simply because they were seen by other tribal actors as members of a rival tribe. A Sunni who wished for nothing more than to bring peace and stability to his nation was looked upon by a Shi'ite death squad not as a rational individual, but simply as another Sunni, and this fact alone was sufficient to warrant his death.

Although it is easy to assume that those who are the beneficiaries of the status quo will be keen to preserve it, historical evidence clearly shows that it is often those most responsible for preserving the status quo who, quite unwittingly, end up leading it to destruction. People do not always know where their best interests lie. Louis XVI, for example, threw his enthusiastic support, backed by plenty of money, to the American revolutionaries who wished to establish a republic of reason in the New World. Less than twenty years later, not long after French revolutionaries had established their own republic of reason in France, he would be condemned to the guillotine.

The Bourbon monarchy under Louis XVI represented what we will call a "self-liquidating legitimacy." This occurs whenever those who are the dominant power in an achieved status quo set about overturning the very world order that is essential if they are to preserve their position of dominance.

Today, the Bush administration's desire to spread democracy throughout the Middle East and the rest of the world may well prove to be the most catastrophic example of a self-liquidating legitimacy in human history. The motive behind this urge to topple the existing world order is no doubt as noble and sincere as that behind Louis XVI's support of the American revolutionaries. Nevertheless it is a classic example of the fanaticism of reason: Instead of ameliorating the evils of the status quo, reason is being used to demolish it, and to create from scratch a permanent and lasting world order in which liberty and justice will prevail for all mankind. Reviewing the American efforts to reconstruct Iraq, for example, there is a feeling that the policy planners were guided by the spirits of the Legislative Assembly and National Convention of the French Revolution: Nothing of the old regime was permitted to remain; all was dismantled, even the army and the security forces; all that was needed was a well-composed constitution, free and fair elections, and a parliamentary assembly, and Iraq would become an oasis of prosperity and freedom, so alluring that other Muslim nations would overthrow their own corrupt regimes in order to imitate the Iraqi model—the same misguided sentiments that led the French revolutionaries to believe that their republic would be copied by the people of the world just as soon as they too threw off their old and corrupt regimes.

The fanaticism of reason that gripped the French revolutionaries ended in anarchy and terror; the fanaticism of reason that gripped the neoconservative revolutionaries in Iraq has had the same result. Yet anarchy and terror are the two great enemies of the status quo—they are the two dissolvents of order, civilized life, and the politics of reasonable compromise. Thus the Bush administration's fanatical obsession with imposing a noble but abstract ideal on the shoddiness of the real world is threatening to bring down the very Pax Americana that the American leadership should seek to preserve. Furthermore, encouraging populist democracy among those who feel a profound resentment of American hegemony is the quickest way to end that very hegemony. By urging the overthrow of corrupt dictators—who are at least willing not to rock the boat—the Bush administration, with the best intentions, is handing power over to people who have no interest in maintaining a status quo dominated by America. Nowhere is this more dangerous than in the Middle East, where a fanatical hatred of the United States and the West has only been increased by the American intervention in Iraq—though even now there is no sign that the leaders of our nation, either republican or democrat, are prepared to recognize this melancholy fact and take the full measure of its significance for the future of our planet.

Our "reality gap" has come about because we have forgotten what it takes to permit the politics of reason to flourish, and we have also forgotten how vulnerable the politics of reason is in the struggle against the politics of fanaticism.

The primary cause of our forgetfulness is that we have forgotten where reason came from. Indeed, we no longer believe that it came from anywhere. We think we are born rational actors. In short, we have mystified reason, and our first task is to demystify it in order to grasp the possibility that cultures of reason could disappear from the world. Reason is not a gift from God or our common biological inheritance, it is a cultural tradition, and like all cultural traditions is subject to the same harsh laws that have swept so much else into oblivion in the human past.

Part Two

Reason, Fanaticism, and the
Struggle for Existence

7

DEMYSTIFYING REASON

T he West today is the victim of a curious illusion. It has created and maintained rare islands of reason in a world otherwise ruled by the law of the jungle, yet it refuses to give itself any
credit for this immensely improbable achievement. By and large,
the West has forgotten that it is an achievement at all. Instead, it
has come to think of reason as an innate faculty of the mind, and
that just as everyone clearly possesses a nose, so all possess reason.
But if this is true, then the problem immediately arises: Why did
reason take hold in the West, while it failed to have any significant
effect in so many other cultures, that is, until they encountered the
West—or, more often, until the West encountered them? If reason is part of our biological endowment, granted to us simply by
our membership in the species significantly called Homo sapiens
("wise" or "knowing" human), then why has it been so little evident in societies untouched by Western influence?

That reason took hold in the West seems beyond argument. Western thinkers have used reason in order to construct increasingly

elaborate scientific theories of the physical world, to develop mathematics, to devise breathtaking technologies that have transformed the ordinary lives of countless human beings. In addition, reason has been used to effect political changes—in modern democracies, political parties must use reason in support of their policies. Even when they are pursuing policies of naked self-interest, they must still offer rational arguments for them— what Karl Marx would call an ideology. Just as hypocrisy is the homage vice pays to virtue, so ideology is the homage self-interest pays to reason.

The West, uniquely, had even used reason to try to prove the existence of God, as Anselm attempted in the eleventh century. Other peoples simply took the existence of the gods for granted. But in the West, it was not enough to be told there was a God; we must be able to convince ourselves, by reason alone, that such an entity existed. What other culture has been annoyed by such doubt?

None of this should be taken to imply that other cultures have not produced reasonable men, or logical thinkers, or scientific minds. Islam, in its heyday, produced a series of great thinkers, such as Averroes, Ibn-Sina, Ibn-Khaldun, to name only the most illustrious. Buddhist thinkers like Nargajuna were capable of dazzling feats of dialectical thinking worthy of the most brilliant West minds. The Hindu thinker Sankara was a profound metaphysician. China had its great sages and wise men, such as Confucius and Mencius. Furthermore, in everyday life, non-Western cultures have used instrumental reason to improve their canoes, devise better weapons, create calendars, and build great monuments.

The Western tradition of *critical* reason, however, does not merely cast reason in the role of a handmaiden, willing to solve thorny problems and to figure things out, indifferent to the purposes involved. Talmudic scholars and learned Muslims have long reasoned about the meaning of their revealed texts; they employ logic and analogy in order to elucidate conundrums presented by their sacred scripture. But it never occurred to any of them that reason itself could be used to attack or criticize the Torah or the Koran, the way the great philosopher Spinoza used reason to judge the accuracy and reliability of Hebrew scripture in his treatise on the Bible. Reason for the scholars of the Koran and Talmud was their tool; for the philosopher Spinoza, on the other hand, reason was his master. Similarly, Confucius used reason to defend and uphold the traditional values of Chinese society as he understood them; but it would never have crossed his mind to argue that reason alone could provide the foundation of an entire social order, as the French revolutionaries were convinced. Al-Ghazali, in his attack on the philosophers, used reason to show that reason was unable to discover the truth without divine revelation, but the whole point of his reasoning was to show the worthlessness of reason alone to provide reliable guidance to the perplexed and erring human race. In short, al-Ghazali, though he made use of reason, had no interest in replacing Islam with the cult of the goddess of Reason.

Yet as the Festival of Reason makes clear, the Western tradition of reason is an ambiguous legacy. The West is unique in preserving, however fitfully, the tradition of critical reason—the reason exhibited by Socrates, for example, in his critique of the Greek pantheon of oversexed and rather adolescent gods and goddesses. Yet the West is also unique in making a virtual fetish of reason, in deifying it, believing that reason and reason alone could be the final judge of all human thought and conduct. This of course is not to say that everyone in the West has shared the same idolatrous attitude to reason. John Calvin called reason "a whore," while the Scottish philosopher David Hume argued that reason "is and ought to be" the slave of our passions. Yet both Calvin and

Hume, however unwittingly, shared the same attitude to reason that has been handed down from Socrates. Both used their own brains to criticize the collective traditions that they had inherited, and to seek out new solutions that were personally satisfying to them. Both were skeptics—Calvin of the claims of Catholicism, Hume of the claims of metaphysics. Neither was content with what he had been taught. Both used reason, even if they were not prepared to admit it, to discover a higher and better truth as they saw it by the lights of their own mind.

The West has also produced great speculative systems of philosophy in which serious attempts have been made to demonstrate that, contrary to appearance, reason really rules the world—either as Divine Reason or as Pure Reason. It is in the West that thinkers first took an interest in showing that the God they worshipped was one who could be counted upon to behave just as reasonably as they did, and perhaps even a bit more. As a result of these great theological and metaphysical systems, many in the West have come to believe that reason is built into the universe, and that humans are by nature creatures of reason.

Yet before the European Enlightenment, reason was looked upon as the distinguishing characteristic of only a small minority of the human race. Aristotle, for example, had argued that slavery was the natural and appropriate condition for most human beings, namely those who had not learned how to control their own impulses. Reason, for the mass of humanity, was not an option. On the contrary, it was the privilege only of those rare human beings who had learned how to master themselves: They alone could benefit from reason. The bulk of mankind could not obtain these benefits by their own efforts; if they were to act reasonably, it could only come about because those who already possessed reason forced them to behave this way. On this view, the majority of humankind was doomed to irrationality, and the only way they could be made rational was through the monopoly of power entrusted to those few who were themselves rational.

Today this is no longer a popular view. It has instead been replaced by the Enlightenment's emphatic assertion that humankind by nature possesses a distinctive faculty of reason.

In this part of the book, I will argue that the Enlightenment's concept of reason as a universal endowment is wrong, and, worse yet, dangerously wrong. Reason, I will try to demonstrate, represents a specific cultural tradition. It is no more an innate faculty than Islam or capitalism. The illusion that reason is universal arose from the fact that, several hundred years ago, in North America and the leading nations of Europe, people began to behave reasonably with each other. Not perfectly, not even fairly or justly, but reasonably. In doing so they created a culture of reason.

Humans are not born rational actors; it takes a whole culture and a deep tradition to make them that way. The civilizing process that ends in producing rational actors must be undertaken at the deepest level, what Norbert Elias called "habitus," or second nature. It must be imparted in terms of visceral imperatives, and not in terms of optional lifestyles. In my *Policy Review* essay "The Future of Tradition," I called this deepest level of acculturation the "visceral code," precisely because it is wired into us at the physiological and precognitive level. For example, when we feel embarrassed, we manifest the physical symptoms of blushing before we ever reach the point of thinking: "I am embarrassed." A person doesn't first think, "I should be embarrassed for what I have done, therefore, I will blush." The same thing is true with the sense of shame and anxiety. To feel shame is not the result of a rational decision of the individual. Shame is first felt at the physiological level, and it is the discomfort and anxiety produced by this automatic sense of shame that polices our conduct far more effectively than moral maxims ever could. Because we do not like to feel the discomfort and anxiety produced by shame, we are reluctant to do those things that trigger the shaming response. Often we do not even need witnesses to deter us from doing something shameful: We have internalized the shaming code to the point that we don't need others to make us feel ashamed of ourselves.

These automatically triggered visceral responses act as a societal defense mechanism. When they operate to keep individuals from committing crimes, there is no need for an external police force. The shaming code that has been wired into the individual acts as a policing agent, and it can be far more vigilant and effective than any secret police. In those societies that have instilled a pervasive shaming code, there will be relatively little need for the state apparatus to interfere in the lives of the individual with threats of coercion or sanctions.

Society has taught us to feel acute embarrassment, panic, anxiety, disgust, and revulsion at certain situations. These unpleasant physiological responses have been systematically programmed into us, in order to inhibit us from doing things that we should feel embarrassed about if caught doing. If you don't want your child to pee in your neighbor's pansies, you must make him feel embarrassed for doing it—it will avail you little to reason with him about other people's rights to their own property.

Yet the visceral code is not an end in itself, but a means to an end. It uses shame and praise as a way of molding certain kinds of individuals. For example, the shaming code of primitive egalitarians will make hunters ashamed to boast about their skills. "Among the !Kung and the Hadza," explains Craig B. Stanford in his book, *The Hunting Ape*, "even the best hunter must be modest. Humility is a strong cultural tradition in nearly all hunter-gatherer societies. This is an extension of the egalitarian nature of these cultures. Attempts to use one's hunting prowess as an entrée to greater ambitions within the society are usually met with stern opposition, ridicule, and attempts to shame the self-promoter. It is preceded by much verbal taunting and badgering from other members of the hunting party."

In a warlike tribe, on the other hand, the shaming code will be used to make boys ashamed of submitting to others without a fight, or of running away from battle. It encourages them to be boastful and arrogant. This is how the primitive pastoralists of the Nilotic Sudan raise their boys. Edward Evans-Pritchard, who studied them, wrote: "That every Nuer considers himself as good as his neighbor is evident in their every movement. They strut about like lords of the earth which, indeed, they consider themselves to be. There is no master and no servant in their society, but only equals who regard themselves as God's noblest creation. Their respect for one another contrasts with their contempt for all other peoples."

The shaming code of middle-class societies, on the other hand, will make boys ashamed to act aggressively. Everything in moderation; no overhastiness in judgment. The shaming code that produces rational actors will make them ashamed to let their emotions and impulses control their conduct. It will shame them out of bullying others, or having temper tantrums, or displaying naked and crude self-assertion.

In short, the visceral code is a technique for producing a society in which everyone will react with the same horror, shame, revulsion, embarrassment, anxiety, and so forth, to the same situations. But as we have seen in the above examples, the visceral code can be used to produce radically different kinds of human beings, from the Spartan warrior to the Quaker pacifist, from lowly serf to the fiery-tempered aristocrat.

Human beings, therefore, are born neither tribal actors nor rational actors; it is the shaming code to which they are subjected that makes them one or the other. Yet, while there is an obvious survival edge in training the young to be tribal actors, it is far less apparent what survival advantage comes by training them to be rational actors. As we argued in the Preface, the rational actor cannot hope to survive in a world ruled by the law of the jungle. Yet if humankind itself has descended from the jungle, by what route did rational actors come into existence? How did they manage to survive, to create societies, and finally, at least during the Modern Age, to dominate those cultures whose shaming code raised its young to be tribal actors?

The Enlightenment thinkers who asserted that reason was an inborn faculty of humanity lived before Charles Darwin's revolutionary theory of natural selection. Man, according to the crude materialism of the Enlightenment thinkers like La Mettrie, was a machine. Diderot certainly thought so, in which case the question, "Where did man come from?" can be answered, He was assembled, perhaps in a stew. He did not have to struggle for survival, just as Rousseau's savage does not have to struggle, always having food and a woman at hand, and not needing to snatch either from someone else.

Yet even before Darwin, some thinkers, such as Herder and Vico, had made daring assertions that humankind, by nature, was much more like a baboon than like the rational depiction of the Enlightenment conceit, and that human reason came about by a process of development from these protohumans to full humans.

But none faced the challenge that Darwin posed—as we shall see, even Darwin didn't face it himself.

We, however, must face this challenge before we proceed. How did animals, caught up in the universal struggle for survival, become transformed into rational actors, capable of controlling their impulses and their passions? How did we learn to hold either our tongues or fists, to take seriously the other person's point of view, to appreciate the worth of cultural traditions that are radically different from our own, and even, on occasion, to exchange ours for theirs? How did we learn to wait our turn, or to follow sensible orders, or to assume that someone else might know more than we do? How did we come to care about how the people around us really felt, instead of being content with having them obey? How did we learn to persuade others to see why we are right, and they are wrong. How did we ever come to wonder—gasp!—if we are really right ourselves?

Charles Darwin, a humane and kindhearted man, observing the natives of Tierra del Fuego during the famous voyage of the HMS *Beagle*, was forced to make the observation:

> Viewing such men, one can hardly make oneself believe that they are fellow-creatures, and inhabitants of the same world. It is a common subject of conjecture what pleasures in life some of the lower animals can enjoy: how much more reasonably the same question may be asked with respect to these barbarians! At night, five or six human beings, naked and scarcely protected from the wind and rain of this tempestuous climate, sleep on the wet ground coiled up like animals. Whenever it is low water, winter or summer, night or day, they must rise to pick

shell-fish from the rocks; and the women either dive to collect sea-eggs, or sit patiently in their canoes, and with a baited hair-line without any hook, jerk out little fish. If a seal is killed, or the floating carcass of a putrid whale discovered, it is a feast; and such miserable food is assisted by a few tasteless berries and fungi.

Darwin goes on to remark: "The different tribes when at war are cannibals . . . it is certainly true, that when pressed in the winter by hunger, they kill and devour their old women before they kill their dogs." When asked why they did this, the answer given was that "Doggies catch otters, old women no." The old women in question are "killed by being held over smoke and thus choked," and the boy who reported this story "imitated their screams as a joke, and described the parts of their bodies which are considered the best to eat."

Darwin goes on to say about the Fuegians: "They cannot know the feeling of having a home, and still less that of domestic affection; for the husband is to the wife a brutal master to a laborious slave." Indeed, not even Richard Dawkins's selfish gene seems to hold any power over the men. "Was a more horrid deed ever perpetrated, than that witnessed on the west coast by [Admiral] Byron, who saw a wretched mother pick up her bleeding dying infant-boy, whom her husband had mercilessly dashed on the stones for dropping a basket of sea-eggs! How little can the higher powers of the mind be brought into play: what is there for imagination to picture, for reason to compare, for judgment to decide upon? to knock a limpet from the rock does not require even cunning, that lowest power of the mind."

In his autobiography, Darwin wrote that "the voyage of the *Beagle* has been by far the most important event in my life," and that "the sight of a naked savage in his native land is an event which can never be forgotten." And yet even Darwin himself found it difficult to escape from the Enlightenment's view of reason as a faculty inherent in all humans. Consider this quotation from *The Descent of Man*, written well after his stay among the natives of Tierra del Fuego.

> As man advances in civilization, and small tribes are united into larger communities, *the simplest reason* would tell each individual that he *ought* to extend his social instincts and sympathies to all the members of the same nation, though personally unknown to him. This point being once reached, there is only an *artificial* barrier to prevent his sympathies extending to the men of all nations and races. (Emphasis added.)

Here we can clearly detect the same historical optimism that inspired the Enlightenment: the inevitable triumph of reason—indeed, the simplest reason—over the "artificial" barriers constituted by different tribal loyalties. It is our common sense of humanity that is most natural to us, while all the narrower bonds that attach us more closely, our family and our tribe, are dismissed as being merely artificial.

Yet immediately after Darwin offers this glowing tribute to the civilizing power of man's inborn faculty of reason, he goes on to register his own misgivings and reservations.

> If . . . men are separated . . . by great differences in appearances and habits, experience unfortunately shows us how long it is, before we look at them as our fellow-creatures. Sympathy beyond the confines of man, that is, humanity to lower animals, seems to be one of the latest

moral acquisitions. . . . How little the old Romans knew of it is shown by their abhorrent gladiatorial exhibitions. The very idea of humanity, as far as I could observe, was new to most of the Gauchos of the Pampas.

If Darwin's "simplest reason" instructs men to be brothers, why have so few of us on this planet figured this out? And why did this new sense of humanity and fellow feeling only come about so late in the development of the human race?

Indeed, we can go one step further. We can ask how this higher moral sensibility could ever have come about in a world that obeys the laws of nature that Darwin himself has illuminated for us. "Nothing," Darwin wrote in *The Origin of Species*, "is easier than to admit in words the truth of the universal struggle for life, or more difficult—at least I have found it so—than constantly to bear this conclusion in mind."

If there is a universal struggle for life, why did it come about that men came into the world as kindhearted as Darwin himself, a man who in his short but charming autobiography confesses, with a quite evident feeling of genuine guilt, that "Once as a very little boy whilst at the day-school, or before that time, I acted cruelly, for I beat a puppy, I believe, simply from enjoying the sense of power . . . this act lay heavily on my conscience. . . ."

How, in short, can we explain the development of a conscience so tender in a world so brutal? Did Darwin inherit a "reason and humanity" gene that the Fuegian boys did not? Or was reason and humanity, far from being a natural endowment, simply part of the very peculiar tradition in which Charles Darwin had been raised— the tradition of evangelical Anglicans who played such a critical role in the great struggle to abolish slavery from the planet?

That reasonable people like Darwin somehow came to exist no reasonable person can deny; yet the process by which this came about eludes us now, as it eluded Darwin himself. What place could even the simplest reason have in the lives of the natives of Tierra del Fuego? And if there was no place for reason among such savages, then at what point in the evolution of our species did reason, and a sense of common humanity, finally emerge?

What chance would a lone Fuegian rational actor have to pursue his own enlightened self-interest, for example, by trying to acquire something of value to himself by his own labor? Darwin tells us that "at present even a piece of cloth given to one [of the Fuegians] is torn into shreds and distributed; and no one individual becomes richer than others." And would not the same fate await the fruits of the labor of a lone Fuegian who tried to behave as a rational actor—assuming that the rational actor himself was not torn to shreds? In which case, we are left wondering, How could the rational actor ever have emerged out of the tribal mind? In such an environment, the rationality of the rational actor would have done him no good, and would most probably have made him an outcast from the tribe, if not a dinner treat for their collective consumption.

T. H. Huxley, the biologist now remembered chiefly as "Darwin's bulldog," was, in many ways, a more acute thinker than the man to whose defense he devoted his enormous talents as a controversialist. In his essay "Evolution and Ethics," published in 1894, Huxley tried to tackle the problem that Darwin hoped to solve with his myth of the simplest reason, and the answer Huxley gives is well worth exploring at this point: In essence, Huxley argues that reasonable behavior is the result not of reason itself, but of a force that we have been taught to regard as irrational, namely shame.

Huxley begins his essay by distinguishing between what he calls the Cosmic Process and the Ethical Process. The Cosmic

Process, as the name implies, rules the universe. It establishes certain laws that operate independently of our own human ideas of right and wrong. Gravity, for example, keeps the moon in orbit, but it also causes airplanes, full of innocent people, to go crashing to their deaths when the engines fail. Does gravity care about their plight? Not in the least. On the one hand, gravity can provide us with hydroelectric power when we dam up a large body of water; on the other hand, it lets toddlers tumble from ninth-story balconies.

For Huxley, however, the part of the Cosmic Process that most caught his attention was the one that his friend Charles Darwin had dubbed the theory of natural selection. Here, too, the Cosmic Process works in utter indifference to our civilized sense of good and evil. Big fish eat little fish—often very cute little fish. Cats kill rodents—often cute ones like chipmunks. The universal struggle for existence, the fundamental axiom of Darwin's theory of evolution, is, by our ethical standards, a totally amoral competition— the victor did not deserve to win; he merely won. The loser does not deserve to lose; he just gets eaten.

When Huxley wrote his essay in 1894, there had developed an influential school of thought called social Darwinism, whose leading figure was the English thinker Herbert Spencer. It was Spencer, not Darwin, who had coined the famous phrase "the survival of the fittest," with its implicit suggestion that the winner of the struggle for survival somehow "merited" his triumph. The survivor survived because he was fitter—and fitter was easily translated into better. After all, in the kind of competition that human beings stage for themselves, like a baseball game or a boxing match, don't we generally assume that it is the best person or team who has won? If a fellow consistently bowls perfect 300s in a bowling competition, while his rivals don't even come close, isn't this proof that he deserves to win the tournament?

The fallacy in this analogy may be quickly seen if we consider the struggle for existence between two cats and the chipmunk they have caught. Yes, it is a competition, but is it what we would call a fair one? When two boxers go into the ring together, every effort is made to see that they are evenly matched—a principle observed in all sporting events. You don't have muscular twenty-year-olds pitted against seventy-eight-year-old women or seven-year-old boys—and if you did, it is unlikely that you would regard the inevitable victor as the better competitor. You would regard him as the bigger brute.

The struggle for existence is not the kind of ethical competition that awards the palm of victory to the best person. Indeed, as Huxley argued in his essay, if another ice age were to return to England, then the struggle for existence might well conclude not in producing the best human, but the best lichen. But would Herbert Spencer regard this exceedingly fit lichen as ethically superior to the unfit human beings whose place they had usurped? Probably not.

For Huxley, it was immensely dangerous to base an ethical theory on the universal struggle for existence. On the contrary, the whole point of ethics was to counter the Cosmic Process—to work against nature, not with it. In short, the Ethical Process was the deliberate attempt to struggle *against* the struggle for existence: to work to keep nature from taking its course. But if ethics means disobeying the laws of nature, what laws are we to obey in their place? And where do these laws come from, if not from nature?

According to Huxley, it was obvious that all human beings were by nature subject to the Cosmic Process. Like Thomas Malthus and Charles Darwin, Huxley saw humankind as locked in the same universal struggle for existence as any other animal. In "Evolution and Ethics," Huxley writes: "with all their enormous differences in natural endowment, men agree in one thing, and that is their desire . . . to do nothing but that which pleases them to do, without the least reference to the welfare of the society in which they are born. That is their inheritance (the reality at the bottom of the doctrine of original sin) from the long series of ancestors, human and semi-human and brutal, *in whom the strength of this innate tendency to self-assertion was the condition of victory in the struggle for existence.*" (Emphasis added.)

What is quite fascinating here is that Huxley, the man who coined the term *agnostic*, is offering a completely scientific and Darwinian interpretation of St. Augustine's doctrine of "original sin." For Huxley, our original sin is that we are born not as humans, but as primates.

Today, many quite intelligent men believe that the doctrine of original sin is sheer nonsense. But what arguments could any modern skeptic use against Huxley's version of original sin, which, unlike Augustine's, does not require us to believe in a fable about talking serpents and forbidden fruit, but simply the matter-of-fact acceptance of the law of natural selection?

If, for Huxley, our original sin is to be born as primates, then the only cure for it is to be made to feel ashamed of our primate nature. It is shame, not reason, that elevated us above the animal. Because Huxley accepted "the reality at the bottom of the doctrine of original sin," he was forced to recognize that any society, if it hoped to cooperate and thereby survive *as* a society, had to develop internal defense mechanisms that could keep in check the human animal's "innate tendency to self-assertion." For Huxley, the only viable societal mechanism that could perform this task was shame—emotionally wrenching and physiologically manifested shame. Children, from a young age, had to be taught to be ashamed of their inborn animal desire "to do nothing but that which pleases them to do." Reason, for Huxley, could not perform this service, because the instilling of shame had to begin long before the age of reason was reached; indeed, unless you first taught children to be ashamed of behaving unreasonably, what chance would you have of ever being able to reason with them? In short, without the installation of a shaming code in all members of a society, the society would merely be an aggregate of different individuals, each of whom sought only "to do nothing but that which pleases them to do, without the least reference to the welfare of the society in which they are born."

Today, in a world where shaming is considered ... well, shameful, Huxley's justification of it goes against our ethical grain. Yet before we reject his argument, we must first understand why, for Huxley, shame was such a vital element in humanity's ethical progress, and to do this we must go back to Darwin's theory of natural selection. In essence, it was shame that led to cooperation, and cooperation to group survival.

For Huxley, it was axiomatic that, all things being equal, an individual who was part of a larger group increased the chances of his survival due to the protection afforded him by the size of the group. In the struggle for survival, loners are losers. But if the survival of the individual depends on the group, then the group that can be depended on the most will give its members an evolutionary advantage over those weaker groups that lack the same cohesiveness. If you are a member of a weak group, all the members of which scatter upon encountering a band of enemies, what advantage does your membership in it give you? It is always better to be a member of a strong group, and a strong group can be defined as one in which all the members have been united by a collective shaming code. It is this code that makes the members of the group *feel* as one. They are disgusted, angered, delighted, and shamed by the same things. This unanimity of their visceral

response is what provides the powerful sense of collective identity: It makes them feel and think as a tribal Us, in contrast to
those tribes who are not disgusted by what disgusts us, or made
angry by what makes us angry, and who feel no shame at what we
think of as shameful. Furthermore, this shared visceral code,
when pushed to the extreme, makes it virtually impossible for the
individual to feel himself as an individual. Our sense of individuality is acquired by our recognition that there are differences between us and other people; but in a tribe where everyone feels
exactly the same things, how could this sense of individuality
emerge?

For example, when British psychologists attempted to give IQ
tests to individual Bushmen in Australia, they were baffled by the
fact that the entire tribe immediately gathered around the individual who was taking the test to help him with the answers. For
the Bushmen there was simply no point in letting an individual
try to solve a problem on his own—the task of problem solving
was a function of the whole tribe. And considering the challenge
of their environment, are they wrong to approach problem solving that way?

What Huxley wanted to focus on was the survival value of the
tribal mind in a world ruled by the Cosmic Process, i.e., the law
of the jungle. A tribe that shares a powerful visceral code that inhibits the natural tendency of the individual to self-assertion will
present a united front against its enemies. It will stick together
and not fragment and dissolve under stress or in the face of conflict. In a strong group, when an individual is given a chance to
desert his fellows in order to save his own skin, he will be inhibited from this act of selfish betrayal by an unbearable visceral
shame. What will keep him loyal to the group is not his higher
faculties of reflection and cogitation—all of which may be
screaming to him, "Run for your life, you fool!" Rather, it is the

physiological reactions that have been programmed into him from an early age through the process of shaming. It is his nervous system, his sweat glands, his bowels that force him to stand and fight with his group rather than to flee at the first opportunity. Yes, it can also be dubbed his code of honor—but a code of honor is just the intellectual assent to the rightness of the physiological responses his culture has implanted in him. A warrior, for example, is first made to feel shame at betraying his comrades in battle; it is only after having been programmed to feel this shame under all circumstances, no matter how adverse, that the warrior can come to take pride in the training and discipline that made him incapable of acting in his own self-interest.

Here is the flaw in any political ethic that is based on enlightened self-interest alone—the most enlightened self-interest cannot counsel a person to die for his group. Enlightened self-interest can give him good advice on all sorts of things. For example, it can counsel me not to buy strawberry milk shakes with my allowance money, but to save it up, and invest it wisely, so that I will be secure in my old age. It can warn me against taking liberties with other people who have the power to injure me. It can tell me to conceal my emotions from others, and it can urge me to feign polite emotions that I really don't feel in the slightest.

There is nothing wrong with enlightened self-interest: wherever it flourishes as an ethos, it makes the world a more civil and decent place. Yet enlightened self-interest is simply raw animal self-interest modified by good manners, and this means it can never violate the basic imperatives of raw self-interest: it can never make a rational actor go to certain death for his group or for his cause. There is no argument in the world so cogent and coherent that upon following it to the finish a person will say, "Yes, now I see—it is in my own self-interest to get mowed down by German machine guns." An individual may be willing to sacrifice himself for his comrades, for his family, for his tribe, for his country, for his cultural traditions, for his religion, but he cannot sacrifice himself for his own good.

In summary, in a world ruled by the law of the jungle, the strongest group, the one in which individuals cooperated the closest, would, all things being equal, dominate over weak groups in which such cooperation was lacking. Furthermore, in a struggle between two highly cooperative groups, that group would dominate in which some of the individuals had been subjected to a system of shaming that made them prefer the risk of physical death to the risk of social death through ostracism and public obloquy. In a life-and-death struggle between two groups, it will take more than enlightened self-interest to win the day. It will require the self-sacrifice that only devotion to a higher cause can provide.

Huxley, in making shame the basis of social cooperation, is defying the English tradition of liberalism that goes back to Thomas Hobbes (1588–1679)—a tradition that attempts to base cooperation on an appeal to reason and to enlightened self-interest. If human beings had to wait until they were reasonable enough to see the advantage of entering into Hobbes's celebrated social contract, they would long since have been made the slaves or become the lean cuisine of those groups whose social unity was based on a primordial and visceral sense of loyalty—a cohesion so intensely felt that it did not need rational arguments to create it. Or, to put it another way, those cultures animated by a high degree of what the Arab philosopher of history Ibn-Khaldun called "group feeling" would eliminate those whose fragile solidarity was based merely on the social contract.

Societal shaming, as we argued earlier, is not random; it is rule-governed, even if those who follow these rules are unaware that they are following mere conventions. Indeed, the whole point of a shaming code is that it makes the person who has internalized this code feel as if it is natural and obvious. He will feel this at the visceral level—shameful conduct will automatically trigger physiological symptoms of panic and anxiety—he will blush, break out into a sweat, have trouble breathing, feel nausea, and so forth. The preemptive judgment passed by the shaming code is not the product of moral reflection—it is like a knee-jerk reaction, but one that has been instilled by society, rather than endowed by nature. Yet it must always seem like nature. Though the shaming code produces what we call second nature, it cannot seem like second nature to the person governed by it: For him, the shaming code must always appear to be right and necessary—so much so that those raised by a particular shaming code will be shocked and horrified by anyone who violates it. The behavior of the violator will seem not merely wrong, but unnatural.

The shaming code can declare itself to us without the need for words; it does not need to be instilled in us through etiquette books or helpful advice—in fact, there is no need for words at all, since slaps and blows and angry faces are often a much more effective way of instilling the shaming code than verbal formulae. Furthermore, the shaming code is shared by others, and so it is not merely a psychological property of individuals. In this sense, the shaming code is like a language—the only difference being that while educated people know that a language is acquired, they are often convinced that their shaming code is inborn and hence natural.

The basis of solidarity in any group is the shaming code that has been instilled into all its members. Thus, any group that instills in its young a code that everyone in the group accepts as law, custom, the Tao, reason, Shari'a, or whatever, will have an evolutionary advantage in the struggle for survival, according to Huxley. It is the shaming code that makes human beings behave reasonably by the standards of their group—i.e., in conformity with everyone's expectation so that conflict will be minimized. Yet this does not mean that all shaming codes are designed to prevent violence; there have been shaming codes in which individuals have been encouraged to use violence. The master class in a society of slave owners, for example, might teach their children to use violence against their slaves in order to keep them in line. According to Evans-Pritchard, among the primitive Nilotic pastoralists called the Nuer, the parents taught their boys to be feisty and ever ready to come to blows with other boys. In the modern liberal West, however, at least among the educated middle class, such training is frowned upon, and, accordingly, people raise their children to think of violence as a visceral no-no. Their children are taught that it is not right to hit others, and that when they do, they ought to feel ashamed of themselves, as no doubt many of them are. They are even taught today that it is wrong to hit others when they have hit you. There is no better proof of the power of the shaming code than its ability to make human beings ashamed even of taking revenge—a triumph that would have made the Arab philosopher Ibn-Khaldun marvel.

In short, where you find a society that is governed by a code of reasonable and nonviolent behavior, you can be sure that the society did not get this way because everyone decided for themselves that such behavior was right; it was rather because everyone had internalized a powerful shaming code that shamed those who resorted to violence and who insisted on bullying others around.

The question, however, then arises, If reasonable conduct is the product of the shaming code, then how reasonable can it be? It has been instilled in us before we had any sense, and certainly before we had sufficient judgment of the world or knowledge of ourselves to decide to accept it. Hence, we could not have chosen it for ourselves—rather, it was chosen for us. That is why so many people find it virtually impossible to cease to be ashamed of those things they were taught were shameful early on. The shaming code is too deeply wired into us. Even when we become aware of it, and are able to criticize it as a rational actor, we are nevertheless still subject to it at a visceral level.

It is this visceral basis that explains why a shaming code, once implanted, becomes virtually impervious to reason. You cannot argue people out of their shaming code, nor change it by an appeal to logic or empirical evidence. The visceral shaming code resists all efforts to repeal it. It is tempting to speak of "the selfish shaming code" as analogous with Richard Dawkins's selfish gene, as the shaming code seems similarly designed to reproduce itself from generation to generation.

This leaves us with a problem. If the shaming code cannot be changed by reason, then it might well appear that it is itself irrational. Yet, though there is some truth to this claim, it overlooks the important possibility that I have already suggested: Just as the warrior's shaming code is designed to produce warriors, so the liberal middle-class shaming code is designed to produce rational actors. In this case, the shaming code instilled in the rational actor has not been chosen by him; it has been chosen for him. Yet while the child did not himself elect to have this particular shaming code instilled in him, the fact that he has been brought up within this code is what makes him a rational actor. Though no child can rationally choose the shaming code by which he will be brought up, there are certain shaming codes, as we have seen, that will raise him to behave and think like a rational actor—they may even raise him to become a person who is capable of thinking critically about the shaming code in which he himself was raised, as happens in the modern liberal West. Yet this is by no means how most shaming codes work. Most are "designed" to infallibly reproduce from one generation to the next what Walter Bagehot called "the cake of custom," by which he meant those rigid, unbreakable, unshakeable taboos from which no member of the society is permitted to escape, and that prohibit the emergence of independent or critical thinking on the part of any individual member. Because the cake of custom creates a uniform and petrified society, we will dub the shaming codes that produce such societies "monolithic" shaming codes. Such codes are employed to reproduce the same tribal mind, with the same tribal values and convictions, from one generation to another.

The monolithic shaming code of the tribe requires a high degree of cultural autarky. Those who obey the shaming code of their tribal culture cannot be open to new ways and customs emanating from outside. The shaming code will demand a xenophobic intolerance of foreign customs, dress, manners, and so forth—in short, what Richard Dawkins has usefully dubbed "memes." The motto of a monolithic tribal culture is that our memes are the only memes worth having; yours are abominations.

The individual, as we have come to think of him, i.e., the rational actor, has no place in any society governed by a monolithic shaming code. What freedom, in our own sense, could he possibly have? He would certainly lack the kind of liberty extolled by John Stuart Mill, namely the liberty to be different, follow your own paths, and make experiments in living your own life. But how do we explain those societies in which individual liberty was stubbornly defended, every man was his own king and thought his own thoughts in his own ways, and did things as he saw fit to do them? If the possession of a powerful group feeling achieved through a monolithic shaming code gives an evolutionary advantage to the individual through the collective protection provided by it, operating on the principle that there is safety in numbers, what becomes of the fate of the lone and rugged individual? Among the Egyptians of Lane's time, an individual who wished to adopt European dress or customs was bound to be a target of public condemnation, ridicule, and perhaps worse: however much the individual in question might have wished to "follow his bliss," and dress like a French dandy, this was not a option for him. But this negation of the individual served a collective purpose: It kept all the members of the tribe feeling viscerally in sync with one another, and prevented the emergence of groups within the community who might splinter and facture its solidarity. According to Huxley, this solidarity gave an enormous evolutionary advantage to those who had obtained it, which would explain why the society would react ferociously to any assault on it. It would act, in a sense, like the immune system of the human body: The moment it detected a foreign agent, it would not ask questions, but would straightaway attack to eliminate the intruder as quickly as possible before it had a chance to reproduce and spread.

Yet this conclusion leads us into a quandary. If a tribe can increase its chance of surviving by suppressing the individual, then what can explain the origin of those societies, like the modern liberal West, in which individualism has been encouraged; indeed, where respect for the individual is the basis of law and custom? Or, to put it in Huxley's terms, How could human beings be free to be individuals, and still cooperate enough to survive?

Those who have attempted to solve this riddle created the great movement called liberalism—liberalism in the widest sense of the word, the sense in which virtually all modern Westerners are liberals, including those who call themselves conservatives. Yet today this question remains up in the air. Yes, liberal societies can survive, because we know that for several hundred years in the West, in England, Canada, the United States, Australia, and France, liberalism has been dominant. But what does this dominance mean? Is it evidence of the irresistible march of liberty and democracy; or was it merely a fortuitous happenstance that created a relatively brief liberal epoch that is destined to pass away, the way feudalism did?

The long global dominance of our culture of reason blinds us to the mystery of its emergence, and makes it seem pointless to inquire how long and under what conditions the culture of the rational actor can survive on a planet where all living creatures, except ourselves, have been doomed to learn of the universal struggle for existence not from reading Charles Darwin, but by observing the world around them.

8

THOMAS HOBBES AND THE
POLITICS OF REASON

Thomas Hobbes, the seventeenth-century English political philosopher, aimed at creating a politics of reason. As the translator of the Greek historian Thucydides into English, Hobbes was well aware of the Greek experiments in creating viable societies in which men would govern themselves by argument and persuasion, and not by brute force. He also knew that individualism, instead of being crushed, was prized by the Greeks. The Greeks admired heroes, wise men, individuals of exceptional prowess—precisely the kind of human beings that the Wanika or the Aché do not want among them. Unlike the !Kung and the Aché, Greeks were boastful—distastefully so from our point of view. They flaunted their individuality. They tried to beat each other in competitions, and they gave praise and wrote lyric poems to the victors.

From the standpoint of a society governed by a monolithic shaming code, this emphasis on the individual's freedom could only seem like an invitation to societal self-destruction. Yet the Greek city-states were formidable contenders in the struggle for survival, and during the course of the Persian Wars, they even achieved the miracle of defending themselves against the threat posed by a great Oriental empire. How was this possible?

The Greeks, it would appear, had hit upon an effective strategy in the struggle for survival, and one superior to the monolithic tribe. What was the explanation of this phenomenon?

The traditional answer has always been that the Greeks discovered reason—not only the reason of their famous philosophers, but the reason of their wise men and political leaders. Thucydides' history of the Peloponnesian war is studded with brilliant set speeches in which various political leaders of the time attempt to use persuasion, argument, rhetoric, and logic in order to convince the other members of their community to follow the course of action that they believe to be right. Here there is no Oriental despot commanding his obedient subjects; nor is there an unthinking reliance on the cake of custom of tribal tradition. True, Thucydides wrote these speeches himself, but this in no way alters the fact that he is providing us a glimpse into a society in which reason, in our sense, is playing a decisive political role.

For Hobbes, the pressing question was, Could reason again become the basis of politics, as it had been among the Greeks? Could the divided English nation of his time listen to logical arguments, namely Hobbes's own, and be persuaded to create a new political order out of the chaos into which they had descended—that is, the Civil War, begun in 1642, that would destroy the old order of hereditary monarchy under the Stuarts.

Writing during the midst of this grave crisis, Hobbes was realistic enough to see that it was no longer possible to get people to obey their sovereign simply because he claimed to be the Lord's anointed: the divine right of kings had suffered a permanent setback when Charles I had been condemned to death by the self-proclaimed representatives of the English people. The Puritan faction had deposed the king by force of arms, and then chopped off his royal head for good measure—a drastic step undertaken for the same reasons that the French Republicans would behead Louis XVI during their revolution. Both regicides were undertaken to make sure that the monarch would never wear the crown on his head again, to guarantee that there was to be no turning back.

Yet in both cases, there was a turning back. In England and France, the monarchy returned: not the deceased monarchs themselves, but their descendants. In England, the Stuarts were returned to the throne, at least for a while, just as in France the Bourbons were restored—though again, only temporarily. In both cases there was an insurmountable challenge: How do you act like nothing has changed when everything has changed? Once the people have seen their king dethroned and beheaded, how is it possible for them ever to feel again the divinity that surrounds a monarch?

Thomas Hobbes anticipated all of this in his masterpiece, *The Leviathan*. Once the myth of the divine right of kings had been demolished in the public imagination, it was no longer possible to base political obedience on habit and custom. The interregnum—the period between the two kings—was an experience that could not be forgotten. For if the king was dead, and there was no immediate shout of "Long live the king!" to compensate for his demise, to whom did his former subjects transfer their obedience? If to no one, then you had anarchy.

Hobbes recognized that the English interregnum posed a unique political problem, difficult to solve. Even if Hobbes himself had accepted the myth of the divine right of kings, he now saw that this was an idea no longer capable of establishing common ground among a ferociously divided English public. But since Hobbes knew that people could not rule themselves without continuous discord and conflict, there had to be some other way of establishing a single ruler who would be in the position of acting as the sovereign authority. Someone had to decide those questions that divided the counsels of the people—otherwise the unity of the group would be fatally undermined.

But who? There had once been a traditional procedure in England for determining who was next in line to be king—a procedure as infallible as an algorithm in mathematics. As in the rules of succession to the presidency in the United States, every contingency was covered in advance, so that, no matter how many kings might die, you would always be able to declare "Long live the King" over someone's head, even if the someone was a three-year-old child. But who do you declare to be the sovereign if you have punctured the notion of the divine right of kings?

Wrestling with this problem, Hobbes saw no way out except through reason. And it was to the politics of reason that he devoted himself in his great work, *The Leviathan*.

Hobbes begins by assuming that every human being would like as much liberty of action as possible—a postulate that is identical to Huxley's belief that all human beings were subject to "the natural tendency to self-assertion," that is, to getting their own way. Further, Hobbes argues that each man's idea of what is right will always mean whatever he has the power to do. For any individual who is capable of forcing another to do his will, might makes right—though the victim of his aggression may feel quite differently. Hobbes goes so far as to argue that man has the "natural right" to do whatever he can get away with doing. Therefore, the only way to keep men under control is to establish an overwhelmingly dominant power that can check our "natural tendency to self-assertion," and the only effective method by which this can be done, Hobbes tells us, is by appealing to the universal human dread of violent death. Threaten to cut off people's heads and they will be far less inclined to play the role of the aggressive alpha male.

Now this is where reason comes in. I may want to do just as I like, but I don't want you to have the same liberty, since you may use your liberty of action against me—and if you are stronger, I am the loser. As a rational actor it is in my enlightened self-interest to find a way of curtailing your liberty of action, as well as that of anyone else who might be a threat to my welfare. But how can I hope to achieve a situation where everyone else except me is willing to have their liberty of action limited? This is a pipe dream. So if I am reasonable, I will recognize that I too must be willing to have my own liberty curtailed at the same time as everyone else's—in which case, the only remaining question is, Who shall have the power to force everyone else to curb and check their natural tendency to self-assertion?

Hobbes's answer is: Someone, anyone. It really doesn't matter who it is, only that everyone acknowledges that same person as the sovereign. We can take a vote on this someone and let him be chosen by a majority. Or we could agree to draw straws and give sovereignty to the person with the longest straw. Or we could choose the individual among us who was the fastest runner, or the best fighter, or the tallest, or the handsomest—it really doesn't make any difference how he is chosen, provided everyone is satisfied with the method of choice. Thus no method of choosing the ruler is more rational than another—what is rational is that there be some method, agreed upon by everyone, by which the ruler is chosen.

The second rational consideration about the sovereign is that he must have sufficient power to govern even the most ungovernable, and the only power that is capable of achieving this objective is the power of life and death. Therefore, the ruler must be granted by the community, if the community is acting rationally, the power to execute those who cannot be persuaded to renounce their natural tendency to self-assertion. Otherwise those who are the most assertive and aggressive will be able to get away with murder—quite literally, not to mention theft and robbery.

Huxley argued that shame was the original factor that curbed men's natural tendency to behave like unbridled alpha males; and, in making this argument, he hit on a brilliant point. Yet the problem with shame as a means of social control is that there can be no escape from shaming if it is to be effective. As we have seen, it must be monolithic in order to be crushing. But once the social fabric of a society has been torn to shreds, once the habits of the heart have ceased to be an infallible guide to conduct, then shaming loses its sting, and shamelessness becomes an option. Thus under disruptive conditions like those experienced during the English Civil War, or during the bouts of anarchy that swept over Greek city-states during the Peloponnesian War, such as the civil strife in Corcyra or the rule of the Thirty Tyrants in Athens, the normal defense mechanism of shame breaks down, and men begin to behave with increasing shamelessness. In such an environment, it is precisely the strongest and most ruthless who, as a matter of course, will become the most shameless.

In Plato's dialogue *The Gorgias*, the young Callicles, in attempting to rebut Socrates' ideas about justice, offers a shameless attack on the institution of shame—an attack that suggests that as a culture gets more intellectually sophisticated, shame can no longer serve its original purpose as a foolproof way of inhibiting the aggressiveness of the strong. "In my opinion," Callicles says, "those who frame the laws are the weaker folk, the majority. And accordingly they frame the laws for themselves and their own advantage, and so too with their approval and censure, and to prevent the stronger who are able to overreach them from gaining the advantage over them, they frighten them by saying that to overreach others is shameful and evil, and injustice consists in seeking the advantage over others. . . . But in my view nature herself makes it plain that it is right for the better to have the advantage over the worse, the more able over the less. And both among all animals and in entire states and races of mankind it is plain that this is the case—that right is recognized to be the sovereignty and advantage of the stronger over the weaker."

Callicles is enunciating social Darwinism without the Darwin. It is right for the strong to dominate the weak. The Cosmic Process works just fine, thank you, and there is no need to invoke the Ethical Process. But when a nimble thinker like Callicles can break free of the social control mechanism called shame, then this raises serious questions about the capacity of Huxley's shame to bring about social solidarity. It can work fine in primitive, hidebound, tradition-dominated societies in which no one is permitted to think independently of his group or to entertain his own agenda; but it ceases to function the moment people are permitted to question, argue, and debate about things. In short, shame can work effectively only until the coming of reason. But once reason emerges, then the efficacy of societal shaming is reduced: People can think for themselves, and stand by their own convictions, without feeling any hint of shame for their departure from communal orthodoxy.

Cooperation produced by shame may have been a necessary stage in the evolution of human societies, but its utility broke down once people began to think independently. Once people have made themselves capable of pursuing their individual self-interest in separation from the collective self-interest of the primordial group, how then are you to keep the individual's pursuit of his own selfish ends from dissolving the society right back to the alpha male anarchy from which societal shame had originally rescued it?

As we noted, Hobbes said the solution is to appeal to everyone's fear of violent death. If it is no longer possible to shame the strong into participating in the Ethical Process, making them desist from their alpha male ambition, it becomes necessary to threaten them with beheading or something along those lines.

Yet does this solution really meet Callicles' challenge? After all, the foundation of Hobbes's argument is that *all* men equally fear violent death, yet as Callicles could easily have argued, this is completely untrue. It is the weak and timid majority who fear violent death. The aggressive and courageous warrior elite do not fear violent death, which is why they can legitimately claim to be the stronger in the first place.

From the sociological perspective, Callicles is merely representing the perspective of the warrior aristocracy who, unlike the timid majority, have been brought up to feel no fear of violent death, and who regard this as their title to privilege. As one of the Spartan generals said in the course of the Peloponnesian War, those who are willing to risk death have the natural right to take the property of those who are unwilling to risk it. If the timid middle class was willing to stand up and fight, they could keep their property and their free status; but because they fear violent death more than dishonor and disgrace, they forfeit the right to be free and independent.

How does Hobbes answer this objection? And can he answer it?

The question brings us to the Achilles' heel of Hobbes's political theory—and, indeed, that of all subsequent attempts to construct a society solely on the basis of the enlightened self-interest of rational actors, i.e., Western liberalism. The warlike and the ruthless are prepared to die, often over what appears to the peaceful to be matters of no consequence at all—a passing slight can cause a duel to the death, an insult will end in the flourish of swords. On the other hand, as we have seen, those who are guided by enlightened self-interest alone can never be willing to face violent death. Violent death, as Hobbes correctly argued, can never be in anyone's self-interest, and, furthermore, it is what all those, except the warrior class, instinctively fear more than anything else, including loss of property and of status. So what happens when a society of warriors goes up against a society whose members are guided by their enlightened self-interest alone?

Hobbes does not deceive himself on this question. Though the sovereign may order his subjects to go into battle against an enemy, and though he may execute those who attempt to flee from the prospect of violent death, the subject himself has no duty whatsoever to face the enemy in defense of his country or his group. The social contract that the subjects entered into with their sovereign was, after all, based on a rational calculation of the subjects' enlightened self-interest. By establishing over them an authority with the power of inflicting violent death on those who could not control their aggressiveness, everyone has benefited from the social contract. It is also to my personal benefit if the sovereign executes all those caught deserting the field of battle, since this may be the only way that the enemy to my homeland may be vanquished—it is in my personal interest to keep the enemy from plundering or enslaving me. Yet can it ever be in *my* personal interest to be one of the ones who gets shot for running away? To say, "Kill the others"—that is in my self-interest. To say, "Kill me" is not.

If my sole reason for entering into the social contract is that it is beneficial to my enlightened self-interest, then I am under no obligation to do anything that violates my self-interest. While I may choose, for whatever reason, to stand and fight the enemy, I am under no moral or ethical obligation to do this. It may be prudent to stand and fight because if I don't, I will be killed; but I have no duty to die for anyone or anything.

Hobbes's appeal to rational and enlightened self-interest marks the end of the feudal system of reciprocal duties. With the collapse of the divine right of kings came the collapse of the subject's absolute duty to obey his sovereign. During the interregnum, when there is no king, to whom would this duty be owed? Who would you be willing to die for? In a world in which everyone is thrown back only on self-interest and personal survival, the only duty left is the duty to look after number one, and no one has ever died to save his own skin. In any society where enlightened self-interest rules, the heroism that is willing to face certain death becomes a moral anachronism. People may still do this, but when they do, they are violating the principle of enlightened self-interest in the name of something else.

But what chance, over the long run, does a society have of surviving if it can no longer produce heroes and warriors who, unlike normal people, do not fear violent death? If you have succeeded in creating a culture where no one is willing to risk his life for anything, then you have obtained one ideal goal at the expense of another—you have created a community of timid but peaceful cowards who won't be unruly or rebellious. At the same time, you have completely eliminated precisely the class of individuals upon whom you must count if your community is to endure in the universal struggle for survival, namely death-defying warriors. Yet if you permit these warriors within a community of the timid and the peaceful, how long will it be before the warriors have established themselves as the ruling elite, as happened among the Greeks and many other cultures as well?

How can reason solve this problem? Or is it a problem that can be solved at all?

For Hobbes, there was one absolute political evil, and that evil, as we have seen, was anarchy. Anything was better than that, because with the coming of anarchy there was a complete loss of political and social stability, accompanied by economic disturbances, not to mention bloodshed and violence. In addition, anarchy produces shamelessness, and this allowed the return of unbridled alpha male aggressiveness, what Hobbes called "the war of all against all," or what we called earlier the decivilizing process. Thus any solution that avoided anarchy was worth taking—and this, for Hobbes, was a maxim that all reasonable people would at once assent to.

The whole foundation of liberal theory is predicated on the notion that all men, being rational actors, would naturally agree with Hobbes's assessment of the horror of anarchy and dread of any interregnum. Yet to see just how illusionary this assumption of the universal horror of anarchy is, let us examine how the Ottoman Empire handled the transition from the rule of one sultan to the next.

Though the doctrine of the divine right of kings may appear to us to be the height of superstitious folly, it did bequeath to us this one invaluable rule: In order to ward off the disastrous effects of an interregnum on the state of society, never let the people doubt for a moment who is their lawful and legitimate ruler. Never, even for a split second, permit the members of a society to debate who is now in charge of them—for such a debate will always be fatal to the preservation of peace and harmony in the social order. You don't want pretenders and contenders for the crown to have to battle it out at the expense of the society.

Compare this prudent system of establishing the succession in advance with the remarkable system that was employed by the Ottoman Empire. There, when the sultan died, the rule was that his sons would have to fight it out among themselves for the title of the new sultan—and because of his many wives, each sultan would, quite naturally, be expected to have many sons. At the death of the sultan, there was no shout of "Long live the sultan," because, during the period in which the various sons conspired to kill each other off with as much cunning and dispatch as they could muster, there was no sultan. In other words, upon the death of the sultan, the Ottoman realm returned to Hobbes's state of nature, at least as far as the sons of the sultan were concerned. Nor was this merely an accidental happenstance; it was, by the proclamation of the mighty sultan, Mehmed II, the law. In short, for the Ottomans, the interregnum was not a regrettable occurrence that they would have eliminated if they had been able to do so; rather, it was their deliberate policy.

This will strike many Westerners as counterintuitive. Yet if we think in terms of the struggle for survival, it begins to make sense—indeed, perfect sense. The sultan, after all, had to be tough and ruthless. Otherwise, how could he hold his vast empire together, let alone try to expand it? But there was no greater obstacle to the cultivation of such ruthlessness than to have been raised in the lap of luxury and security, without a worry in the world, and without an enemy to one's name. The French dauphin, the heir to the throne, was brought up in a world in which everyone knew that he would one day be king—all he had to do was simply not die of smallpox or in a hunting accident. Furthermore, in order to get people to do his will, he had only to ask them nicely, and everyone around him immediately jumped to. Thus, when the ill-fated Louis XVI ascended the throne, he did so without bloodshed. He simply stepped into inherited power—it was given to him by others, and this meant that he did not have to seize it for himself. Nor, given Louis XVI's nature and education, could he have seized it for himself. As a boy, his tutor had been Fenelon, who had filled his head with noble images of the ideal king whose sole passion in life is to look after the good of his people. Thus everything conspired to make Louis XVI the kind of man who, when given the choice between civility and ruthlessness, automatically rejected the latter in the hope of maintaining the former. When he was advised to open fire on the mob during the initial riots of the French Revolution, Louis XVI protested that he could not shoot his own people, any more than he could have shot his own children—for in his mind his people were his children, and he was their father. The same humane failing would, two generations later, force Louis Philippe, the citizen king, to abdicate the throne rather than open fire on his people.

Now here we can at once see the advantage of the Ottoman system. When the new sultan had at last secured his position by murdering all his siblings and their collaborators, he was pretty much guaranteed to be a good bit tougher and more ruthless than a hereditary monarch who had obtained his crown peacefully and without contention. All Ottoman sultans, no matter how privileged their upbringing, would be forced by both custom and law to learn the secret of seizing power for themselves—and to seize it in the most violent and brutal way possible, namely by killing off all rivals.

It is as if the Ottomans had said to themselves, "Listen, we must at all costs prevent our rulers from becoming soft and decadent. If we just let them take power, then they will not know how to keep it—in order to know the secret of keeping power, you must first learn the secret of seizing it. Let us only bestow power on the one who is most accomplished in getting his bloody hands on it." In short, the Ottomans, rather than dreading anarchy as the worst of all possible ills, domesticated it for their own purposes: They used it to create an artificial struggle for existence that could be relied upon to make sure that the new sultan obtained his throne in accordance with the principles of natural selection.

This brings us back to a weakness in Huxley's criticism of the social Darwinists of his time. In "Evolution and Ethics" he argues, *contra* Spencer and his followers, that it is impossible to determine in advance what human qualities will be the "most fit" in the future. Eugenics, the alleged science of producing a superior race, is for Huxley not only ethically abhorrent, it is also scientific nonsense. As his lichen example indicates, no one can say today what biological traits will be best adapted to the environment of the future. Since we do not know the challenges our society may face over the next generations, we cannot tell what traits and characteristics in our children we should select for, and which ones we should eliminate.

Huxley poses his scientific objection in the form of a challenge. Suppose you have before you a number of boys in their early teens. You can examine them, look at them, talk to them. Yet can you decide on this basis which of them will contribute more than the others to the survival and well-being of your society one or two generations from now? For example, let us suppose that you come across a boy who is severely crippled. Do you eliminate him on the basis of his disability? You might, of course. But suppose that the child in question was the brilliant engineer Charles Steinmetz, a terribly disabled man whose inventions helped to create the technological superiority of the modern West. Or what about the always frail and sickly Darwin—by eliminating him as a boy, would you have notably improved the English race?

In dealing with an advanced and sophisticated modern society, Huxley's scientific arguments against social Darwinism are quite compelling. As in Aesop's fable of the mouse and the lion, it may look as if the mouse could never hope to repay the lion who had so generously spared him, but once the lion was in the hunter's net, he saw the error of his ways. He owed his life to the mouse's tiny but sufficiently sharp teeth. But can Huxley's argument be applied to all societies universally? The answer is no.

Consider the struggle for survival among the sons of the sultan. In this case, if you were to examine the various boys and young men who were about to embark upon their life-and-death battle for king of the mountain, you could make reasonable estimates of who was likely to survive and who was not. The timid, the passive, the slow-witted, the kindhearted, the noble, the generous, the peacemaker, the coward—these probably would not make it through the first several rounds of the brutal competition. On the other hand, those sons who displayed the opposite qualities would no doubt reap the reward of their ruthlessness, duplicity, and low animal cunning.

More significantly still, the entire political and military system of the Ottoman Empire was based on the conviction that it was possible to select the best boys, i.e., best *for the purposes of the Ottoman system*, at precisely the relatively tender age that Huxley proposed for his own thought experiment, namely, boys in their early adolescence. Furthermore, this theoretical conviction was amply proven in fact: The fundamental bulwark of the Ottoman Empire's fabulous expansion and endurance for the course of many centuries was the famous Janissaries, an elite military fraternity made up of the boys who had been selected for their "fitness." Again, though, it must be stressed that this fitness was not measured by some metaphysical standard, but was defined in practical, concrete, and instrumental terms.

Devçirme is the Turkish word for the process of culling the best, brightest, fittest, and handsomest boys from their non-Muslim subject populations. By the seventeenth century, the Greek population, whose boys were one of the favorite targets of the Ottoman *devçirme*, had coined their own word for the process, *paidomazoma*, which literally means "boy taking."

The process was precisely like Huxley's challenge. At varying periods over the years, agents of the Ottoman Empire went from village to village in the Balkans, examining the Christian boys of these regions to find those who would be the most valuable in filling important positions within the Ottoman Empire. The boys so chosen not only made their way into the Janissary corps, but were often enlisted in the Ottoman administrative bureaucracy. Up until the reign of Selim III (1789–1807), the position of a Janissary could not be passed from father to son; each new Janissary was to be freshly recruited from the subject Christian population. This restriction was designed for several good reasons—it destroyed the possibility of nepotism, but just as importantly it was essential to the Janissary's discipline and training in fanatical loyalty to the sultan. The bodyguard of Janissaries "had the task of protecting the sovereign from internal and external enemies," writes scholar Vasiliki Papoulia. "In order to fulfill this task it was subjected to very rigorous and special training, the janissary education famous in Ottoman society. This training made possible the spiritual transformation of Christian children into ardent fighters for the glory of the sultan and their newly acquired Islamic faith."

Because the Christian boys had to be transformed into single-minded fanatics, it was not enough that they simply inherit their position. They had to be brainwashed into it, as we would say today, and this could be done most effectively with boys who had been completely cut off from all family ties. By taking the boys from their homes, and transporting them to virtually another world, *devçirme* assured that there would be no conflict of loyalties between family and duty to the empire. All loyalty would be focused on the group itself and on the sultan.

Ironically, the so-called slaves culled from the Christian population flourished at the expense of the native Muslim population of the Empire. As Papoulia observed, the institution of *devçirme* "functioned as a leveling instrument on the social status of all subjects and created the necessary institutional frame for the elevation of these slaves to the status of the ruling class for more than three centuries, discriminating to the detriment of the native Muslim element. It must be noted that no native Muslim rose above the rank of *sanjakbey* for a considerable time span." Indeed, even by the time of Mehmed II, the conqueror of Constantinople, the Janissary army had acquired such political clout that Mehmed, who was himself no shrinking violet, was twice forced to accede to their clamorous demands for a raise. He had no choice.

The worldly success of the *devçirme* would appear to challenge Huxley's attempt to refute the social Darwinists. Yet, as was stressed above, the culling of boys was done for a quite specific utilitarian purpose—to get the toughest and ablest corps of males available in order to train them to defend the sultan, the empire, and Islam. They were not looking for boys who would grow up to be billionaire computer geeks, brain surgeons, professors of quantum physics, or brilliant inventors, they were looking for boys who were the adolescent equivalent of the alpha male, what we will dub "alpha boys," the kind of boys who today, in our modern educational system, would most likely be drugged with Ritalin.

The culling of these alpha boys had two effects, both of them good for the Ottoman Empire, both bad for the subject population. By filling the critical posts in the Ottoman Empire with boys who had been selected on the basis of their intrinsic merit, and not on their family connection, the Empire was automatically creating a meritocracy—if a boy was tough, courageous, intelligent, and fanatically loyal, he was able to work his way up the Ottoman hierarchy; indeed, as we have seen, he become a member of the ruling elite, despite having the formal title of being the sultan's slave. The Ottoman Empire was both strengthening itself through acquiring these alpha boys, and weakening its subject population by taking their best and brightest. Thanks to the institution of *devçirme*, the more "fit" Christian boys who would be most likely to be the agents of rebellion against the Empire become the fanatical Muslim warriors who were used to suppress whatever troubles the less "fit" Christian boys left behind were able to cause.

Of course, it is impossible for those who value and respect what Huxley called the Ethical Process not to shudder at the very idea of stealing other people's children, forcibly converting them, training them to be fanatical and ruthless warriors, and employing them to suppress the communities of their biological origin. Yet from the point of view of the Cosmic Process, the system was a machine of ruthless efficiency in the struggle for survival and supremacy, and it well explains the immense power that the Ottoman Empire was able to wield as long as it remained true to this ethically repugnant (to us) institution.

Reflecting on the success of *devçirme*, the social Darwinist can reply to Huxley: You have a point about modern societies. You may well be right about liberal societies in which people depend on reason, persuasion, and logical argument rather than brute force to get their way. But you don't have a point if we are discussing a world in which the Cosmic Process is still dominant—a world in which the universal struggle for existence is the name of the game. In such a world, it is quite easy to pick which of the adolescent boys you want to have on your side—the high-energy alpha boys who display guts and loyalty. Boys who, instead of being loners and isolated dreamers, feel an intense camaraderie among themselves, who have team spirit, and think in terms of the All for One, and One for All maxim of Dumas's Three Musketeers. The boy who wanders lonely as a cloud, or who doesn't like the rough play of the alpha boys—they are the ones that you can leave behind in the village. So long as you can keep the alpha boys on your side, you will dominate. That is, so long as you are still living in a dog-eat-dog world.

Huxley pointed to shame as the mechanism by which the alpha male in us all was to be curbed and controlled; but in the system to which the Janissaries were exposed, shame was used to produce the opposite effect. Here the alpha boys were made to feel ashamed of failing to act the part of the alpha male. They were made to feel shame at the fear of even the most violent death. And the same was true for the boys who were trained in the Spartan *agôge* as well as boys brought up to be samurai warriors in feudal Japan. In all these instances, shame, rather than promoting egalitarian harmony, was employed to give a warrior class an indispensable confidence in their own ethical superiority, the all important psychological sense of entitlement. If they did not feel superior, they would not act superior—and if they did not act superior, they could not fulfill the essential function of any ruling elite, which was to make other people *feel* their own abject helplessness and by their own visceral response to acknowledge their inferiority. Brute force is never enough to sustain a ruling class—those who are ruled must genuinely feel their own lowliness and inadequacy.

Here too we can see clearly another weakness in Hobbes's attempt to create a politics of reason. Hobbes's sovereign is in the same pickle as the sultan. He is only one man. Theoretically, Hobbes's sovereign is an autocrat—his word is everyone else's command. Yet how can one single man hope to have this kind of power? As Jean-Jacques Rousseau (1712–1778) pointed out in his essay on the origins of inequality, even the strongest man must eventually fall asleep—and his sleep would liberate even the most cringing slave: hence physical strength cannot give anyone this immensity of power. So by what means can the sovereign play the role that Hobbes intends for him?

Hobbes says that everyone else in the community agrees to turn over their own power to him; but that, again, is merely in theory. This voluntary acceptance of the sovereign by the community is still an expression of the will of the community—it is not an indication that the members of the community viscerally feel their own abject wretchedness in contrast to the sovereign's equally visceral conviction of his own inherent superiority. Instead, the social contract is an arrangement made by the members of the community—it is purely instrumental, and it in no way establishes the all important psychological sense of entitlement in the sovereign, and a sense of abject helplessness in the subjects. The psychological relationship is not that of master and slave, or aristocrat and peasant, but of a CEO and the other head officers in a modern corporation.

This lack of a visceral foundation for the superiority of the sovereign undermines his hold on power. His subjects do not obey out of a visceral sense that they are worthless and that he alone is entitled to rule—his subjects obey merely because it is in their enlightened self-interest to obey. But what happens when it is not in their enlightened self-interest to obey? Yes, we have all agreed, as rational actors, that it is reasonable for there to be one man in absolute control, since he can overawe troublemakers; but what happens if I am the one accused of making the trouble? Will I feel that it is reasonable for him to overawe me? Or will I feel it reasonable to resist him as best I can? Especially if the sovereign is threatening me with his trump card, namely, the certainty of a violent death. Am I to resign myself to my own beheading? Of course, if *you* are the troublemaker, I can easily resign myself to *your* beheading—your beheading is in my enlightened self-interest, since it is a guarantee of order and stability in my community. But, once again, how can my own beheading ever claim to be in my enlightened self-interest?

Furthermore, let us suppose that I am part of a group, all of whom have been condemned to death by the sovereign. Do we calmly say, "It is in our long run best interest to all hang from a gibbet?" Or do we follow the new course that our enlightened self-interest now strikes out for us, and try to overthrow the sovereign? When presented with a life-or-death option, even the most enlightened self-interest must choose life over death, in which case the exact same reason that originally urged us to obey is now urging us to rebel.

And why not rebel against the sovereign? Recall that, in Hobbes's politics of reason, the sovereign exists only for the utilitarian purposes of providing for law and order. Unlike a king or a sultan or a pharaoh, there is nothing intrinsically special about him. *We* have chosen him—but, having chosen him, are we not free to change our minds? Yes of course, we did promise and make a contract. But, Hobbes argues, no one can rationally make a contract that requires him to die in order to fulfill it.

This line of thinking leads directly into *The Second Treatise on Government* by Hobbes's successor, John Locke (1632–1704). Locke held that the people have the "natural" right to dismiss their rulers at will—to chase a king from his throne, and to invite another one to take his place, as the English did during the Glorious Revolution of 1688. But wasn't this revolutionary thesis simply the logical consequence of Hobbes's notion of the social contract? If the sovereign originally derives his power from the

rational consent of the governed, and if he retains his power only
so long as they virtually all continue to consent to his governance,
what happens when the governed change their minds? The consent was given in the first place out of utilitarian calculations—to
have a single authority would be in the general welfare. But if the
single authority is no longer in the general interest, then what is
to keep the people from rebelling—and doing so for the same
reason that they entered into the original social contract? Thus,
the politics of reason that Hobbes hoped to construct can never
provide the stability that Hobbes was hoping to achieve—the
kind of stability that was secured by the doctrine of the divine
right of kings. If legitimate authority was ordained by God, then
it was beyond the reach of mere human beings; if it was conferred
by human beings, it could also be taken away by human beings.
But in this case, on what can the sovereign rely to maintain law
and order? If reason cannot support his authority, then what
choice does he have but to resign, or to defend his authority by
brute force, relying upon the maxim that governs the struggle for
existence: Might Makes Right?

In summary, when the politics of myth fails, then there is no
choice but to turn to the politics of reason. With the collapse of
the myth of the divine right of kings, Hobbes was compelled to
turn to reason. But as we have just seen, the politics of reason ends
by justifying rebellion against any and all forms of authority. Yet
recall why Hobbes originally turned to reason—it was in the
hopes of restoring order during periods of anarchy. A divided society is a society where individual life was fraught with danger; it is
also, however, a society that was collectively at a great disadvan-
tage in a struggle against an enemy that was not torn apart by civic
conflict and feud. A house divided against itself cannot stand—one
of the oldest pieces of mankind's accumulated political wisdom.
But how can a house not be divided against itself if every one of its

inhabitants is pursuing his own rational self-interest, instead of each putting his all at the service of the house itself?

The critical sense of tribal solidarity cannot be created by a social contract. The independence and autonomy of the rational actor disqualifies him from the capacity to feel and think as one with his tribe. Essential to the evolutionary success of the tribal mind, however, is precisely a radical distinction between the tribal Us and the dangerous outsiders who were Them. This Us versus Them mentality creates the rigid distinction between friends and enemies that is characteristic of the tribal mind, and along with this distinction comes the establishment of two totally different rules of conduct and engagement. Within the tribe, members will cooperate; they will not steal from or kill each other. They will generously offer assistance to other members of the tribe when the need arises. They will avenge the death of their own tribesman, and they will feel that this is one of their most sacred duties.

This same ethos is at work in the artificial tribe, like the Janissaries, and indeed may be said to reach its peak of perfection only in the artificial tribe. Artificial bands of brothers, bound by a sense of group loyalty, are often far more united than quarrelsome and sometimes fratricidal biological brothers. Furthermore, their division between Us and Them can often be far more radical. The Ottoman Janissaries intensely felt themselves to be the elite and the elect.

But there is a further advantage to the artificial tribe. Because it does not depend on biology, there is virtually no limit to the size that can be attained by the artificial tribe. A blood tribe can produce only as many warriors as can be made out of the raw material provided by the male offspring of the women of the tribe. But an artificial tribe, as we have seen in the Ottoman example, can tap into the biological reservoir of all the peoples and tribes that they have under their control. By taking other people's sons, and instilling in them the shaming code of the Janissary, the Ottomans could create an army that far surpassed the manpower that even the largest blood tribe could produce.

The fanaticism of the artificial tribe is the key to understanding the remarkable success of Islam. Islam began as an artificial tribe that was highly self-conscious of its difference from the blood tribes from which it recruited its new members. Gustave E. von Grunebaum describes the early phase of Islam: "Gradually men of position in Mecca joined the community of slaves, derelicts, and foreigners dedicated to the service of the one merciful and omnipotent God. . . . Common creed and common suffering welded the group together. Their loyalties went out to their co-religionists rather than to clansmen. The prayer ritual that set them apart drew them together."

The artificial tribe cannot depend for its solidarity and cohesion on mere biological affinity. It must find another way of making the various individuals who join it feel and think as one. The Islamic solution to this problem was to create a set of new traditions and customs that required the fanatical allegiance of the new converts to the artificial tribe. The worldly success of the tribal mind demands a rigid Us versus Them distinction, but the Us versus Them distinction in Islam could not be the product of biology; it had to be created by instilling a rigorous visceral code that commanded Muslims to do what other people did not do, such as perform the Islamic prayer rituals, while at the same time ferociously prohibiting many things that other people felt were perfectly acceptable, such as drinking alcohol or burying female infants in the sand.

The nineteenth-century French historian and philosopher Ernst Renan is among the rare liberal thinkers who has attempted to make sense of fanaticism as a historical and cultural phenomenon, and to view it with genuine sympathy. In his *History of the Hebrew People*, Renan argued that fanaticism has played a dialectically necessary role in human ethical progress. Yes, he admits, the Hebrews were fanatics; yet without their fanaticism, how could they have preserved their high ethical standards from being diluted by a misguided toleration of those with lower standards? The same thing may be said about early Islam. It was only by implanting a code of fanatical devotion to the religion of Allah that Islam could fight against the natural tendency of its new converts to backslide to their native tribalism: A convert to Islam had to renounce his own tribe, both physically and spiritually. Yet this fanatical code was also the secret of Islam's ability to expand far beyond the limits of the largest blood tribe. It was not a man's blood or race that made him a Muslim; it was his willingness to follow fanatically the customs and traditions of Islam. In the artificial tribe of Islam, it was fanaticism that replaced biology as the foundation of group feeling and solidarity. But clearly such fanatical devotion to Islam demands that the individual submits and rejects the rational actor. The rational actor, because he insisted on his independence, could never fuse with the artificially created tribal mind of the Islamic faithful—he would remain an outsider, and as such, an enemy.

According to the myth of modernity, the rational actor represents a higher stage of social or psychological evolution than the tribal actor. But against this optimist scenario, the social Darwinist has a powerful objection. The optimist scenario assumes that the rational actor will be living in an environment where the law of the jungle has been virtually repeated. He does not have to struggle against fanatics, let alone against disciplined troops of fanatical warriors, like the Janissaries. But what if he suddenly finds himself in the midst of the jungle once more?

Rational actors, and communities made up of them, want law and order, stability and predictably. They will be the natural enemies of anarchy, and the use of lethal violence to impose one's will on others. But as we have seen from the Ottoman example, there is nothing natural about this horror of anarchy. On the contrary, anarchy is the way for the violent and the ruthless to get ahead. If these techniques work for you, why not employ them? The Ethical Process might disapprove, but the Cosmic Process is sure to absolve you.

Here is one of the illusions that is most difficult for the rational actors of the modern liberal West to understand. There are those who thrive on anarchy, because it opens doors to them that would otherwise be closed by the status quo. They do not have the same universal dread of anarchy that Thomas Hobbes tried to make the basis of the liberal state. They seek it out and stir it up. They do not enter into social contracts in order to avoid it, but rather are willing to tear up all promises and pledges if it helps advance the cause of disorder and confusion. To us, anarchophiles represent the Radical Other, which is why we are so reluctant to recognize their existence.

The rational actor finds the social contract theory of the state quite convincing; but then this is because it suits his needs and purposes as a rational actor. But by its very nature, the social contract can never ask the individual to make the ultimate sacrifice. The fanaticism of the artificial tribe, on the other hand, requires that the faithful be prepared to make just this sacrifice, which brings us back to the challenge posed by the Chechen terrorists: Who will win in the end, the rational actor or the fanatic?

In summary, the politics of reason, as conceived by the rational actor, would appear ultimately to be a prescription for suicide in an environment in which the Cosmic Process was dominant and the struggle for existence was the law that governed all. It would fragment and divide, just when there was a need for unity and cohesion. It would urge individuals to pursue their own selfish good precisely at the moment when they should be preparing to sacrifice for the general welfare. The politics of reason may not be a rational adaptation to the law of the jungle. On the contrary, it becomes the height of irrationality when viewed from the perspective of group survival.

Yet as we all know, the modern liberal West, composed of rational actors engaged in the politics of reason, has come to dominate the world. But this could only have come about if, at least in certain parts of the West, entire cultures had been able to lift themselves out of the jungle, abolish the rule of the Cosmic Process, and institute the Ethical Process as the norm. Yet by what set of miracles did this come about?

We can accept that the West is unique; we can even hold that it is ethically superior; but this still leaves one big question outstanding. What does the triumph in the West of societies of rational actors mean in terms of the overall pattern of history? Does it represent an irresistible trend, or the hand of providence? Or is it simply a peculiar cultural configuration that, like other societies, will have its day in the sun, then disappear from history as a living form?

Basically, there are two ways of answering this question.

First, there are those who have argued that the universal destiny of mankind is to escape the law of the jungle, i.e., the Cosmic Process, and to enter into a golden age in which the lion lies down with the lamb, and the Ethical Process governs all human affairs, without exception. On this reading, the triumph of reason in the West is simply a predestined step on the ladder of civilization: The West is unique in having reached this rung first, but all others will inevitably follow in due course. This optimistic view of human history was the one embraced by many thinkers during the period known as the Enlightenment, and in particular, by Condorcet.

Second, there are those who have argued that the West's escape from the law of the jungle was a fluke. On this reading, societies dominated by rational actors, far from representing the universal destiny of mankind, will always be the exception and not the rule. There is no reason to expect that the human future will differ very much from the human past in this respect. True, there may be times when the Ethical Process has clearly gotten the upper hand; but these are seen only as temporary respites, before the return of the jungle brings with it a resumption of the Cosmic Process.

Which view is right?

The myth of modernity is an expression of the optimist view. But there have been philosophies of history, such as those developed by Ibn-Khaldun, Giambattista Vico, Oswald Spengler, and Arnold Toynbee, among others, who have argued the pessimistic view that mankind will cycle forever between periods in which the Ethical Process is in the ascendant, and those in which the Cosmic Process again sweeps away all before it.

Though the question may seem to be a debate between philosophers, there are few questions more deserving of urgent inquiry than the one I have just posed. If the myth of modernity is right, then the worst that can await us in the future are merely a few more inconsequential clashes between the modern West and those who are futilely resisting inevitable modernization. But if the myth of modernity is wrong, then we may well be facing a crash of civilization that will result in a full-scale return to the law of the jungle and triumph of the Cosmic Process in human affairs. And what question can possibly be more important than that?

Today the challenge to the myth of modernity is not arising from philosophers quietly meditating on the meaning of history. It is arising from the fanaticism of radical Islam, and it is operating on the same principle that every warrior culture has adopted. It is teaching and training alpha boys to be willing to die. It is steeping them in myths of heroic self-sacrifice and martyrdom. It is producing a new generation of Muslims who bitterly resent Western modernity, and who have dedicated themselves to destroying it. Radical Islam does not speak the language of the balance of power, but of conquest. If it succeeds, and the West fails, then the fate of the rational actors will be grim.

In Part Three, we will go back and examine the origin of the myth of modernity in the European Enlightenment, when intelligent thinkers first argued that humankind had reached a point where ethical progress would become inevitable. Among these arguments we will come across much that is naïve and overly optimistic, yet we will also find something that many "enlightened" intellectuals today will find deeply offensive—namely the idea that certain nations of the West had reached a state of ethical and moral progress that was far and away superior to that which had been reached by any other culture in human history, and the West therefore had a duty to help the rest of the world to become like itself.

Today we regard as enlightened those who emphatically deny the ethical superiority of the West. Yet the men who first enlightened us did not feel this way themselves. On the contrary, they had no doubts whatsoever that their culture was superior to all the other cultures in the world, in which case it is hard not to wonder, Who speaks for the Enlightenment today?

Part Three

The Origins of Popular
Cultures of Reason

9

CONDORCET'S TENTH STAGE

A cardinal tenet of the Enlightenment was that, thanks to the Enlightenment itself, mankind had reached a point where reason was no longer in any danger of disappearing. A corner had been turned, and there was no going back to the Dark Ages. Reason, once it had shone forth in the world, could never again be eclipsed. Though the cultures of reason established in the ancient world—the Greeks, the Romans—may have been overwhelmed by barbarism, superstition, prejudice, and folly, this could never occur again. History, instead of cycling back and forth, would now have a straightforward trajectory.

Modernity begins with the proposition that, even if all men are not born reasonable, they can be made so with the proper education. No longer would cultures of reason be restricted to an elite; they could be indefinitely extended to all the members of society, and indeed to all the people in the world. There were no more natural slaves. All human beings were born to be free, and it would be reason that freed them.

To us this proposition has become a platitude, but to many intelligent thinkers of the eighteenth century, it seemed like a paradox. It assumed that reason would be able to hold sway over the masses, even though these same masses were at the time filled with violent prejudices and subject to irrational superstitions. Who could take seriously the idea that the masses could become enlightened?

Prior to the French Revolution, the French philosophes had uniformly assumed that if the world was to become enlightened, this could only occur through the agency of "enlightened despots." To us, this very phrase sounds like an oxymoron, but we must recall that Voltaire put his hopes in Frederick the Great, while Diderot enthused over Catherine the Great; both leaders controlled their nations with an iron fist. Yet why did Voltaire and Diderot single out despots as the vehicle by which enlightenment would be brought into the world? Why couldn't democratically elected leaders fill the bill? Or even constitutional monarchs? What made it necessary to place their hope in absolute despots, over whom the people exercised no control whatsoever?

The answer was, the people themselves. It was their ignorance and prejudice that made the enlightened despot necessary. If you asked the people how they thought their society would be organized, they would insist on retaining those very traditions, prejudices, and superstitions that enlightened thinkers sought to uproot and destroy forever. The people, if left to themselves, would reject enlightenment and vote to maintain their bondage under a religious authority for which they held a superstitious respect. In order to liberate the people from this subjection, you could not ask for their advice or their

approval, or even their consent. You had to force enlightenment on them—as the Austrian emperor Joseph II attempted to
do during his tumultuous reign. The enlightened despot had to
make the people take enlightenment the way an adult makes a
child take medicine.

The justification for this approach was that, ultimately, enlightenment was in the interests of the people. Yet the short-term
backlash against such high-handed attempts to impose new models of society upon intransigent people made it plain that even the
most sincerely motivated of enlightened despots was limited in
his power to reshape a culture. But if despots armed with the
power of the modern European state could not enlighten their
own subjects, who could?

It was Condorcet, the French philosophe, who attempted to
solve this riddle. He was among the first to argue that public education, undertaken by a secular state, should be used to wean children away from the superstition, prejudice, bigotry, and
fanaticism of their parents. Condorcet provided the first great
practical design to create not merely isolated pockets of reason,
such as existed among the Greek ruling elite, but an entire culture of reason. Reasonableness would be the shared ethos of all
members of the society, and not merely an enlightened elite—
though it was the job of the enlightened elite, needless to say, to
direct and guide the process of popular enlightenment.

Significantly, Condorcet was also the first thinker to challenge
the pessimistic view of history—and to base his own historical optimism on what he considered the "inevitable" triumph of reason
over superstition and prejudice. It was reason that provided an escape from the historical pessimism of an Ibn-Khaldun or a Vico,
because reason, being a universal endowment of all humankind,
needed only to be liberated from the shackles of superstition and

the dead weight of tradition in order to usher in the final stage of history.

Marie-Jean-Antoine-Nicolas Caritat, Marquis de Condorcet, was born on September 17, 1743, the son of a French aristocrat who had married a wealthy middle-class widow. He was sent to a Jesuit preparatory school at Rheims, and was subsequently enrolled in the Jesuit College of Navarre in Paris. When he was sixteen, Condorcet gave a brilliant defense of a mathematical thesis before a group of mathematicians, and at the age of twenty-two he published his first work, *Essay on Integral Calculus*, followed by several other works in the same field that were admired by the leading mathematicians of his time, including Jean-le-Rond d'Alembert and Joseph Langrange. At twenty-six, Condorcet was elected to the prestigious Academy of Science, and his admirers saw him as a potential rival of the great Descartes and Pascal in the field of mathematics. Yet at age twenty-eight, Condorcet abandoned mathematics and turned his attention to the problems of social science, though he did so in the hope of applying the rigorous logic of a mathematical mind to the conundrums posed by human existence. In short, Condorcet became a philosophe, devoting himself to economics and to dreams of reforming the world along the lines that we today clearly recognize as liberal. For example, in 1781 Condorcet published an essay attacking slavery and the slave trade, while in another pamphlet he came down on the side of religious tolerance by urging the elimination of legal discrimination against French Protestants.

A friend of Condorcet wrote that his face "plainly showed that goodness was the most distinctive and the most decisive characteristic of the man's soul." He was very kind to animals, and though he enjoyed hunting, he gave it up because his sensitive nature could not tolerate the cruelty. In a letter to his daughter,

Condorcet told her to guard "in all its purity and strength the sentiment which makes us sensitive to the pain of all living things. Do not limit yourself to sympathy for human suffering but let that sympathy extend to the sufferings of animals." Another comment on Condorcet's nature again showed him as the passionate reformer. "His usual calmness and moderation was transformed into fiery ardor when it was a question of defending the oppressed or of defending what was even more dear to him, human liberty and unrewarded virtue." Liberalism was, for Condorcet, not a set of ideas, but a temperament, a sensibility, a way of life.

When the French Revolution came, Condorcet did not play a major role on the order of Marat or Danton, but he was unique in being the only significant French philosophe who played any part in it—many of the earlier philosophes, like Voltaire, Diderot, d'Alembert, Turgot, and others, were long dead by the time the Bastille fell. During the period of the Constituent Assembly (1789–91), Condorcet's political opinions were quite advanced. No longer content with the ideal of a constitutional monarchy, he advocated the creation of a French democratic republic based on universal manhood suffrage—a radical idea at the time. Furthermore, in 1790, Condorcet, with the dauntless consistency of his mathematically trained mind, took what seemed to him to be the next logical step, and wrote an essay titled *On the Admission of Women to the Right of Suffrage*, in which he argued that, since women were also human beings, they possessed the same natural rights as men. Therefore if all men had the right to vote, so too should all women. Here Condorcet was anticipating by several generations the argument that John Stuart Mill would make in his essay, *On the Subjection of Women*, and, in this respect, Condorcet clearly represented a position that, while shocking even to his revolutionary contemporaries, has become a commonplace of our time.

Perhaps Condorcet's most significant contribution to the liberal legacy of the French Revolution came when he wrote the report on education that had been requested by the French Assembly—a report that is universally regarded as "a landmark in the history of education." In this report, Condorcet outlines the program for education that, while revolutionary at the time, has been universally adopted by all Western nations. In many ways, it is precisely this program of education that constitutes the modern liberal West, though it took more than a century before it could be achieved, even in advanced nations like the United States or England. Condorcet's proposal was straightforward: The government should establish a national system of education. It should cover primary, secondary, and higher education. It should be free, secular, and offered both to boys and to girls equally.

Up until Condorcet's program, it was assumed that education was the natural function of the Church, and that the whole point of education was to instill a respect for traditional authority. This had certainly been the kind of education that Condorcet had received from the hands of the Jesuits, though it was emphatically not the kind of education that he wanted to establish in the future France that the French Assembly had set out to construct. But what kind of education did he want?

To us, the concept of public, secular education has long been stripped of its revolutionary associations. It is the norm, and, like all norms, it arouses no passions, either for or against. But in eighteenth-century France, Jesuit education was not only the norm, but the rule; there were no alternatives, except to hire a private tutor. That is why the first French thinker to propose the idea of secular education, Réné de le Chalotais, in his *Essay on National Education* of 1763, had an explicitly polemical purpose in mind: He wanted to used the state's own secular system of education to combat and oppose the immense educational influence of the Jesuits. In other words, the point of national education was not simply to educate children; it was to keep the Jesuits from miseducating them.

Jesuit education was designed to serve the purpose of the Church. It was a form of indoctrination. Its goal was not to teach young people to think for themselves, but to control their minds—to brainwash them. Or such, at least, was the attitude of those who were vehemently opposed to that system, foremost among them Condorcet, himself the product of the Jesuits. Indeed, Condorcet, like modern liberals, was vehemently opposed to any form of religious instruction taking place in the public schools, and to make absolutely certain that public education remained secular, Condorcet's proposal recommended that priests be forbidden from teaching in the state-operated schools.

At the same time, Condorcet was opposed to using public education for any form of indoctrination, political as well as religious. As J. Salwyn Schapiro has admirably summed it up in his book, *Condorcet and the Rise of Liberalism*, for Condorcet "the aim of all education was to produce a type of mind, free, liberal, and critical, that would be able to carry on the progress of mankind without the hindrances of tradition and faith. To him, as to the other philosophes, the past was not the light of experience but the darkness of prejudices, from which the eighteenth century had succeeded in emancipating itself. He feared the creation of another past, equally vicious, unless every generation was taught to evaluate the existing ideas and institutions in the light of the latest scientific knowledge. Instruction should, therefore, be given in a critical, and not in a conforming spirit ... the teacher should encourage his pupils to study in a spirit of *libre examen* in order to avoid traditional ideas and consecrated attitudes that are generally favored by those who wish to perpetuate existing abuses."

Whereas education had previously been the transmission of traditional authority, its new goal for Condorcet and his followers became the exact opposite. The whole point of secular education was to get students to question authority, to open their minds, to dare to think for themselves. In Condorcet's words: "The aim of education is not to instill admiration for the existing political system but to create a critical attitude toward it. Each generation should not be compelled to submit to the opinions of its predecessors, but it should be enlightened so that it could govern itself by its own reason."

In addition, Condorcet also insisted that public education should not be aimed at the elite, but at enlightening the masses. "Public education is a duty that society owes to all citizens," Condorcet's report begins. Its objectives are "to assure to each one the opportunity of making himself more efficient in his work; of making himself more capable of performing his civic functions; and of developing, to the highest degree, the talents that one has received from nature, thereby establishing among the citizens actual equality in order to make real the political equality decreed by law." Public education, in short, was to be "the door of opportunity" through which everyone, even the poorest children, could pass in order to reach the highest degree of development of which he was capable.

Yet there was another political virtue of universal education that Condorcet stressed. It was the only surefire method by which the dangerously volatile mob mentality could be permanently eliminated from the body politic. "Only by means of education could a turbulent, unruly, superstitious populace be transformed into an orderly, enlightened, and self-contained people," as J. Salwyn Schapiro put it, again summarizing Condorcet's position. In short, according to Condorcet, public education would be the cure for the social pathology known as fanaticism and intolerance, mob violence and irrationality. By instructing the children of a society to think for themselves, question authority, overthrow superstition, and examine each issue critically, the day would come when the entire populace of a nation would no longer need to be guided and ruled by an elite, but could "govern itself by its own reason." And with the disappearance of the last ruling elite, the era of true liberty, fraternity, and equality would descend upon the planet.

Many enthusiasts, in the early years of the French Revolution, thought that this millennial day had already arrived. So convinced were they that a new epoch of humankind had commenced that they discarded the old Christian calendar and instituted a new one; 1793 became the Year One. Yet that same year, the Revolutionaries were becoming bitterly divided between political factions and ruthlessly ambitious individuals. The Jacobins and the Girondins engaged in ferocious battles from which Condorcet vainly tried to distance himself. Robespierre attacked him as "a timid conspirator, despised by all parties, who works ceaselessly to darken the light of philosophy by means of the perfidious rubbish of his paid-for rhapsodies." Marat called Condorcet "a consummate Tartuffe wearing the mask of frankness, an adroit intriguer who has the talent to grab everything in sight, a shameless impostor who endeavors to reconcile opposites."

Note that in the violent language of Marat, the mere endeavor to reconcile opposites has become a political crime. Extremism and fanaticism alone have been respectable political virtues. Moderation and reasonableness are signatures of the criminal, the timorous, those lacking resolve. Both may even be looked upon as downright treasonable.

The crisis for Condorcet came when the Jacobins used the Parisian mob to expel their rivals, the Girondins, from the Convention. Power, at this point, had come to depend entirely on who was best able to manipulate the volatile collective emotions of "the turbulent, unruly, superstitious populace." For Condorcet, this new form of fanaticism, with its political sloganeering, was no more acceptable than the old style of fanaticism, with its religious veneer—both were equally deplorable. Condorcet immediately set to work writing a pamphlet attacking the Jacobins' appeal to mob violence in order to destroy their rivals and to impose their own dictatorial regime. The expulsion of their political enemies was an act of violence, indeed, an act of treason against the state. It was nothing less than a coup d'état.

On July 8, 1792, Francois Chabot, a Jacobin deputy to the Convention, launched a virulent attack on Condorcet and advised an immediate order for his arrest. The Convention agreed, and Condorcet's august name was added to the list of those who had already been proscribed by the triumphant Jacobins. His friends made arrangements to hide him, and he found safety in the house of a Madame Vernet, where he spent the final nine months of his life. It was under these circumstance that Condorcet began the work for which he is most remembered today, his *Sketch of the Intellectual Progress of Mankind*.

No Christian martyr, approaching the end, could display a more serene faith in his God than Condorcet displayed toward Reason. Knowing well that the chance discovery of his whereabouts would lead him directly to the scaffold and the waiting guillotine, Condorcet was still able to write these remarkable words: "I have the good fortune to write in a country in which neither fear, nor expectation, nor respect of national prejudices has the power to suppress or to veil any universal truth. . . . There now exists a country where philosophy can offer to truth a homage pure and free, a worship purged of all superstition, hence a description of the progress of mankind can be written with complete freedom."

In the final chapter of his book, Condorcet, who has examined human progress up to the present, looks ahead to glimpse the future of the human mind. "Our hopes for the future condition of the human race," he writes, "can be subsumed under three important heads: the abolition of inequality between nations, the progress of equality within each nation, and the true perfection of mankind."

Condorcet's hopes, when stated abstractly, sound remarkably lofty, and frankly utopian. Yet, in the next line Condorcet rephrases his hopes in a far more realistic vein. "Will all nations one day attain that state of civilization which the most enlightened, the freest and the least burdened by prejudices, such as the French and the Anglo-Americans, *have attained already*?" (Emphasis added.) Here Condorcet is not building his own cloud-cuckoo-land out of whole cloth; he is asking whether the other nations of the world can one day achieve the level of civilization that has already been achieved in three nations: France, England, and the American Republic that he deeply admired. Far from setting up an unobtainable ideal that no society made up of real human beings can ever hope to achieve, he is presenting to the reader a concrete and embodied ideal, and this fact cannot be stressed enough.

If Condorcet was merely devising utopias that exist only in the world of fantasy and dreams, it would be easy to dismiss as chimerical the hope he is holding out for mankind's progress. But he is not doing any such thing. He is in fact pointing to three nations—flawed in many ways, as he was well aware—representing in his mind a state of civilization that is, relatively speaking, enlightened, free, and unburdened by the weight of superstition and prejudice. Thus, though he may speak of the perfectibility of mankind, it is critical to keep in mind that he is not speaking of an utterly unworldly ideal. Instead, he is asking whether it might be possible for all mankind to enjoy the same state of civilization that was enjoyed in his time by France and the Anglo-American nations.

Though Condorcet is arguably the father of Western Liberalism, it is obvious that he is not a multiculturalist. His comments continue with two questions: "Will the vast gulf that separates these people [i.e., the French and the Anglo-Americans] from the slavery of nations under the rule of monarchs, from the barbarism of African tribes, from the ignorance of savages, little by little disappear? Is there on the face of the earth a nation whose inhabitants have been debarred by nature herself from the enjoyment of freedom and the exercise of reason?"

Condorcet does not pretend that there is not a great gulf between the civilized state and that of the barbarian and the savage. For him, it would be impossible not to notice this immense divide. Yet the fact that such a gulf existed was not, for him, proof that the difference between these states arose from the natural qualities and defects of the peoples themselves. To use the language that would become popular in the nineteenth century, it was not race that explained this gulf, as the French thinker Arthur Gobineau would postulate, but culture. It is their culture that keeps men barbarians and savages; that fills them with prejudice and superstition; that deliberately raises them to be ignorant tools of a manipulative elite.

For Condorcet, it is culture that is the enemy of human progress, for culture is simply the sum of those traditions that are mindlessly passed on from one generation to another. The past is the greatest obstacle to future progress—and that is why reason is so critical. Reason always starts from scratch. It takes nothing on authority, and it is determined to be guided by its own insights. Reason represents the ideal condition "in which everyone will have knowledge necessary to conduct himself in the ordinary affairs of life, according to the light of his own reason, to preserve his mind free from prejudice, to understand his rights and to exercise them in accordance with his conscience and creed. . . ."

In a clash between cultures, Condorcet cannot be neutral. If one culture represents a state of genuine civilization, such as had been obtained in his time in France, England, and America, and the other represents the lower stages of barbarism and savagery, then Condorcet will favor genuine civilization because it is more enlightened. This, however, does not mean that the superior civilization had the right to brutally dominate or exploit those still trapped in the state of barbarism and savagery—after all, those caught up in these inferior and backward cultures have not chosen their fate; rather their fate has been thrust upon them by accident and contingency. Who in his right mind, Condorcet might have asked, would wish to have been born in Mecca or Bombay or Baghdad when they could have been born in Paris or London or Boston?

The proper attitude of those who represent the superior state of civilization is to approach inferior cultures as friends, brothers, and mentors. Condorcet writes that "vast lands are inhabited partly by large tribes who need only assistance from us to become civilized, who wait only to find brothers amongst the European nations to become their friends and pupils." But, Condorcet adds with frank realism, there are lands inhabited "by races oppressed by sacred despots or dull-witted conquerors, and who for many centuries have cried out to be liberated." Still other lands on the globe are inhabited "by tribes living in a condition of almost total savagery in a climate whose harshness repels the sweet blessings of civilization and deters those who would teach them its benefits." Finally, there are the lands occupied "by conquering hordes who know no other law but force, no other profession but piracy."

These last two groups of humankind pose the most serious challenge to Condorcet's optimistic scenario of human progress, and he is well aware of this challenge. Accordingly, he writes that "the progress of these two last classes of people will be slower and stormier; and perhaps it will even be that, reduced in number as they are driven back by civilized nations, they will finally disappear imperceptibly before them or merge into them." In short, as mankind progresses, the recalcitrant savage hordes and the barbarian conquerors will have the choice: extermination as a people, or the loss of their ancestral traditions and ways of life.

There is, however, one event that gives Condorcet pause—the one event that could prevent the completion of the great human revolution that he sees as being another "inevitable result of the progress of Europe" and America. This threat he refers to as "a new invasion of Asia by the Tartars," i.e., the Mongols or the Turks of Tartary—an invasion that would imperil European civilization with the old specter of conquering Asiatic "hordes who know no other law but force, no other profession but piracy."

Condorcet quickly adds that such a catastrophe is no longer possible, then goes on: "everything forecasts the imminent decadence of the great religions of the East, which in most countries have been made over to the people, and, not uncontaminated by the corruption of their ministers, are in some already regarded by the ruling classes as mere political inventions; in consequence of which they [i.e., the great religions of the East] are powerless to retain human reason in hopeless bondage, in eternal infancy."

Here, perhaps for the first time, a Western liberal has confidently expressed the conviction that the East could become like the West, and inevitably *would* do so. For Condorcet there is no Kiplingesque "East is East, and West is West, and never the twain shall meet." On the contrary, according to Condorcet, nothing could be easier than the mass conversion of those who have long been held in the hopeless bondage and eternal infancy of the great Eastern religions, such as Islam and Hinduism.

"The progress of these people," Condorcet writes in a moment of exceptional breathlessness, even by his standards, "is likely to be more rapid and certain than our own because they can receive from us everything that we have had to find out for ourselves, and in order to understand those simple truths and infallible methods which we have acquired only after long error, *all that they need to do is to follow the expositions and proofs that appear in our speeches and writing.*" (Emphasis added.) In short, the way to rid a Muslim or a Hindu of their fanatical intolerance and their centuries of accumulated and encrusted superstition is to provide them with copies of Euclid's *Elements*, Descartes' *Discourse on Method*, Newton's *Principia*, the French *Encyclopedia*, the French declaration of the Rights of Man, Tom Paine's *Common Sense*, the American Constitution, and, no doubt, Condorcet's own *Sketch for a Historical Picture of the Progress of the Human Mind.*

To read such a naïve and arrogant assertion is to wonder whether Condorcet could possibly have believed what he was writing. Did he really think that "the time will come when the sun will shine only on free men who know no other master but their reason; when tyrants and slaves, priests and their stupid or hypocritical instruments will exist only in works of history and on the stage; and when we shall think of them only to pity their victims and their dupes; to maintain ourselves in a state of vigilance by thinking on their excesses; and to learn how to recognize and so to destroy, by force of reason, the first seeds of tyranny and superstition, should they ever dare to reappear amongst us."

Yet of what avail to Condorcet was the vaulted force of reason while he scribbled his last manuscript in his hiding place *chez* Madame Vernet? The guillotine had been busily chopping off the heads of the Girondins whom he had defended. The force of reason did nothing to stop it. On the contrary, the men who kept it going day after day were themselves the devotees of reason, and their actions were committed in its majestic name. Condorcet was not tormented by the thought of his own death at the guillotine, but he was horrified to think that the woman who had hidden him might pay the ultimate price for giving sanctuary to a fugitive like himself. One morning, he evaded her watchful guard, and escaped from her pension wearing a disguise that granted him a few more days of precious liberty as he roamed about the quarries in Clamart, on the outskirts of Paris, hungry and weary, with only a copy of the Roman poet Horace in his pocket to console him. When he entered an inn to beg for food, suspicion was aroused by his appearance and behavior. He was arrested and taken to the prison of Bourg-la-Reine. On the following morning, April 8, 1793—or the Year One, as it was then designated—Condorcet was found dead in his cell, a little less than five months since the Festival of Reason.

What killed Condorcet is something of a mystery. He was examined by a medical officer, who stated that the philosopher had died of a blood congestion, a plausible enough explanation considering his exhausted physical state and mental anxiety. But one of his early biographers, Francois Arago, made the claim that Condorcet carried a ring with him that contained a poison, and that he had used it to commit suicide, thereby cheating the guillotine of at least one of its consecrated victims.

However Condorcet may actually have died, there remains a distinctly suicidal element to his tragic fate. A devout worshipper of reason, a zealous missionary in its cause, a faithful propagandist for its triumphant future, Condorcet was the embodiment of the reasonable man. He lived by the standards of reason; he trusted in its power; he believed that ultimately the force of reason would overcome all the obstacles that prejudice and superstition put in its path. Yet his final destiny compels us to ask, Is this what happens when too much faith is placed in the power of human reason? Does reason commit suicide when it blinds itself to the reality and the power of the irrational? By placing too much confidence in it, do reasonable men, such as Condorcet, condemn themselves to become the victims of fanaticism, prejudice, and superstition? Do these dark forces overpower them simply because reasonable men lack the imagination to take them seriously, and can see in them only childish errors and infantile mistakes— errors and mistakes that can be easily swept away by the friendly counsel and advice of reasonable men like themselves?

Today the great nations of the West have, through an extraordinary series of serendipitous miracles, fulfilled beyond his wildest hopes the dreams and visions of the Marquis de Condorcet. We are all his children; we all subscribe to his ideas; they live in us, and we live through them. To be a modern Westerner is to be a spiritual descendant of Condorcet, and this is true no matter whether we call ourselves liberals or conservatives. Who in the leading nations of the West today is opposed to free public education for all children, both rich and poor? Who wishes to revive slavery or the slave trade? Who believes that secular education is an evil to be stomped out? Who is opposed to universal manhood suffrage or free and fair elections? Who wishes to deny women the right to vote? The nineteenth-century European reaction that swept down upon the ideals of the French Revolution— Condorcet's ideals—has been vanquished by the geopolitical triumph of those nations in which Condorcet placed hope for the expansion of human progress: France, England, and the United States. Indeed, with the collapse of the Soviet Empire, the liberal West sincerely believed that it was on the verge of actualizing Condorcet's Tenth Stage of Human Progress—a fact attested to by the enormous popularity and influence of Francis Fukuyama's *The End of History*.

Yet in reviewing Condorcet's life and his ideas together, it is impossible not to feel the tragic tension between the reality of the world as it really was and Condorcet's lofty expectation for it—lofty because of his profound trust in reason. Reason for him, as it was for many intellectuals during the French Revolution, was a new religion, with its own deity, its own scriptures, and its own commandments, the moral laws that all reasonable men were bound to agree on, establishing their common sense of identity. Reason, according to Condorcet, is not just for survival, it is for the improvement of the race. It is not that men have a better chance of surviving if they are reasonable, but because, being reasonable instead of unreasonable, they have become better men. The reasonable man is a higher form of life, just as the lion is a higher form of life than the jackal.

What was it about reason that made for better human beings? According to Condorcet, it was because reason gave them independence and autonomy. Reason gave freedom—the only genuine kind of freedom, namely the opportunity to think for yourself and to control your own life. Reason freed us from bondage and slavery to others. It allowed us to be individuals.

This is a lofty and ennobling view of reason, but there are two questions that we must raise about it. First, how realistic is it? Is Condorcet indulging in another flight of utopian fancy, like his belief in the perfectibility of mankind, or is there a core of solid sense to it? Second, if human beings can be taught to think and act independently, how will it be possible to hold a society together? If the visceral solidarity of the tribal mind is conducive to success in the struggle for survival, then the independent and stubborn individual who refuses to think and feel as others feel would appear to threaten the all-important cohesiveness of his tribe. Even worse, in a society where there are only individuals, and no tribes, how can such a loose-knit aggregation hope to defend itself against an enemy who is united by their visceral solidarity, who are prepared to kill and to die for their tribe, without giving a thought to their individual self-interest?

10

REASON AND AUTONOMY

At first glance, Condorcet's vision of teaching everyone how to think for themselves may appear as an exercise in utopian fantasy. Indeed, it is difficult not to suspect that Condorcet was committing the common human error of supposing that everyone else's mind is preoccupied with the same kind of stuff as his—the worst possible mistake that a philosopher or philosophe could make. For Condorcet, it may well have been impossible to understand how people could fail to think for themselves, since, as long as he could remember, and despite his Jesuit education, he had been thinking for himself about all sorts of things. The fact remains that most people have absolutely no interest in thinking for themselves in the way that philosophers like Condorcet do. Why should they? The overwhelming number of people who do think for themselves on abstruse issues are ridiculously wrong. A man who feels that he is on the verge of perfecting his perpetual motion machine is obviously a man who thinks for himself, but he would do better taking the word of Lord Kelvin on the subject.

Yet this is not what Condorcet is really saying. To create a popular culture of reason it is not necessary to get everyone to think for themselves like philosophers and other intellectuals do. Otherwise, there could be no popular culture of reason, and reason would be the domain of a select elite, as it was among the ancient followers of Pythagoras and Epicurus.

For Condorcet, the goal of a popular culture of reason is not to make everyone a philosopher; it is to make everyone independent and capable of judging those matters that personally interest and concern them. Condorcet writes: "The degree of equality in education that we can reasonably hope to attain [in the Tenth Stage], but that should be adequate, is that which excludes all dependence, either forced or voluntary." By dependence, Condorcet means the dependence of one human being upon the opinions and beliefs of other people whom they deem as their cognitive superiors, and to whose authority they automatically accede.

Condorcet, in an admirable passage, gives us a portrait of the common man as a man of reason, though by no means what anyone would call an intellectual. "We can teach the citizen everything that he needs to know in order to be able to manage his household, administer his affairs and employ his labor and his faculties in freedom; to be acquainted with his duties and fulfill them satisfactorily; to judge his own and other men's actions according to his own lights and to be a stranger to none of the high and delicate feelings which honor human nature; not to be in a state of blind dependence upon those to whom he must entrust his affairs or the exercise of his rights; to be in a proper condition to choose and supervise them; to be no longer dupe of those popular errors which torment men with superstitious fears and chimerical hopes; to defend himself against prejudice by the strength of reason alone; and, finally, to escape the deceits of charlatans who would lay snares for his fortune, his health, his freedom of thought and conscience under the pretext of granting him health, wealth, and salvation."

Another way of putting it is that Condorcet looks upon enlightened education like taking lessons in self-defense, only unlike karate or judo, which deal with physical self-defense, enlightened education is the effort to teach people to defend themselves against those who would entrap them by beguiling their mind or corrupting their judgment. Rather than being a catechism that tells you what you must believe, enlightened education becomes a kind of mental training that permits one not to be taken in by those who happen to be better with words, or who possess a more powerful imagination, or whose cunning is more profound. It is a mental training that is necessary if I am going to be able to protect myself from those who, frankly, are smarter than I am.

Here again, Condorcet is not asking for miracles. He wants to make skepticism second nature to the entire population, so that no one in the society can be duped into becoming a follower of someone else. Once men who were formerly independent become the followers of others, then the society goes from being a culture of reason to one of fanaticism.

The essence of fanaticism is to follow blindly the collective mind without question or criticism. It is the negation of individual thinking that pays off in terms of the capacity of a group tradition to survive in competition with other traditions. The fanatic is the person who is willing to follow blindly, and to trust implicitly, and never to doubt or to question the authority of the group customs and traditions. He may never throw a bomb or burn a heretic at the stake or behead infidels, but he is still a fanatic all the same. And it is the fanatic that Condorcet's enlightened system of education is aiming to eliminate. That is its whole purpose. Eliminate the fanatic from human society, and your problems are over—everyone who is left will be reasonable enough to create at least cultures as civilized and reasonable as the France, England, and America of Condorcet's time. Without fanatics, there will be no blind followers, and thus no despot to order them around and use them to gain power and control over others. The way to protect human liberty was to eradicate fanaticism. A man would be deemed reasonable enough so long as he lacked the capacity to become a fanatic. He did not have to be a philosopher; he just had to be a stubborn individual.

The whole point of stubborn individualism is not to become someone else's dupe or patsy. It is to resist the will of others, and especially that of the imperious alpha male—the power salesman who uses every available technique to manipulate you to do what he wants you to do, to buy his bill of goods.

This explains why Protestant Dissenters played such a critical role in the formation of popular cultures of reason in England and especially in America, which they founded. Protestant Dissenters encouraged everyone in the community to be stubborn individualists. By dissenting to the opinion of those in established authority, they cultivated and passed on a visceral aptitude for intellectual independence. Dissent was in their blood, and the courage to dissent was part of their character. Carrying on their inherited tradition of independent thought, how could it be expected that they would not prove capable of questioning even the tradition of dissent itself? You cannot raise your children to be called Dissenter, and then criticize them when you discover that they disagree with you. If you teach them to follow the light of their conscience, there is nothing you can do to prohibit them from following it. Even when they disagree with your opinions, they are still honoring your commandments.

Condorcet himself recognizes the important role of the Protestant Reformation in the freedom of thought, but he emphasizes, quite rightly, that this was no part of the intention of the reformers themselves—it was completely serendipitous happenstance. This is his explanation:

> The spirit that animated the reformers did not lead to true freedom of thought. Each religion allowed, in the country where it dominated, certain opinions only. However, as these diverse beliefs were opposed to each other, there were few opinions that were not attacked or upheld in some part of Europe. Besides, the new religious assemblies had been forced to relax somewhat their dogmatic strictness. They could not without crudely contradicting themselves limit too narrowly the right of free inquiry since it was by appeal to this very same right that they had justified their own separation from the established religion. Even if they refused to give reason its full freedom, they yet allowed its prison to be less narrow; the chain was not broken, but it was less heavy and less constricting.

Yet this admission on the part of Condorcet raises an intriguing problem. An enormous step has been made in the progress of reason. With the Protestant Reformation, the goal has not yet been reached, but it is coming within sight—though, as Condorcet stresses, the increased liberty of thought is an accidental by-product of the polemical struggles of theological disputants. They wanted to impose their dogma, but could only argue for it instead—and by arguing, they invited counterarguments, and before they knew it they had created a culture of reason—a culture in which people in conflict used arguments and reasons, even if we would not admit these arguments and reasons ourselves.

What this means, though Condorcet fails to notice this point, is that here is a religious tradition, namely Protestantism, that has paved the way for the emergence of the full intellectual freedom of inquiry that became the watchword of the European Enlightenment. Protestantism was, though by accident, the vehicle of historical progress, as Condorcet defines it: It took fateful steps in the liberation of reason. For Condorcet, Protestantism was, a bit paradoxically, a progressive tradition. It was a religion that ended by producing the rare popular cultures of reason in England, America, and in revolutionary France. As Condorcet puts it: "in those countries where it had been impossible for one religion to oust all others, there was established what the dominant cult in its boldness dared to call tolerance, that is, a license given by men to other men to believe what their reason inclined them to believe, to do what their conscience orders them to do, and to give to their common God the homage that they believe will please him best. One could then profess any tolerated doctrine with a more or less complete frankness."

Then Condorcet goes on to make a remarkable statement: "In this way there arose in Europe a sort of freedom of thought, not for all men, but for all Christians; and indeed if we except France, it is only Christians who enjoy this freedom today." On the other hand, Condorcet says that "the religion of Mahomet . . . seems to condemn the whole of that vast area of the earth where its empire has held sway to eternal slavery and incurable stupidity."

Yet here is a riddle for Condorcet's own theory of history. He has stressed the difference between reason and tradition, and he has clearly indicated that he thinks tradition the enemy of reason. But here was an inherited culture—indeed, a religious tradition—that had laid the foundation of tolerance and freedom at least in

Europe, though this was not part of the intention of those who developed this religious tradition. In the case of the Protestant tradition, reason and tradition are not opposed to each other, but rather the Protestant tradition of dissent guaranteed that the battle cry of the Enlightenment was not in vain: Reason, tolerance, and humanity had already been established as a way of life for ordinary men and women in France, England, and America before anyone thought to elevate them as social ideals of universal application and import.

The chief defect of Condorcet's vision of humankind's future moral progress lies in his failure to grasp the powerful hold that the tribal mind will always command over those who have been raised by the tribal shaming code. It will not be enough for someone brought up by his tribal code simply "to follow the expositions and proofs that appear in our speeches and writing." As we argued in Part Two, the shaming code produces a visceral attitude that is impervious to reason.

For example, the early-nineteenth-century Yankee missionaries to the Hawaiian Islands tried to prevent the natives from celebrating their feasts in their customary way, namely by baking dozens and dozens of dogs, along with a good supply of pigs. Of course, the pigs were fine—despite the fact that the Old Testament quite clearly condemns the eating of pork. But eating dogs—that was too ghastly for the Yankees to contemplate. Not only could they not abide the thought of eating dogs themselves; they couldn't abide the thought that dogs could be eaten at all, by anybody.

Yet when the Hawaiian converts to Christianity asked the missionaries to explain why they wished to impose this unheard-of taboo on eating dogs, the missionaries could not even quote a biblical passage in support of this odd new commandment, Thou Shalt Not Eat Dogs. They were taken aback themselves at their own visceral revulsion. The Yankee missionaries were at a loss to explain, both to others and to themselves, why people should refrain from eating an animal that tasted good, and which was in plentiful supply. Yet, for us, the answer is self-evident: eating dog was against the visceral code that had been implanted in all Americans. Eating dog was disgusting and unthinkable—not because it was irrational, but because it was a violation of the Yankee's visceral code.

In short, Condorcet had a grossly exaggerated faith in the power of reason and argument, proofs and demonstrations, to change the deeply entrenched visceral and shaming codes of non-Westerners. He also failed to grasp that you could not make children into rational actors or morally independent agents simply by having them read proofs and demonstrations either. Here again, the making of rational actors required installing from an early age a visceral code that made children ashamed of acting like animals; ashamed of unreasonable outbursts, temper tantrums, impulsive acts of aggression, immoderate expressions of emotion, inconsiderate conduct toward others, and so on. But again this was a visceral code that parents in a community of rational actors had to instill in all their children, while the community at large had to back them up. It required, in other words, the preexistence of men and women who already lived by the visceral code of the rational actor. Yet this code, though it could be reinforced by formal education, could not have originated from formal education: instead it was the product of a unique and serendipitous set of specific historical, geographical, and cultural circumstances. The rational actor was able to emerge in certain cultures only because individuals in these cultures did not need the tribe to protect them.

But what kind of cultures permitted the individual to escape the tribe? It is this question that we will take up in the following chapter.

11

LIBERAL EXCEPTIONALISM

Senator Albert Beveridge, in his classic 1916 biography of John Marshall, describes the setting in which the future Supreme Court Chief Justice grew up.

> In the back country bordering the mountains appeared the scattered huts of the pioneers. The strong character of this element of Virginia's population is well known, and its coming profoundly influenced for generations the political, social, industrial, and military history of that section. They were jealous of their "rights," impatient of restraint, wherever they felt it, and this was seldom. Indeed, the solitariness of their lives and the utter self-dependence which this forced upon them, made them none too tolerant of law in any form.
>
> These outpost settlers furnished most of that class so well known to our history by the term "back-woodsman," and yet so little understood. For the heroism, the sacrifice, and the suffering of this "advanced guard of civilization"

have been pictured by laudatory writers to the exclusion of its other and less admirable qualities. *Yet it was these latter characteristics that played so important a part in that . . . great experiment of making out of an inchoate democracy a strong, orderly, independent, and self-respecting nation.*" (Emphasis added.)

Future president James Madison discovered one of these less admirable qualities the first time he ran for an elective office. The custom at the time was that a candidate would provide enough alcohol to get his constituency properly drunk before they voted for him. Madison, fresh from Princeton and full of his high Republican ideals, disdained to stoop to such means to procure votes for himself. He lost by a landslide. The next time he did not make the same mistake. The voters, after all, were not interested in voting for a man who thought he was better than they were.

This is not, of course, our own idea of how free and fair elections should be carried out. But a candidate who was able to win over a crowd of drunken and disorderly frontiersmen obviously had to have tact and charm: He had to come across, even in the intimacy of alcohol, as one of the boys.

According to Beveridge, the American capacity for republican self-government arose from these far from admirable habits and mores of the backwoodsman and the pioneer. It was not because Americans were more rational than the French, or more artistic than the Italians, or more courageous than the Germans—it was because they were more stubborn, more impatient of restraint, more insistent on standing up for their rights. The primitive and coarse Americans simply refused to bow down to or follow anyone. As foreign travelers to the United States during the nineteenth century testified, there was a shocking dearth of servants in America, especially "decent" ones. Why? Because no one in the United States wanted to take orders from anyone else. To these crude early Americans, their feisty independence meant everything, and even the law was often looked upon as an infringement of their natural liberty.

At the same time, Beveridge is also offering an explanation for these early American cultural habits, traditions, and mores. The stubborn individual pioneers did not need to depend on each other in order to defend and protect their civic freedom, though they might rally together temporarily to form a militia. These militias were purely voluntary, and no one had any duty to the organization—men often served in a militia at their own good pleasure, leaving it whenever they disagreed with a commander or simply wanted to go home.

Among the early settlers in America, there was no need for that intense group loyalty that a community must feel if it is to survive in a dog-eat-dog world. Indians posed a problem for those who lived along the frontier—but it was not the same kind of threat that arises when a community of farmers is confronted by the professional army of an empire intent on turning them into tribute-paying subjects. Thus, early Americans could live in stubborn independence because they could get away with it—their pursuit of their natural liberty did not render them vulnerable to a superbly organized warrior class whose specialty was the subjugation of the unprotected. They had successfully escaped the nightmare of history, left behind in the Old World.

Beveridge's pioneer knew how to "manage his household, administer his affairs and employ his labor and his faculties in freedom," and yet he might never have stepped foot in a schoolroom. In addition, he was "acquainted with his duties" and he could "fulfill them satisfactorily." Furthermore, he could judge, and indeed he insisted on judging "his own and other men's actions according to his own lights." Nor was the rugged pioneer "in a state of blind dependence upon those to whom he must entrust his affairs," assuming that he was prepared to trust his affairs to anyone. Finally, he was able "to escape the deceits of charlatans who would lay snares for his fortune, his health, his freedom of thought and conscience under the pretext of granting him health, wealth, and salvation."

Condorcet believed that, under his system of centralized secular education undertaken by the state, everyone could be "taught" to be the kind of stubborn and skeptical individualists that the American pioneers managed to become virtually without any education at all. But can this kind of individualism really be taught as part of a school curriculum, the way world geography or chemistry is taught? Can such a spunky and obstinate attitude be taught like algebra? Isn't this like supposing that you can teach a timid and shy boy to be boisterous and aggressive?

Indeed, the question can legitimately be raised whether the pioneer's feisty independence could have tolerated anyone arrogating to himself the power to shape and mold his mind, not to mention his children's, in the accordance with someone else's enlightened ideal. After all, despite Condorcet's insistence that the aim of universal secular education was to create intellectual independence, he knew there was always the threat that the educators would use their power to influence their pupils to think the way they think. The educators themselves do not even have to be aware of the influence they are wielding; they may quite honestly think that they are helping to liberate their students from superstition and prejudice. But can they be trusted not to become a kind of new Jesuitical order, intent on imposing their own convictions and ideals on their pupils, instead of encouraging them to think for themselves?

Condorcet had argued that much of the credit for the success of the European Enlightenment was due to the emergence of "a class of men who were concerned less with the discovery or development of the truth than with its propagation, men who whilst devoting themselves to the tracking down of prejudices in the hiding places where the priests, the schools, the governments and all long-established institutions had gathered and protected them, made it their life-work to destroy popular errors rather than to drive back the frontiers of human knowledge—an indirect way of aiding its progress which was not less fraught with peril, nor less useful." Yet the enlightened educator, because he is concerned with propagating the truth discovered by other men, is not likely to question or criticize these truths himself: He simply accepts them, and sees his mission in life to propagate them to his pupils. His role as an enlightened educator further requires him to uproot the prejudices that stand in the way of his pupils' acceptance of the truth that he is committed to propagating. But, at this point, what a fine line divides the enlightened educator from the committed propagandist of a creed: the educator is not interested in thinking for himself, but in spreading the new revealed truth. Furthermore, he will seek to indoctrinate this truth in his pupils, and will have no interest in getting them to think for themselves. If the educator believes he already possesses the truth, then, by encouraging his pupils to think independently of him, he will not be freeing their minds, but leading them into error. In short, the enlightened educator will end, if he is successful, in weaning his pupil away from their cognitive dependency on their inherited tradition, but only to instill in them a new dependency on the enlightened elite for which the educator has become nothing more than a propagandist. The ultimate result of enlightened education, according to this method, will not be the creation of stubborn individuals, insistent on thinking for themselves, but

the mass production of ideological clones of the enlightened educator, who himself will be the ideological clone of the enlightened
elite on whom he is himself dependent for the latest and most up-
to-date revelation of the truth.

Herein lies the danger lurking behind Condorcet's vision of
the triumph of reason through universal, secular education. Instead of creating a nation of stubborn individuals, who can't be
pushed around intellectually, it ends by creating a new priesthood
dedicated to the mass production of faithful followers, all of
whom will automatically accept as gospel whatever party line is
fashionable at the apex of the priesthood. Right thinking has replaced real thinking as the goal of modern secular education—a
sobering reminder that what makes a priesthood so dangerous to
intellectual independence is not the creed that is being indoctrinated, but the principle of indoctrination itself.

Beveridge notes the importance to the formation of the American
Republic of the stubborn individual, who insisted on doing all his
own thinking. But where did this trait come from? Was it because
the pioneers and frontiersmen carefully followed the development of advanced European thought of the time? No, the only
book they all read was the Bible. And because the American pioneers were mainly made up of Protestant Dissenters, they each
were fully convinced that they themselves could determine what
the Bible meant, and how to apply its message in the conduct of
their own affairs. They did not need priests or experts to tell
them what the Bible said: No matter how simple and uneducated
they might be, they had been raised to believe they could figure
out what the Bible said for themselves.

Strange as it may sound, the Bible idolatry of the Protestant
Dissenters played a critical role in the formation of America's culture of reason. As we discussed in Chapter 10, the tradition of the

Protestant Dissenter is one in which each child has not merely a right but a duty to make up his own mind. The American Baptists, for example, did not believe in forcing the child to submit to his parents' religion; children had to accept Christianity into their own hearts; it was not permissible to ram it down their throats.

For Condorcet, as for Thomas Jefferson, democracy could only exist in a community made up of stubborn individuals, who did not follow party lines or vote as their leaders or priests or mullahs told them to. Therefore, the existence of a society of stubborn individuals was a precondition of democracy—a fact that challenges the optimistic idea that Jeffersonian-style democracy could be made to work in any society that lacked an abundance of these obstinate and willful men.

Alexis de Tocqueville, after his famous visit to America, had been mesmerized by the idea that the march of democracy was inevitable and irreversible, and had published these views in his famous book, *Democracy in America* in 1835. "The gradual development of the equality of conditions is . . . a providential fact, and it possesses all the characteristics of a Divine decree: it is universal, it is durable, it constantly eludes all human interference, and all events as well as all men contribute to its progress. Would it, then, be wise to imagine that a social impulse which dates from so far back can be checked by the efforts of a single generation?" But what if in America the "development of the equality of condition" has not represented a providential fact, but a number of geographical, cultural, and historical flukes, unique to the conditions found in early North America?

A decade before de Tocqueville published his famous book, the German philosopher Georg Wilhelm Friedrich Hegel, who had never visited America, came to a far more skeptical conclusion concerning the viability of taking the libertarian communities of

North America as representing the irresistible wave of mankind's political development. For Hegel, the North American experience was altogether unique and exceptional; and this fact made Hegel question the wisdom of trying to plant liberal North American political institutions in other parts of the world. Today, in the wake of America's ill-fated intervention in Iraq, many people have come to share Hegel's skepticism about America's mission to bring liberal democracy to the world. Often, however, this skepticism is based on the dangerous and erroneous idea that we in America are "better" than the Iraqis. In fact, Hegel's argument is that we were just luckier. America was born into the right traditions, at the right time, and in the right place. America could not have come into existence except when it did, where it did, and how it did.

Hegel stresses the fact that the people who first settled North America were overwhelming Protestants, and most of these, Protestant Dissenters. For Hegel, this just happened to the right tradition for a people who aspired to create libertarian societies. It was not that Protestants were better individuals, or smarter, or more likely to get into Heaven; it was not that their dogma and doctrines were theologically more sound than Catholics'. It wasn't because their God looked after them providentially better than Allah looked after the Muslims. It was simply because, first, as stubborn individuals, Protestants tended to make up their own minds, and believed themselves to be competent to do so—a result of their widespread Bible idolatry. Second, because as Dissenters they did not belong to the Roman Catholic Church or to any of the state-controlled established Protestant churches, so they had no choice but to create their own congregations and to run and manage them on their own resources. Indeed, they were quite insistent about this. Travelers from England who came to the United States in the nineteenth century were often confounded to find that Protestant congregations would arbitrarily dismiss perfectly good and learned divines for no reason—as it seemed to the travelers. But, of course, there was a reason: It was that the Protestants were fearful that their ministers, instead of ministering to them, would become spiritual virtuosi, dominant alphas who might acquire a following. Again, Protestants had a repugnance for followers. Hence their violent indignation when the Mormon prophet Joseph Smith began to attract them—and not only attract them, but form them into a paramilitary organization that would obey his every command. How can the stubborn individual survive in a world where one man has ten thousand followers who are willing to die and kill for him? The WASP horror of Mormonism only deepened with the revelation of the reinstitution of plural marriages. In their eyes, with good reason, Smith was establishing himself as an Oriental despot, complete with his harem of females and his bodyguard of loyal janissaries. Who wanted the revival of Oriental despotism in the libertarian wilderness of North America? Thus Mormonism was condemned for the same reason as popery, and just as violently. It was not an argument about theology, but about what kind of society the WASPs wanted to live in, and their answer was emphatic: A libertarian community in which no one was a follower, but everyone thought for themselves. Joseph Smith, on the other hand, insisted that he had a special relationship with God, who personally revealed truth to him, just as Mohammed had claimed. This was unacceptable to Bible idolatry because it meant that the Bible did not have all the answers; thus the Protestant scorn for the Koran-like Book of Mormon. It was not religious bigotry that led to the murder of Joseph Smith, it was the same instinctive horror that all alpha males feel when one of their numbers begins on the path toward despotism.

In North America, the triumph of Protestant Dissent was a historical accident. There was nothing inevitable about it. Indeed, the question may be raised whether the tradition of Protestant Dissent could have survived in the Old World, if there had not been a New World where it was able to flourish and prosper. In the Old World, Protestant Dissenters were either expelled from their homes, as when Louis XIV revoked the Edict of Nantes, or they faced persecution for refusing to worship in the established churches. That is why they fled to America, where they could find places in which to set up their own communities and congregations, namely in the midst of the wilderness.

The early Americans could get away with an ethos of stubborn self-dependence because in the New World there were no external threats that would have forced the rugged pioneers to abandon their individualist way of life. They could survive as individuals because they had no need to unite. Yet this, too, was not the result of the inevitable progress of reason; it was the result of geographical and historical good fortune. In the New World, the Protestant Dissenters were exempted from the cultural struggle for survival and supremacy that was the rule in the Old World, and especially in the oldest parts of the Old World, like the Levant. The New World, in short, provided an exception to the laws that had operated against stubborn individualism, and that had naturally given the survival advantage to those cultures in which the group and the tribe took precedence over the individual. In the New World, as was noted by both Hegel and de Tocqueville, people were prone to go off the deep end on questions of religion, but with the exception of Mormonism and other cults they did this acting as individuals. The New World was the home of new religions, and the wild proliferation of sects, cults, and congregations in North America is the best evidence of how completely free individuals were to customize and craft religions to their own specifications.

But if liberty of thought and conscience triumphed in America, once again, this was not because of some inevitable march of reason and freedom. It was due to the exceptional circumstances found only in North America. The success of America, therefore, did not prove that human progress was inevitable, and that all mankind would one day achieved the Tenth Stage of Condorcet. On the contrary, it suggested the exact opposite, namely that human beings can only attain to this stage when there is a serendipitous combination of freakish conditions.

This was also Hegel's conclusion: The peculiar culture found in America says nothing about the general course of human progress. In fact, for Hegel, what was most important to understand about America was its historical exceptionalism. There human beings were not locked in the brutal struggle for survival and supremacy that had long dominated life in the Old World.

"America," Hegel tells us, "is the country of the future, and its world-historical importance has yet to be revealed in the ages which lie ahead. . . . It is a land of desire for all those who are weary of the historical arsenal of old Europe. . . . It is up to America to abandon the ground on which world history has hitherto been enacted. What has taken place there up to now [i.e., circa 1830] is but an echo of the Old World and the expression of an alien life; as a country of the future, it is of no interest to us here, for prophecy is not the business of the philosopher."

Yet what gave America its exceptional status lay in several big facts that had nothing to do with the cultural tradition they brought with them, such as Protestant Bible idolatry or the Anglo-Saxon's mystical reverence for written contracts. These were all the results of geographical and historical good fortune.

First, North America was not just a New World—it was a young and fresh world, virtually free of the usual burden of history. There were no established empires to topple, only primitive native tribes to exterminate or chase off into the wilderness. Thus there was no need for a strong state for external defense. And because America was a land of opportunity for everyone who came there, the state was not charged with the job of keeping the resentful and discontented in their place.

> As to the politics of North America, the universal purpose of the state is not yet firmly established, and there is as yet no need for a closely knit alliance; for a real state and a real government only arise when class distinctions are already present, when wealth and poverty are far advanced, and when a situation has arisen in which a large number of people can no longer satisfy their needs in the way to which they have been accustomed. But America has a long way to go before it experiences tensions of this kind; for the outlet of colonization is fully adequate and permanently open, and masses of people are constantly streaming out into the plains of the Mississippi. By this means, the principal source of discontent has been removed, and the continued existence of the present state of civil society is guaranteed.

By civil society, Hegel meant the kind of minimalist Lockean government that was the ideal of Thomas Jefferson. It was the loose libertarian form of government that did not require the normal apparatus of the state. Hegel's argument is that, as long as

America had outlets for its discontented, there would be no need for the emergence of an oppressive state. Because America had a convenient remedy for those who were dissatisfied with the status quo, there was no danger that those who were deeply resentful with their position in the world would pose a political threat to the stability of the social order. Instead of rebelling against the status quo, they simply left it behind and went in search of a better life for themselves in the frontier—potential rebels became pioneers. "If the ancient forests of Germany still existed, the French Revolution would never have occurred. North America will be comparable with Europe only after the measureless space which this country affords is filled and its civil society begins to press in on itself."

In other words, in America resentment of the status quo could be relieved by moving into virgin territory where there was yet no status quo. Therefore, every man could be his own master, provided he was willing to be a pioneer. It was the land of dreams for the restless and discontented alpha boys—a land of so many hills and mountains that it seemed that virtually everyone could become the king of their own.

There was also a second factor that permitted America "to abandon the ground on which world history has hitherto been enacted," and this was its immense geographical separation from the Old World. In America, there was no need for standing armies, or for dictators, or for military elites. The only cultural predators, the native Indians, were still stuck at the stage of the tribe—and in order to deal with them there was no need to train up a special class of warriors and soldiers: Those men who knew how to use guns would be able to organize themselves into a voluntary militia, and the basis of this organization would be none other than enlightened self-interest. No need to instill a fanatical code of group loyalty in an elite class of boys—the adults, acting as Hobbesian rational actors, could deal with any threat that the native Indians posed. Therefore, as we earlier saw, stubborn individualism in the general population was not a prescription for national suicide.

The lack of cultural predators in the New World and its geographical separation made America unique and exceptional, as Hegel and many other Europeans recognized in the nineteenth century. It could permit individual liberty to flourish to an extent unthinkable in a nation surrounded by immemorial tribal enemies waiting to devour it. When you are surrounded by tribal enemies, you become a tribe—whether you want to, or not. That is your only guarantee of longevity. In North America, because a man could remain a stubborn individual, he could also learn to behave like the rational actor of liberal theory: he could calculate his own self-interest, permitting him Jefferson's "pursuit of happiness," and, of course, property.

Yet, once again, both the lack of formidable enemies among the natives as well as the geographical separation provided by the great oceans was not the achievement of those who emigrated to America. It was a gift of serendipity.

There was, however, a third factor that made American exceptional and unique—one that is often overlooked. In North America, the Anglo-Saxons did not find a population that was organized into anything like the complex imperial organization of the Aztecs and Incas. There was no grand moment signalizing the conquest of the American Indians, analogous to Cortes' entry into Mexico City, or Pizarro's triumph over the Incas. More importantly, because there was no conquest in America, there were no conquered people. In North America, there never emerged a class of docile American Indians who were willing to become serfs and slaves of the white conquerors. They either died or were forcibly removed—and this meant that there could be no natural demographic basis for the development of the odious institution of peonage or serfdom. The horrors of the African slave trade to the Americas was brought about because there was otherwise no preexisting servile class to do the hard and dirty work, especially in the South.

America's work ethic has often been explained by the famous Protestant work ethic. America was the promised land of Protestant Dissenters, who brought over with them the noble concept of the sanctity of hard work. There is, of course, an element of truth in this. But it must be recalled that the Afrikaners brought to South Africa the no less rigorous work ethic of the Dutch Calvinists. The Dutch, after all, lived on land that had not come to them by conquest, but by hard work—they had literally dredged their *Lebensraum* up from the bottom of the sea, and by means of an elaborate system of dikes. Everything they had had been gained by their own diligent labor. Yet when the Afrikaners came to South Africa they immediately became slave owners. Their Dutch Calvinist work ethic notwithstanding, the Afrikaners could not resist the temptation of exploiting the slave labor that had been traditional in African cultures. This reliance on slavery would later became a point of bitter contention between the Afrikaners, who thought the institution of slavery both necessary and just, and the English abolitionists, who thought that it was an abomination that should not be tolerated.

In North America, on the other hand, there was no temptation to force involuntary servitude on the native population because the colonists found that it was impossible to do this. Furthermore, when some of the more enlightened Anglo-Saxon newcomers attempted to help out the Native Americans by providing them with land to work for themselves, the way the Anglo-Saxon farmer did, they discovered that the Native Americans had no more interest in laboring for themselves than in laboring for others. Often they survived by selling off everything of value on their land, and finally selling off the land itself. Their motto was, Anything but work; and this had been the same attitude displayed by the native populations of the Caribbean whom the early Spanish conquistadors had vainly tried to exploit, but with disastrous effects.

Chasing people off their ancestral lands, or even exterminating them ruthlessly—neither of these constitutes conquest. To be a conqueror it is necessary to come across a people who, unlike the natives of North America and the Caribbean, are willing to provide involuntary labor for their conquerors. The easiest way to do this is to discover a people who had been previously conquered by someone else. For example, when the Arab conquerors seized the reins of the Byzantine Empire in Syria and the Sassanian Empire in Persia, they found a docile peasant population that had been long accustomed to sharing the fruits of their own labor with the ruling class—often most of the fruits. The reason that they were so accustomed to their involuntary servitude is that in the Levant no one could remember a time when there wasn't an empire by conquest that ruled over them. True, these empires were ruled by different powers, e.g., the Assyrians, the Babylonians, the Persians, the Byzantines, to name a few; but in essence, all the imperial systems worked along the same principles. There was an immense base of peasants who were exploited; there was an elaborate administrative system that, from early on, had been controlled by that indispensable tool of all Levantine empires, the eunuch, whose job was to keep the day-to-day operation of the empire running smoothly and efficiently. Finally, there was the ruling class itself, whose position in the empire had originated either directly from conquest, or else by inheriting the conquest of their ancestors. The sole job of the ruling class was to keep others from conquering what they or their ancestors had already conquered. It was to hold on to what they already had, and if possible to expand their empire in order to increase the base of the tribute-paying class.

Here again we can see the uniqueness of North America. It could only be peopled, not conquered. Unlike the Arab conquerors, those who arrived in North America did not discover a convenient peasantry just waiting to be exploited by a new set of warlords. Military prowess and supremacy, in North America, were not the key to wealth, as they were in Mexico and in Peru, and as they have always been in the Middle East since the time of the first great military empires. In North America you could not use your sword to get others to work the plow for your benefit. If a man wished his fields to be plowed, he had to start by plowing them himself. In fact, he normally had to start by cutting down the trees in order to make space enough for his field. In North America, in short, there was no ready-made division between masters and slaves, landowners and peons. Slavery, when it came to North America, had to be imported from Africa, where it had long been a thriving institution, as the Afrikaners discovered.

Those who have been accustomed to doing all the hard work feel bitterly resentful and hostile to those who set themselves up as masters by brutalizing an inferior population. It was this resentment that ultimately led to the American Civil War, and not a humanitarian interest in the welfare of the slaves. Both Lincoln and Grant wanted to see the liberated slaves exported back either to Africa, Lincoln's idea, or Haiti and Martinique, Grant's plan. The reason they had for wishing to get rid of the slaves was not, in essence, racism. It was the fear that a population that had been trained up to be slaves would always remain servile—a class that could be exploited by men who preferred brutalizing their fellow men to working with their own hands, men who found it easier to hold a whip than a plow.

For the American pioneers on the frontier, freedom and liberty of action were natural—indeed, they were the most natural things in the world. So too was the right to keep to yourself, wholly undivided, the fruits of your labor. A man who worked hard profited from his hard work, and could thereby make a better life for himself—and this, too, remarkably enough, came to appear to be the "natural order" of things.

Yet this was a complete illusion. In the Old World, and especially in the oldest part of it, to labor on the land was to be either a slave or a serf. There the natural order was that the peasant did all the drudgery, while the ruling class divided among themselves the fruits of the peasants' labor. That is how things had worked since the formation of the first great empires of the Near East. The world was divided into two types of human creatures: the beasts of burden who worked the land, and those who worked the beasts of burden.

There is a hadith of Muhammad that captures perfectly the natural order that existed in his world from time immemorial: "The plough brings submission into the house." In other words, be a farmer and you lose your freedom. The path of hard work is the path of slavery and servility; if you wish to avoid the curse of the former, you must pick for yourself a way of life that avoids hard work. For example, if you wish to be free, you must become a raider, a band of thieves, or warrior conquerors—in short, to be free, you must figure out a way to live off the hard work of others, and to exploit them ruthlessly. In the Old World, the only way to play the dominant alpha male was to be a warrior, or to have ancestors that hed been.

Over the concentration camp at Auschwitz was a sign that quoted an old German proverb: *Arbeit macht frei,* or "Work makes free[dom]." In the post-Holocaust world, it is hard to read these words without thinking of the sadistic irony that guided Rudolf Höss to come up with this particular slogan—but, had it been applied to most of human history, the sadism would have been a bit muted, though no less present. For throughout most of history, work did make freedom, not for the workers themselves, but for those who exploited the workers and looked upon such socially productive labor with complete contempt.

Yet the original meaning of the German proverb had been direct and sincere. It was an expression of faith. It meant, quite simply, that a community in which everyone was prepared to work hard to support himself and his family would in fact be a free community because there was no one in it who wished to make his living by exploiting others. But such a community could only come into existence if it eliminated all those who, historically, have not been content to support themselves by hard work. For example, you could not allow gangs of hoodlums and thieves to get organized; nor could you permit a priesthood that used its formidable power over the human imagination to hoodwink people out of the fruits of their labor; nor could you permit a king or a prince to live in luxury off his hardworking subjects; nor could you permit him to support a retinue or bodyguard by providing them with the dole. Nor would you allow someone to make a living by lending out money at interest. Nor would you put up with a class of beggars. And, of course, horror of horrors, you could not permit slavery and peonage, because both inevitably end by demeaning the status of the person who labors freely.

Perhaps too much emphasis has been put on the idea that the Protestant work ethic taught personal salvation through hard work, and not enough on the fact that a community made up exclusively of hard workers would liberate human beings from the natural order in which a few members of the ruling elite live in idleness supported by the exploited laboring masses. The intolerance of idleness, and the insistence that everyone should work hard, including even those who didn't need to, so characteristic of Puritan New England, is often mocked by us nowadays; but this is because we fail to see the deeper objective of this intolerance: it is the desire to make sure that Puritan communities did not revert to what they saw as an ethically inferior stage that had dominated every aspect of human existence in the Old World. Yet, as Werner Sombart has argued, the same intolerance of idleness could be found in Italy before the coming of the Protestant reformation—it was part of the ethos of the middle-class burgher. Sombart, in quoting the maxims of the Florentine merchant Alberti, notes how many of them echoed the advice offered by Benjamin Franklin in eighteenth-century America.

No wonder that John Locke became the dominant philosophical voice in the New World. Here liberty did appear to come from nature herself.

In his enormously influential *Second Treatise on Government*, John Locke had offered a model libertarian society in which there was no military caste, or ruling elite, or priesthood, or subjugated peasants. Instead, all the members of the community would be independent, stubborn individuals, each of whom labored for himself and intensely wished to preserve for his own benefit the fruits of his labor. Each member, furthermore, insisted on his own liberty of conscience and was prepared to tolerate that of other members of his community, so long as they refrained from trying to impose their own religion on the community. Thus, for Locke, religious tolerance was not extended to the Roman Catholic Church, because, historically, it had refused to recognize the Protestant doctrine of the priesthood of every man. Needless to say, he would equally have objected to the toleration of Islam. In short, in Locke's model community, a man may follow his own conscience, but he must never be permitted to become a fanatic determined to impose his own religious faith on others.

The security of the community would be left up to the ordinary members of it. There would be no standing armies; if the society needed to defend itself, the ordinary males of the community would come together in militias. If a ruler needed to be selected, his authority would be entirely dependent on his selection by the independent, stubborn-minded males of the community. If he acted inappropriately, then the community could remove him from his position of authority at their discretion and appoint another in his place. Because each of the males in the company was keen on preserving his individual rights, they could be trusted to check any attempt at usurping power by the man they had placed in authority over them. Because there was no standing army, however, there would be no opportunity for a political leader to become a military chieftain.

In Locke's model community, each man went his own way. There were no leaders and no followers. There were no exploiters and no exploited, no idle ruling elite and no laborers keeping them in the lap of luxury, no priests and no hoodwinked masses filled with superstitious awe at their powers of salvation. Furthermore, in Locke's community there was no need even to eliminate such social pests. They didn't exist because, according to Locke, his model community represented mankind's "state of nature" before the arrival of military elites, priesthoods, subjugated peasants, slaves, slave armies, or religious fanatics.

In *Second Treatise*, Locke was describing to a T, with some idealistic embellishments, the actual historical communities that the English settlers were creating for themselves in North America. Yet these communities, as we have argued, did not represent man's state of nature: They were freaks of nature—communities where people could start afresh, without being crushed by the burden of history that weighed so heavily in the rest of the world. In North America, the right to keep the produce of one's labor did seem to be part of the natural order. Yet this conclusion was based on a complete illusion. Yes, it was part of the natural order "round these parts," but it was certainly not part of the natural order in the rest of the world. Protestant North America was an exception to the rule. As Hegel argued, America had given the Old World a chance to start over again—and nothing could be less natural than that.

American liberalism was the result of a society in which every individual had the right to the fruits of his labor. But obviously those in the community whose labor had produced the most fruits would be the ones who had the deepest vested interest in maintaining a society that was primarily concerned with defending property rights—and who would want to defend property rights more than those who owned property, namely, the middle class? Thus, due to the exceptional circumstances of the settlement of America, the foundations were set for the triumph of the middle class.

Here we must admit that Karl Marx's critique of liberalism was substantially correct. A liberal society, according to Marx, was nothing other than the cultural hegemony of the middle class. It was through the achievement of this hegemony that the middle class was placed in a position to control the education of the children of the entire society, and to instill into them the "respect for other people's property" shaming code by which the middle class has always raised its own children.

Condorcet put his faith in secular education to lead the moral progress of the human race; the Protestant middle class, however, did not need to be told this. They wanted to keep maximum control over the education of their children, and they did not want a priesthood to indoctrinate them. For the Protestant middle class, the aim of education was to pass on its own values to its children. They wanted them to be stubborn, independent individuals, like themselves. They did not need to be converted to Condorcet's ideal of education. It was their own ideal. They wanted an education that "excludes all dependence, either forced or voluntary." They wanted an education that stressed the teaching of facts and the imparting of skills, especially those skills useful in a capitalist society.

Bourgeois societies also demanded that the lower classes be subjected to the same rules as the middle class themselves, even if this required the brutal and draconian punishment meted out by the gallows, as in liberal England in the eighteenth century. The middle class would not rest content until everyone observed the same uniform code of behavior that had worked so successfully for them. They believed that it was only by imposing this code universally that they could be assured of maintaining and preserving the cultural dominance of their traditions and values within the entire society. The warrior ethos did not have to be universalized to cover the entire society—on the contrary, to do so would have been in direct opposition to the interests of the warrior elite, who wished to keep the secret of their power to themselves. You didn't let slave boys listen to Homer so they could aspire to be Achilles. Yet the middle class were forced to universalize their own traditions and values, for their own security. Otherwise, how could the middle class, with its pacific and hard-working ways, hope to survive in the struggle for survival against those who preferred to live by violence, theft, and gross exploitation?

The middle-class businessman was accustomed to thinking in terms of his enlightened self-interest; it was his natural mode of experiencing the world. Thus for men of this mentality it was possible to think of cooperation as arising out of contracts. Such men would see the advantage they could gain from cooperating with others, provided there was a quid pro quo that would secure some mutual advantage to the other party. Thus in any society in which such men had achieved dominance of the status quo, it was entirely possible for them to conceive of large-scale cooperative projects in which all parties could expect to benefit. Out of this specific way of organizing their own lives, the middle class conceived of the idea of organizing an entire society around the concept of enlightened self-interest. There could be a politics of reason that could dispense with all the myths that had hitherto served as the basis of social cooperation, such as the divine right of kings, and could, at the same time, dispense with the necessity of coercion as the basis of the state. The state would not need to coerce to enforce obedience; virtually everyone in the society would see that it was in their enlightened self-interest to obey the laws that were of benefit to one and all, such as the laws protecting life, liberty, and property—or, in general, the autonomy of individual action.

Yet there was a problem in this. Could such a society actually satisfy everyone in it? Or was it merely a contrivance, as Marx argued, by which a select class had gained for itself the control of state power, to use for its own selfish interests, acting in much the same way that the warrior elite had always acted, namely by asserting that its own peculiar virtues were the right and necessary ones? After all, in both cases, the domination of one group appeared to come at the cost of other, often much larger groups—the peasant in the case of the warrior elite, the working class in the case of the capitalist elite.

A historian of French liberalism has said that during the heyday of bourgeois liberalism, i.e., the reign of the citizen king Louis Philippe, "liberalism acquired a bad name in France; it was branded as the philosophy of a selfish, capitalist oligarchy. Parliament was distrusted as a bourgeois institution, especially by the socialists who avowed their purpose to destroy, not to reform it." Yet this kind of attack misses the point. Bourgeois liberalism was indeed the philosophy of a capitalist oligarchy, namely the middle class; but its origin in the middle class was precisely what created the necessary conditions for the emergence of popular cultures of reason. No other class could have produced an ideology that elevated middle class conduct into a universal rule. No other class would have promoted as cardinal virtues such unheroic and unglamorous traits as reasonableness, moderation, prudence, thrift, and sobriety—the boring virtues, from the point of view of the aristocrat or the working man. It is quite true, as Marx argued, that these middle-class values were not universal values. Yet these were the values necessary to create a society in which violence and fanaticism, despotism and mob rule, could be eliminated. Only through the hegemony of the middle class could a society be made safe for the rational actor.

But what about those who were not members of the middle class? How would they react to the attempt to make middle-class values the foundation of a social order that left them out in the cold? In Europe, the working class turned to socialism of one sort or other, and what united these diverse reactions against middle-class hegemony was a violent rejection of middle-class values.

Here again America offered an exception to the rule. In a book published in 1906, Werner Sombart asked the question, "Why is there no socialism in America?" At the time socialism was wildly popular in France and in Germany, among other European nations, and yet, as a political movement, it never got off the ground in the United States. What, in Sombart's mind, explained this curious lack of enthusiasm for socialism in America?

Sombart's answer was that basically Americans were quite satisfied with their capitalist system. Enough of them were genuinely convinced that by working hard, or by striking it lucky, they could indeed get rich under the existing system; therefore, there was no resentment at the status quo, since it was perceived to offer most people a way to improve their lot in life. A decade before Sombart made his observations, William Jennings Bryan had made much the same point during the famous speech that handed him the Democratic nomination for president in 1896. Attacked by the business interests of the East as an anarchist and a socialist, the liberal and progressive Bryan responded: "We say to you that you have made the definition of a business man too limited in its application. The man who is employed for wages is as much a business man as his employer, the attorney in a country town is as much a business man as the corporation counsel in a great metropolis; the merchant at the cross-roads store is as much a business man as the merchant of New York; the farmer who goes forth in the morning and toils all day—who begins in the spring and toils all summers—and who by the application of brain and muscle to the natural resources of the country creates wealth, is as much a business man as the man who goes upon board of trade and bets upon the price of grain; the miners who go down a thousand feet into the earth . . . and bring forth from their hiding places the precious metals to be poured into the channels of trade are as much business men as the few financial magnates who, in a back room, corner the money of the world."

In short, in Bryan's America, there was no working class, no capitalist class: All Americans were equally businessmen, that is to say, rational actors and economic calculators, though obviously some had made cleverer or perhaps just luckier calculations than others. No doubt, there were many who had fallen far short of success in their various business enterprises, but by no means enough to spark off a widespread desire to overthrow the capitalist system and replace it with an experiment in socialism. Even after Frederick Turner declared the frontier closed, and there were no more empty spaces to occupy, young and ambitious alpha boys, like the heroes of the popular Horatio Alger novels, could still make a name for themselves and leave a mark on the world, and many did. America drew from all over the globe precisely those young men who wished to improve their lot by escaping the crushing burden of history so characteristic of the Old World. In America, as Henry Ford put it so well, "History is bunk."

But what about France? After the collapse of the Bourbon monarchy, France went through the empire of Napoleon, the restoration of the Bourbons, a bourgeois monarch, another revolution, another empire, and finally the Third Republic, which lasted until Hitler's conquest of France in 1940. Yet as the French say, *"Plus ce que ca change, plus ce que c'est la meme chose"* (The more things change the more they remain the same). Albert Sorel argued that there was a profound continuity underneath all the surface upheavals in French history from the reign of Louis XIV to the Third Republic, and foremost among these was the fact that there was always a powerful central government in France.

De Tocqueville had participated actively in the revolution of 1848, and his experience with the short-lived Second French Revolution sobered considerably his assessment of the providential triumph of democracy. He wrote in his *Memoirs*, speaking of his attitude toward the events of 1848: "I did not then think, any more than I think now, that a Republican form of government was the best one suited to the needs of France, meaning by 'Republican government' an elected executive branch. Where the habits, traditions, and mores of a people have assured such a vast sphere to power for the executive, its instability will always, whenever troubled days come, lead to revolution, and even in peaceful times such instability will be uncomfortable. In any case, for me a republic is an ill-balanced form of government, promising more freedom and giving less than a constitutional monarchy." In another reflection on the Second Republic, he remarks that: "In France there is only one thing that we cannot make: a free government; and only one thing we cannot destroy: centralization."

In France, the divine right of kings had been preserved in the tradition of the divine right of the central government. The uniquely powerful central state that had been achieved by the Bourbons, while unfavorable to political freedom, was immensely valuable to the full development of the rational actor. A strong state gave the individual security. It would defend both him and his property. Where you can call the police and trust them to defend you, you do not need a tribe. Furthermore, the French state, no matter what form it assumed, was always anxious to have the middle class behind it. Louis Philippe was a bourgeois monarch, the Second Republic was a bourgeois republic, and Louis Napoleon created a bourgeois empire. Therefore, in France, no less than England and America, the triumph of the middle class was secured, and cultures were created that were safe for the rational actor.

In sum, the necessary material and historical conditions for the creation of popular cultures of reason have been the domination of the social order by the middle class and the imposition of their own particular values upon the rest of society. Wherever this stage has not occurred at some point in a society's past, then no popular culture of reason has been able to emerge.

In those societies, however, where the political hegemony of the middle class has been able to create popular cultures of reason, there has been an inevitable tendency to forget this success was the product of a number of happy accidents. It did not represent an inevitable march of mankind toward the same destination.

It did not portend the wave of the future. It was, in short, the most unnatural order possible on the planet.

France, England, and America, the three nations that Condorcet regarded as representing the highest stage of civilization, were flukes. Each had developed cultural traditions favorable to the emergence of the rational actor. These cultures were not created by rational actors; these cultures created an environment in which the rational actor could emerge and flourish. Yet because all three of these nations adopted Condorcet's program of education, it is easy to mistake cause and effect. Secular education did not make rational actors; secular education was the kind of education that the middle-class rational actor wanted for his children. He did not want them brainwashed or indoctrinated; he wanted them to think like a good middle-class businessman, tolerant, cautious, independent, critical.

Yet today the goal of secular education in America, England, and France has been radically transformed from its original objective. It has become the aim of enlightened educators to "liberate" their students from the middle-class traditions that created the first cultures of reason, and to instill in their place the same enlightened values held by the educators themselves, most of whom are contemptuous of the values and traditions of the middle class. Even worse, the enlightened values that are being taught to our young are not the same values that Condorcet or the other leading thinkers of the Enlightenment held.

Today Condorcet's belief in the superiority of the West has been replaced by what is called multiculturalism. Yet the problem with multiculturalism is not that it teaches us to respect other cultures and disrespect our own. The problem is that the multiculturalists have a profoundly shallow concept of culture: They see cultural differences as if they were merely differences in consumer tastes and preferences. Some Americans like Thai food, others prefer French cuisine. Some prefer Tide to Cheer, Chevrolets to Fords, Elton John to Eminem, Sax Fifth Avenue to Kmart, Dell to Apple, and so on. Why can't we all have what we want?

Modern multiculturalists celebrate diversity. But this ideal diversity is merely the reflection of the ethos of the society in which the multiculturalists live. In a consumerist society, of course diversity is celebrated. The consumer is king, and he demands that his own personal and individual preferences be satisfied. Henry Ford said you could have any color of Ford you wanted, so long as it was black. Alfred Sloan, his inventive competitor at General Motors, offered people their choice of color. He celebrated diversity, because he knew it would sell more cars, which it did. But the diversity of General Motors was successful because the consumer wanted it. They didn't want to have a choice of just black—they wanted a palette of colors. Today in the consumerist West, people are simply dazzled by the number of choices they have been given. Buying even a bottle of V8 juice—low sodium? spicy? regular?—presents a challenge. And so too with all other consumer items: Businesses customize their product to match the consumer's personal tastes, and everyone is happy.

Multiculturalism is the natural anthropology of a consumer-friendly economy. Because our own lives are filled with personalized choices, each made according to our unique tastes, we have come to approach culture in the same spirit. For us, a culture is like an individual choice of a consumer product: If a man owns a Volvo, you can assume that it was his choice to own one. If a man prays to Mecca five times a day, or celebrates Christmas with a big tree, or bathes in the Ganges, these are all viewed as if they were personal choices—like the way we choose where to spend our vacation.

In sum, the multiculturalist treats all differences in human culture as if they were analogous to a preference for pasta over couscous—that is, mainly a difference in consumer tastes. This view, however, is radically different from the view that cultures are themselves weapons in the struggle for survival and supremacy of those who carry on those traditions. In a society that is not consumer based, there will be few, if any, choices given to the individuals. Henry Ford's maxim will prevail: You can have any kind of culture, so long as it is the inherited culture of your tribe or sect. Perhaps a bit of leeway is allowed in nonessential matters, but when it comes to the core traditions of a culture, its foundation, such tolerance will simply not be permitted. Experiments in living will be summarily condemned.

The consumerist multiculturalist approach overlooks the critical fact that every culture has both core values and incidental ones. The core values cannot be challenged; the incidental ones may be. Preferring couscous is an incidental value of Muslim societies; but excluding females is a core value. It is a tradition that cannot be altered without bringing the whole edifice of the culture tumbling down. A culture that adopts pasta in place of couscous will remain pretty much the same. A society, however, that stops excluding women becomes a radically different society. Going from couscous to pasta will not appreciably alter a culture's ability to keep its core traditions intact, and to survive. But can the same be said of abandoning the exclusion of women?

Progressive-minded women have frequently claimed, in justification of their cultural influence, that they are pacifying agents. They make men less warlike and aggressive. They civilize them. But suppose the aim of a culture is precisely to keep the boys and men from becoming too civilized and too pacific? The Ottomans had no interest in reducing the natural aggressiveness of the alpha boys they inducted into the Janissary corps; on the contrary, they did everything to stimulate it, and one of the primary methods by which this was done was to segregate the young Janissaries from females. To us this may seem frightful, but if a culture is concerned with survival under violent conditions, then it must figure out a way to preserve and augment the natural ruthlessness and ferocity of their alpha boys. Hence, in such a culture, those institutions that achieve this purpose will be protected and guarded; they will form part of its inviolable core traditions.

Today, however, our modern system of education refuses to recognize that the modern liberal West might also have core traditions that cannot be overturned without destroying the foundation of liberalism itself. Here again the consumerist model is implicit in our theory of educating children: They are taught to think of themselves as ideology consumers, picking whatever religion or politics appeals to them. Inevitably even the most intelligent consumer, especially a child, will be unconsciously swayed by the clever sales techniques of those peddling their own brand-name ideology, just as they are swayed when buying footwear and blue jeans. Indeed increasingly our education system is being turned over to teachers who are frankly salesmen for the ideological brand that is in vogue among the intellectual elite.

If we could awake the spirit of Condorcet and ask him to visit our classrooms, what conclusion would he draw? Would he think that we are teaching our children how to defend themselves against intellectual charlatans, or would he condemn us for entrusting such charlatans with our children's education?

Condorcet objected to the Jesuit system of education because it consisted of teaching children to accept a specific creed, not merely at the intellectual but at the visceral level as well. For Condorcet, on the other hand, the whole point of enlightened education was to enable children to resist the imposition of ideas and values that other people wished to impress upon them. Nor did it matter whether these ideas were right or wrong; what was wrong for Condorcet was the passive acceptance of someone else's creed. Condorcet's aim was to teach people to be independent in both their thoughts and their actions. But is this really how we are educating our children today? True, we give lip service to the ideals of Condorcet, but do we really practice them?

Today in the West there is an educated elite that is entirely convinced that it has all the right answers to every question imaginable. Furthermore, because this elite entertains no doubts about its own rightness, it has no qualms in eradicating ideas that seem to represent wrongness. It is, of course, quite possible to look on our intellectual elite as carrying out the noble goal of liberating children from the claims of the tribal mind by getting them to think for themselves, just as Condorcet argued that educators should do. Yet all too often in contemporary education, the goal seems less a question of getting children to think for themselves than of indoctrinating them with ideas and values that are currently fashionable among the intellectual elite. Often this indoctrination seems more like the tribal initiation rites than the cultivation of independent thinking. The goal is not to provide the tools by which a student can discover answers for himself; rather the objective is to induce the student to have the right subjective attitude. For example, instead of analyzing the concept of racism, studying the history of its development, and the ambiguity of its meaning, students are taught that what is important about racism is that a person shouldn't have racist feelings, and that anyone who has such subjective attitudes is a racist.

This form of indoctrination aims not so much at producing a uniformity of thought as a uniformity of sentiment. What the student thinks matters less than how he feels—and what matters most is that the students should feel about things the same way that his teachers feel. If the teacher feels that war is wrong, or that sexism is a terrible thing, his primary duty will be to get his students to feel the same way about these things. What matters is to impart conviction: The politically committed scholar must encourage his students to adopt his own subjective attitudes and feelings about politically important questions, since he takes for granted that his are obviously the correct attitudes and feelings to have. Thus we have created a situation in which a shaming code is being imposed by an enlightened elite upon the unenlightened masses—though, strangely enough, neither the active nor the passive party seems to have any clue about what is taking place. Instead of teaching our children to think and act for themselves, our enlightened educators work hard to make children ashamed of entertaining feelings or ideas that are not approved by their teachers as politically correct—whatever the fickle standard of political correctness happens to be at the moment.

The problem with our enlightened elite is that they assume that in order to create a liberal, tolerant, and reasonable society you need only cultivate the personal virtues of liberalism, tolerance, and reasonableness. It assumes that the task of educating is finished simply because students have been given the right subjective attitude, so that they themselves will not be intolerant of others, or act unreasonably with them. But a tolerant society needs more than citizens who are themselves personally committed to tolerance: It needs to produce citizens who, in addition to being tolerant themselves, feel that they have an unconditional duty to insist that everyone else in their society be tolerant as well. Somewhat paradoxically, in order to secure a tolerant society, you must teach the young that there are times when they have a civic duty to be intolerant, namely, when dealing with those who refuse to play by the rules that are necessary for the creation of a tolerant society. If you teach the young that they should never be intolerant themselves, because intolerance is always wrong, then you will be making your society immensely vulnerable to those who themselves practice intolerance. In order to get it right, you must encourage personal tolerance, but at the same time make it clear that there are situations when one's own preference for tolerance on a personal level may need to be checked by a sense of duty to society as a whole. In short, education in a liberal and tolerant society must teach children not only to have the right subjective attitudes, but that there are rules everyone in a liberal and tolerant society must obey, and that must be impersonally enforced, even if we might personally prefer to make an exception in this or that particular case.

For us, tolerance has become purely a matter of a person's subjective attitude. An intolerant person is a person with intolerant opinions and attitudes. True, he may do nothing whatsoever to injure gays or blacks by his behavior, but that, for us, does not make him truly tolerant. So long as he entertains negative feelings about other groups, we still regard him as a bigot, even if he manages to keep these feelings largely to himself. Here again all that matters is subjective attitude and personal sincerity.

By this logic, those who wish to be tolerant must cleanse themselves of any negative feelings toward other groups. It is not enough simply for a man to put up with people whom he personally doesn't like; what counts is not his public behavior, but his private and subjective attitude. Hence to be truly tolerant, by this standard, a person must rid himself of all forms of subjective prejudice against other groups. A society is tolerant if and only if it is made up of individuals who have no personal prejudices against anyone or any group.

In the modern liberal West, we have been taught to be ashamed of intolerance, to look upon it as a personal failing. On the other hand, we have been encouraged to tolerate different cultures and different traditions from our own, often to the point of admiring other societies more than our own. We are praised for having an open mind, being willing to try new foods and new fads, to listen to the music of other lands, and to see all men as our brothers. Furthermore, we have been taught to look askance at Western claims to ethical superiority—though this claim, as we have seen, was a cardinal tenet of the Enlightenment. All in the name of tolerance.

Yet what happens to an enlightened culture, in which everyone has adopted tolerance as a personal virtue, when it comes into conflict with a society that is fanatically intolerant of those who do not share its own inherited traditions and customs? The spread of enlightened values throughout the general population of the liberal West, brought about both by our systems of education and by our popular culture, has made the modern, liberal West the most tolerant culture that has ever existed. Yet, as I have argued in this book, in the struggle for survival and supremacy among cultural traditions, the advantage will invariably go to those who are most fanatically committed to maintaining and expanding their own cultural traditions, and who, because of this commitment, are united by a powerful sense of group feeling. Yet in the liberal West today, the whole point of enlightened education is to shame children out of any sense that they belong to a superior group that possesses a superior set of ethical values and traditions. This was not Condorcet's idea of education. Furthermore, this is not how children are brought up under Islam. Nor, as we will see in the next chapter, is there any reasonable possibility that Muslim cultures would tolerate any effort by an enlightened, secular elite to assault and undermine the religious and cultural traditions that Muslims have defended with such formidable tenacity and, yes, fanaticism.

The goal of popular enlightenment, according to Condorcet, was to eliminate popular fanaticism—and in the West, this goal has been achieved to an astonishing degree. The question, however, is whether this remarkable success story will turn out to be the prelude to the end of history, as Condorcet hoped, or a prescription for cultural suicide.

Part Four

The Challenge of Islamic Fanaticism

12

The Logic of Fanaticism

To Western liberals, logic and fanaticism seem like antithetical terms. A fanatic is someone for whom logic and rational debate mean nothing. Yet, though fanatics may themselves be impervious to logic, there is still a method in their madness, for, as we argued earlier, fanaticism is what produces the "group feeling" of the tribal mind, and creates men who look with contempt upon the rational actor because he is only concerned with calculating his own enlightened self-interest. It is due to the fanaticism of such men that empires have been toppled, religious tradition uprooted and destroyed, cultures turned upside down. That is why this kind of fanaticism must be taken seriously, and why its dramatic return to the world stage cannot be ignored. If we wish to understand our era, we must neither deny fanaticism, nor simply condemn it from our own ethical perspective. We must, above all, grasp its logic and power.

Those who, out of a misplaced sensitivity to Muslim feelings, wish to deny the populist Muslim tradition of fanatical intolerance, fail to comprehend the simple fact that Muslim fanaticism works, and throughout the centuries it has worked with spectacular success. Considered from a purely pragmatic point of view, the political and cultural achievements of Muslim fanaticism represent one of mankind's more ingenious and brilliant solutions to the age-old problem of group survival in a hostile and unfriendly world. Other religions have failed in the task of maintaining their ethical traditions in a world full of enemies. Christianity died out before the wave of Islam in the Byzantine Empire, in Egypt, and in North Africa. Zoroastrianism suffered the same fate in Persia. Islam, on the other hand, has succeeded in making permanent conquests in every part of the world into which it has expanded, with only three exceptions: Spain, Sicily, and certain parts of the Balkans. Yet these exceptions to the rule serve only to prove the pragmatic efficacy of the ethos of fanaticism, since the only cultures that have succeeded in driving back the inroads of Islam have been those cultures that have adopted the Muslim principle of fanaticism to serve their own purposes. The Catholic reconquest of Spain, for example, could only have been achieved by a religion that had adopted the same ethos that had animated Islam. Indeed, the Spanish victory over Islam may be seen, from the perspective of Ibn-Khaldun, to fit the cyclical pattern whereby an imperial and reasonably tolerant culture, such as flourished under the Islamic rulers of Spain, was overthrown by men whose zealotry far exceeded that of those whom they conquered.

Their fanatical intolerance made Muslims in the realm of Dar el-Islam utterly impervious to all outside efforts to change their fundamental way of life. Kenneth Latourette, in his definitive *History of Christian Missions*, provides ample documentation of the complete and utter failure of Christian missionaries to make even the slightest inroads among Muslims. In few other cultures on the globe did Christian missions fail so abysmally to make converts—

a bad thing from the point of view of the Christian missionaries, but quite obviously a good thing from the point of view of devout Muslims. The Ottoman Empire, itself Muslim, nominally ruled over the Arabs for centuries, and yet they never succeeded in changing the fundamental ethos of this proud and stubborn people. Various European colonial powers, including Italy, France, and England, also found that they were completely unable to transform the nominally subject populations to their own European ways. In these cases, popular Muslim fanaticism acted as a societal defense mechanism against alien influences, operating as automatically as the body's immune system operates when it comes into contact with foreign microbes. Or to use the language of Richard Dawkins, popular Muslim fanaticism functioned as a method for expelling or eliminating those dangerous foreign memes that, if permitted to invade Dar el-Islam, might sooner or later bring about a disruption of their collective tradition.

This is a point where our modern Western notion of the isolated fanatic is apt to lead us astray. For us, fanaticism is synonymous with disruptions of the social order, instability, and violent upheaval, because in Western societies the fanatic is represented by individuals or groups that oppose the status quo. But when an entire society shares in the same collective fanaticism, when fanaticism *is* the status quo, then the effect is quite the opposite. In this case, popular fanaticism operates as a way of assuring a complete consensus of values and homogeneity of thought in any culture that adopts it as an organizing principle. Since no foreign ways are permitted to infect any segment of the population, there is no risk of a division between those who accept the old tradition and those who wish to discard this tradition and establish cultural innovations. Where collective fanaticism is the rule there can be no culture war between the "backward" masses and an "enlightened" elite, which explains why, from time immemorial, the elite

of Islamic clerics have invariably acted as the spokesmen for popular sentiment and have put themselves forward as leaders of the
people—quite unlike the intellectual elites of the modern West
who often seem intent on representing those values and ideas that
are most bitterly opposed by the masses.

During those periods where the Muslim world has been on the
defensive, their tradition of collective fanaticism has worked with
astonishing success at protecting Dar el-Islam from foreign and
potentially disruptive cultural influences. Furthermore, it has created societies that have throughout history made it virtually impossible for any foreign power to dominate them culturally or
even militarily. True, in certain cases, especially in modern times,
there will be small groups of Muslims who advocate the adoption
of what they perceive as the superior ways of a more advanced
foreign culture, but such advocates of Westernization or modernization often find themselves in the same position as the Spanish
liberals who wished to bring the benefits of the Enlightenment to
their own backward fellow Spaniards—though they may be
looked upon as heroes struggling to bring progress to their country by their liberal sympathizers in other nations, they are often
viewed as cultural traitors within their own.

As we observed in Chapter 1, collective fanaticism, when operating on the defensive, might well be compared to a policy of cultural protectionism—it works to assure the continuation of
cultural autarky within any society that has embodied an ethic of
collective fanaticism. In the eyes of modern liberals this may
smack of backwardness, but it is impossible to deny that such
backwardness has a pragmatic value to those whose primary anxiety is to preserve their cultural traditions intact and free from foreign contamination.

Toward the beginning of this book, we noted that in the 1820s
E. W. Lane had predicted that "the fanatical intolerance" of Mus-

lims toward Western ways and customs would diminish, but after a longer familiarity with the modern Egyptians of his time he was forced to confess that his prediction had not yet been fulfilled. In 2006, the so-called "cartoon riots" that broke out in various parts of the Muslim world were a shocking reminder of the continuing intensity of the Muslim fanaticism among the "religious and learned profession" and "the bulk of the population." What to liberal Westerners appeared to be a harmless cartoon led to outbreaks of lethal violence in Afghanistan and in Nigeria, where Muslims seized and murdered Christians in the streets—and yet what did these Nigerian Christians have to do with a cartoon published in a hitherto obscure periodical published in Denmark? In the United States, our children routinely watch animated cartoons, such as *South Park*, *Family Guy*, and *The Simpsons*, in which nothing is sacred. It is fun to ridicule Jesus, and to mock Christians—and who riots about that?

Fundamentalist Christians in the United States are often cited by leftist intellectuals as examples of the same kind of religious fanaticism that animates Islam. But the mere fact that Christian fundamentalists hold beliefs that are considered to be silly or irrational by the intelligentsia does not make them fanatics: They may be deluded fools, but they are peaceful deluded fools. In 2005, for example, when the high courts decided to remove by force a copy of the Ten Commandments from a courthouse in Alabama, there was a throng of Christian fundamentalists who, with sullen faces and angry placards, exercised their right of peaceful assembly to protest the removal. None lifted a finger to stop the process, nor did the removal of the Ten Commandments spark off mass rioting among Southern Baptists. No one was killed; no one received a scratch. Among those who regard themselves as progressive thinkers, it is common to argue, "The Muslims have their fanatics, but we have our fanatics, too." Perhaps, but our fanatics don't seem to get that the whole point of being a fanatic is to be prepared to go to any extreme in order to defend your traditions. Our so-called fanatics don't recall the fact that real fanaticism *works*: rioting and going on bloody rampages have historically proven to be a far more effective way of defending a cultural tradition than sullen faces and angry placards. Muslims understand this: Their fanaticism has protected them not only from foreign influences, but from any attempts by an intellectual elite to impose its own more progressive and enlightened values on the bulk of the population.

Another example of the persistence of the fanatical intolerance of Muslims came to the world's attention in the same year as the cartoon riots. A Muslim in Afghanistan had converted to Christianity—the same Afghanistan that the United States had liberated from the fanaticism of the Taliban. But fanatical intolerance in Afghanistan clearly did not require an organization like the Taliban to keep it alive. Here again, it sprang up quite spontaneously from the religious and learned mullahs and from the bulk of the people. Islamic law demands that an apostate from Islam should be executed, and there were cries for blood that again took the form of riots and outrageous pronouncements from Muslim clerics, one of whom urged that the apostate be torn limb from limb by the people themselves. Fortunately, due to pressure from the West, the man was flown out of Afghanistan to sanctuary in Italy. Remarkably the Bush administration was initially content to look upon the convert's fate as a purely domestic affair to be decided by the Afghanis themselves—another example of the triumph of multiculturalism over liberalism even in a White House derided by the Left for its supposed Christian fundamentalism.

To the liberal West, the cartoon riots could not but appear shocking. Yet there is nothing uniquely Muslim in either event.

In the middle of the nineteenth century, the bloody Sepoy rebellion was set off in India among Hindus over a completely unfounded rumor that the English had deliberately used the grease from cows in the casing of the bullets they provided to their native army, the Sepoys. Muslims also rebelled, because the rumor added that grease from pigs had been combined with the grease from cows—but here the Muslims were only doing what other religious fanatics had done since time immemorial.

The same thing can be said about the Afghan convert. During the Sassanian Empire of Persia, the Zoroastrian priesthood, the Magi, transformed what was once a reasonably tolerant religion into one that was fanatically intolerant: Death was the punishment for apostasy. But then the Catholic Church had no problem condemning to death heretics who departed from the orthodox faith, and John Calvin in Geneva had few qualms about burning Miguel Servetus because of the latter's questionable theological notions about the Trinity. In all of these cases, the execution of apostates and heretics was looked upon as a collective duty that must be discharged in order to protect the community from the spread of ideas and values that threatened to undermine and dissolve its solidarity and homogeneity.

Fanatical intolerance, when undertaken to protect the existing cultural and religious traditions of a people, is thus by no means a phenomenon unique to Muslims. It is simply that the Muslims still retain this cultural defense mechanism in a world in which fanatical intolerance is no longer the practice of the other great religions.

The Western approach to this defensive intolerance can vary. Some may believe that the course of wisdom is to make no effort to reduce the defensive intolerance of Muslims—simply accept it and work with it as best you can. Others believe that the West should try to reduce it as a necessary stage in bringing modernization to the Islamic world. Yet the question for those who take this point of view is simple: How do you reduce it? If Lane's original prediction has not yet been fulfilled in 2006, when will it be fulfilled, and by what process will this transformation come about?

The brilliant Italian Marxist Antonio Gramsci wrote in a newspaper article in the 1920s that the Enlightenment would come to America in the twentieth century, as it had earlier come to Europe. His words have proved prophetic. But in both cases, the method by which the bulk of the population was enlightened remained the same as that envisioned by Condorcet: You sent out an enlightened elite whose first task was to attack and combat the prejudice and superstitions of the bulk of the population. Education had to be thoroughly secular and cosmopolitan, in order to uproot the religious and ethnocentric prejudices that children quite naturally pick up from their parents and family. Yet if popular enlightenment can only be brought about by the agency of educators whose own beliefs and values are far more advanced and progressive than the masses', then what chance is there that the Muslim world could ever achieve popular enlightenment when its schools and educational system are entrusted to the very people who are keenest to keep religious prejudices and intolerance alive?

Here we can see the profound contradiction between contemporary multiculturalism and classical liberalism. For Condorcet, it was self-evident that you could only enlighten the bulk of the population through an education that was emphatically secular and cosmopolitan—one that was designed to prevent fanatical adherence to inherited traditions. Had Condorcet and those who subscribed to his ideas followed the path of the multiculturalist, then they would have been forced to repudiate their own vision of education—they would have argued that it would be disrespectful to the cultures of Catholicism and Protestantism to insist on taking the education of children out of the hands of priests and clergymen. But if this view had prevailed, then the fate of the

Enlightenment would have been very different. Enlightenment would have remained isolated to small sects and cults—it could never have been diffused through the general population.

Here, too, we can see the contradiction in the liberationist strategy of the Bush administration in the Middle East. It was deemed permissible to liberate Iraq from Saddam Hussein, but it would have been culturally insensitive and politically incorrect to insist that the education of Iraqi children could no longer be entrusted to mullahs and clerics, but should rather be turned over to people who espoused the values of the European Enlightenment. Of course, it is also quite likely that such an attempt to impose popular enlightenment on the Iraqi people would have lead to an explosion of fanatical resistance and resentment among both the religious professions and the bulk of the population—but here again we return to the challenge of how to overcome a cultural defense mechanism that had worked so well to keep Islamic traditions alive from generation to generation.

This challenge, however, is quite an old one; and it is one that has been faced by all those who, like E. W. Lane, hoped to see that day when the fanatical intolerance of Western ways would be "materially diminished" in Muslim countries. Today, on the other hand, we are facing quite a different challenge, and few things are more important than to keep these two challenges distinct. It is one thing to try to change them; it is another matter to try to keep them from changing us. It may simply prove impossible for us to change them in their own lands—the dream of the inevitable modernization of Islam may turn out to be a utopian illusion. But unless it is possible to keep them from changing us, then the Western tradition of reason is in serious trouble indeed.

This new challenge to the West is the revival of the institution of jihad among those who represent what has come to be known as radical Islam. And it is to this challenge that we will now turn.

13

The Legacy and Future of Jihad

The Islamic institution of jihad has become a source of debate in the post-9/11 era. What does jihad mean? How great a threat to the West does the current revival of jihad represent? How do we defend ourselves against terrorists who see themselves as following in the footsteps of the Islamic holy warriors of their heroic past?

Earlier we noted that what has been most astonishing about the intellectual response to 9/11 was the striking failure to come to terms with the return of Islamic fanaticism, even when it came to our attention one beautiful September morning when the Twin Towers collapsed. Instead of thinking, Here is something new and important, most Western intellectuals attempted to fit this catastrophic event into the paradigms they had embraced prior to the morning of 9/11. Few took seriously the idea that the West was watching the revival of an ancient institution that most Westerners had come to believe was long dead. Just as few took seriously the idea that Mount Saint Helen's, so long dismissed as a dormant volcano, could ever erupt again, so few grasped the significance of the revival of jihad in the Islamic world.

In 2005, Boston physician Andrew Bostom published a thick volume titled *The Legacy of Jihad*, an indispensable work for anyone who wishes to understand that "peculiar institution" of Islam called jihad. Though his book is the product of exhaustive scholarly research, it is nevertheless a book written with a profound sense of urgency. Bostom wants his readers themselves to grapple with the historical evidence, and to come to their own conclusions about the significance of jihad. Yet the reader can have no doubt that for Bostom there are few challenges facing the liberal West today greater than radical Islam's revival of the classical ideal of jihad. In his acknowledgments, Bostom expresses the poignant wish that his own children and their children may "thrive in a world where the devastating institution of *jihad* has been acknowledged, renounced, dismantled, and relegated forever to the dustbin of history by Muslims themselves."

Yet after reading and pondering Bostom's book, it is difficult not to ask the question, Why should Muslims renounce and dismantle an institution that, while it may have been devastating to those who have been its victims, has nevertheless been the historical agent by which Islamic culture has come to dominate such a vast expanse of our planet? What would prompt any culture to abandon a tradition that has permitted it not only to expand immensely from its original home, but which has made permanent and not merely temporary conquests of so many hearts and minds?

Yet before we can address this question, let us first note the curious challenge that Bostom faced in simply getting his contemporaries to recognize that Islamic jihad is a peculiar institution in the first place—an institution quite unlike any other known to us. In our current climate of political correctness, there has been a reluctance even to acknowledge the most obvious facts about the nature of jihad. Indeed, just as there are Holocaust deniers, there is a contemporary tendency to deny the historical evidence relating to jihad, though as Bostom's book amply demonstrates it is scarcely lacking from any number of sources through every century from the original wave of Arabic conquest to today's headlines. Generally speaking, the approach of the jihad deniers, both Muslim and non-Muslim, is to refuse to recognize that there is anything historically distinctive and peculiar about the Islamic concept of jihad.

For example, some have argued that the "true" meaning of jihad is the struggle within the soul of each Muslim to overcome his own failings and sins: On this view, jihad is a spiritual war declared by a Muslim upon himself, and not upon infidels. Furthermore, it is a personal campaign and thus not a campaign waged by the entire Muslim community collectively, and on this reading, jihad becomes akin to the Protestant's classic and agonizing struggle with his own conscience. On the other hand, Khaled Abou El Fadl, a professor of law at UCLA, argues in a paper written in 2002 that "Islamic tradition does not have a notion of holy war. *Jihad* simply means to strive hard or struggle in the pursuit of a just cause." Note that on both these interpretations jihad is not only rendered nonviolent, it is also identified with traditions that are shared by other cultures and religions. Jews, Christians, Buddhists, Hindus—all struggle against the darker forces within themselves; they also, along with ethical atheists, strive hard in the pursuit of a just cause.

Those who follow a particular religion are of course free to adapt its historical traditions in light of their own needs and modern ideals. The twentieth-century Jewish theologian Martin Buber provides an example of this kind of idealistic and modernizing revision in his handling of the Hebrew theme of the Chosen People—an idea that in its primitive formulation resonates with the arrogant sense of superiority found among all warlike bands. We were chosen because we are the best. According to Buber, however, the ancient Hebrews were not chosen because they were inherently superior to other tribes; on the contrary, they were chosen because they were the most insignificant of tribes— mere slaves in the land of Egypt. Yahweh did not choose the Jews for their merits or abilities; he chose them in an act of grace—an interpretation of the ancient Hebrew concept that is clearly derived from the Protestant doctrine that God's saving grace is not dispensed upon the meritorious, but upon weak and unworthy sinners, and in a wholly arbitrary fashion—at least, arbitrary from the human perspective.

Such modernizing revisions of traditional religious concepts can be useful in weaning the followers of a religion away from the primitive and often barbarous ethos out of which many ancient religions arose, and in this manner, these revisions may serve a civilizing function. They allow a member of a religion to believe he is being true to his faith, while, at the same time, radically altering the content of this faith. Thus, for those who wish to see Muslims repudiate the classical tradition of jihad, it may be beneficial to encourage the illusion that jihad has always meant an internal struggle against sin or a fight for a just cause, and that any other interpretation of jihad is contrary to the "real" message of Islam.

Yet for those who are seeking to understand the nature of historical Islam, it is imperative to come to grips with what jihad has actually meant to Muslims throughout their history, and especially during those periods in which Islam expanded itself, not only by conquering new territory, but by transforming utterly the cultures of those who fell under its sway. The Norman Vikings, too, were ruthless conquerors; but, like many other warlike people, they adapted to the culture of those they conquered, acquiring the language and customs of their subjects, while abandoning their own—the same pattern followed by many of the barbarian invaders of the Roman Empire in the West. The Arab conquerors, on the other hand, not only retained their own language and culture, but were able to impose them on those they conquered. Furthermore, the cultures the Arabs transformed were not primitive cultures existing on a far lower plane of social organization, but cultures that were more civilized and sophisticated than that of the camel nomads who toppled them. Two examples of this process are the conquest in the first century of Islamic expansion of the Byzantine Empire in Syria and the Sassanian Empire in Persia. How did this remarkable achievement come about?

The answer lies in what Andrew Bostom calls "the historically unique institution of *Jihad*"—an institution that his fascinating and thought-provoking book examines from a host of different perspectives. Tracing the development of the concept of jihad from its origins in the Koran, Bostom devotes a hundred pages of his book to an anthology of various Muslim commentators from Ibn Abi Zayd al-Qayrawani in the tenth century, through Ibn-Khaldun and al-Ghazali, to Sayyid Qutb in the twentieth century. Letting these Muslim thinkers and scholars speak with their own words, Bostom is able to demonstrate beyond any doubt that the historical institution of jihad did not mean a personal and individual struggle against evil or the nonviolent pursuit of a just cause, as some contend today, but rather a collective and violent struggle by the entire Muslim community against those outsiders who were not Muslims. Jihad, in other words, was the project of the whole community, not of a single individual.

Yet what kind of collective struggle was Islamic jihad?

E. W. Lane, in his book *Modern Egyptians*, explains that he once thought of jihad as being purely a war of aggression, but that after discussing the matter with a local Muslim scholar, he persuaded himself that jihad meant what we in the West, since the time of St. Thomas Aquinas, have called a just war. Curiously, the French scholar Jacques Ellul, in one of the most compelling essays in Bostom's book, argues that in fact the medieval concept of a just war was itself derived from the Islamic notion of jihad, and that the Crusades were simply a jihad directed by Christians against their own infidels, i.e., the Muslims. For Ellul, however, both just wars and crusades were equal betrayals of the true Christian ethics, which required a complete renunciation of any form of violence, including the violence of so-called just wars.

But was Islamic jihad the same thing as what Medieval and later European thinkers regarded as a just war?

The very concept of a just war only makes sense where there is an established and settled order of nations, each of which implicitly recognizes the right of other nations to exist. The underlying assumption is that there exists a more or less stable balance of power between the various players on the geopolitical stage. This rough stability represents the status quo, and all the players are expected to accept it precisely for the sake of the stability and order it provides. Any player who challenges it, therefore, is properly seen as a threat. For example, if a nation decides to take a chunk out of its neighbor's territory, this will upset the balance, and for order to be restored it will be necessary to force the offending player to return to its own borders. When the force required to achieve this goal is the deployment of arms in what we call a war, then the struggle is a just war; by the same logic, the war waged by the aggressor is an unjust one. Thus, the whole concept of a just war is dependent on the acceptance of the legiti-

macy of a preexisting status quo—what is unjust is any distur-
bance of this status quo; what is just, on the other hand, is the attempt to restore the status quo.

Here again Bostom's book completely dispels the notion that jihad is a just war in the sense recognized by the European concert
of nations. Islamic jihad, from its commencement, refused to recognize the legitimacy of any status quo other than that which has
been achieved in Dar el-Islam, or the domain of peace. Outside
the domain of peace, there was only the domain of war, i.e., the
law of the jungle, and here no entity could hope to be treated as
representing a legitimate order, for the simple reason that no order not based on Islamic law could ever be recognized as legitimate in the eyes of Muslims. Just as the French revolutionaries
refused to recognize the legitimacy of the European status quo of
their time, and called upon the people of Europe to overthrow
their ancien regimes in order to transform their culture into repli-
cas of France, so Muslim jihadists refused to recognize the legitimacy of any political status quo achieved by infidels, and called
upon the infidels to convert to Islam and join the Muslim domain
of peace—the only status quo that could be truly genuine, since all
mankind was born for the purpose of living as Muslims.

The concept of jihad, therefore, explodes the popular "clash of
civilizations" paradigm that is often used to describe conflict between Islam and the West. As we earlier argued, in the clash of
civilizations model, each player will try to improve his position
within the framework of a settled order, but none will seek to demolish and annihilate this framework. A nation will go to war with
another to achieve certain political goals that cannot otherwise be
achieved, as Clausewitz argued. But no nation will embark on a
course not merely of completely conquering another nation, but
of transforming its culture into a replica of its own. Yet this is precisely the goal of jihad—to destroy the status quo of those outside

the realm of Islam, in order to create an expansion of the realm of Islam—a realm in which Muslim culture would completely transform the old cultural traditions, as occurred repeatedly during those periods of Muslim expansion. For that is another unique feature of jihad: Islam did not conquer territories to create a colonial empire, but to expand its own domain over mankind. The Romans, the British, the French—all represented empires that were content to leave the conquered peoples their own gods, customs, and traditions. But Islam had a mission, and this mission was not the creation of empires, but the spread of Islam.

Empires, by their very nature, require a high degree of tolerance of differences. What is looked for in the subject population is docility and tranquility, not turmoil and rebellion. Hence, it makes perfect sense that during the heyday of the Islamic empires those who ruled these empires would exercise prudent and politically savvy toleration of the diverse peoples and culture over which they ruled—just as the Romans had done centuries before them and as the British would do centuries afterward. Yet while those who governed the Islamic empires might have wished to achieve a normal empire, built upon the basis of a clear-cut distinction between the rulers and the natives, the unique institution of jihad worked against the natural multicultural tolerance that had been sagely adopted by virtually all other great empires. Had jihad only been designed to conquer people in order to turn them into slaves and tributary subjects, then there would have been nothing distinctive about it. But the aim of jihad was not just conquest—it was conversion. Its goal was not to rule over a multicultural domain, but to create a single unified culture under Islam, and in carrying out this mission jihad was stunningly successful. Once Islamic culture sunk in, it became virtually impossible for any foreign cultural influence to make headway against it—and here again we can see its profound difference from those ephemeral military conquests that, while capturing territory, are unable to capture the hearts and minds of those who have been conquered.

Bostom devotes a large segment of his book to accounts of various historical jihads, and provides overwhelming evidence of the fanaticism, brutality, and ruthlessness of the Muslim holy warriors. Indeed, the book contains several narratives of the horror unleashed by Islamic jihad that, to our modern sensibilities, are simply revolting. Yet it is important to remember that there is nothing historically unique about this nauseating beastliness. During the Seven Years' War in eighteenth-century Europe—the Age of Reason—one witness wrote that "We are surrounded by hanging corpses, and the soldiers do not hesitate to massacre women and children as well if they resist the ransacking of their houses." In 1788 the highly civilized Prince Potemkin began a siege of the Ottoman city of Otchakof that lasted for six months. Later the French ambassador to Russia, Comte de Segur, wrote in his *Memoirs*: "The fury of the Russian soldiers was such that two days after the assault, when they found Turkish children hidden in forts and underground refuges, they seized them, threw them in the air, caught them on the points of their bayonets and cried, 'These hostages will never do harm to Christians.'"

Man has always been wolf to man, and there is sadly no atrocity committed by the holy warriors of classical jihad upon their infidel enemies that was not committed by European Christians on each other at some point in the past—and the quite recent past at that, as Hitler's wars of conquest sadly proved.

The comparison with Hitler, however, highlights precisely the factor that made Islamic jihad unique. A Russian Jew who fell under Nazi domination did not have the choice of converting to Aryanism. An inferior race could not change its status by changing its faith or behavior. But in the case of jihad, there was always an alternative to subjugation and extermination—you could convert to Islam, and it made no difference who you had been before or what race you belonged to or what language you spoke. Islam was, from the start, an artificial tribe; it was an escape from the biological tribe. Even the bitterest enemy was offered the opportunity to convert. For example, during the siege of Khartoum, the Mahdi assured General Gordon that his life would be spared if he simply converted to Islam—something that Gordon, a devout, if somewhat unorthodox, Christian, obstinately refused to do. More recently, and even more remarkably, the late al-Qaeda leader, al-Zarqawi, sent a message to George Bush saying that all would be forgiven if Bush himself simply converted to Islam. Indeed, as Andrew Bostom observes, a person who converted to Islam could be absolved of even the most heinous crimes—once he sided with Islam, all was forgiven.

Needless to say, to those who have been brought up in the liberal tradition of the modern West, the choice "Believe what I believe, or die" is not an acceptable mode of persuasion. Yet at least it is a choice—a choice that Joshua did not give the Canaanites, nor the Nazis the inferior races who fell into their hands after the invasion of the USSR. To many in the West, this may not appear to be much of a difference. For us it is axiomatic that no one may threaten another man with death in order to make him change his religion or cultural traditions. But in terms of designing a successful policy of conquest over new territories full of new people, this distinction is fraught with enormous world historical implications.

If a conqueror gives the conquered people a choice between becoming one of them or being subjugated or even eliminated, he will immediately gain an enormous advantage over those who do not offer such a choice. If the conquered people know that they have no choice but to accept their status as slaves and chattel, their hearts will continue to be rebellious. They may obey, but it is only out of fear; they will never come to feel that the conquerors represent legitimate authority. They will certainly never be willing to fight to defend the conquerors' position of supreme domination, but will rather work to subvert and undermine their hold on power.

Things will go quite differently, however, if the conquered people know that, by converting to the faith of their conquerors, they will be able to escape the humiliation of servitude and subjugation. If those who choose to convert are looked upon as members of the community of the faithful and no longer as infidels, then there will be a powerful incentive among people who, if not given this option, would necessarily be forced to remain in permanent opposition to their conquerors. It is difficult to imagine any method by which a quicker pacification of a conquered people could be achieved than by allowing them to make a swift and easy transition from being outsiders to being insiders—a transition that only required a person to accept the simple principle, "There is no God but Allah, and Mohammed is his Prophet."

Finally, by converting to Islam, a former subject was accorded a set of rights that no mere military conqueror would ever think of bestowing on his conquered subjects: No Muslim would be a slave, nor were Muslims expected to pay tribute. In short, the mission to spread Islam often worked against the interest of the ruling elite at the apex of empire. As the subject population became Muslims, the all-important distinction between the conquerors and the conquered vanished, and a single homogenous culture emerged, one that was often difficult to govern.

By accepting Islam, of course, it was also necessary for the new convert to accept the fanaticism that came with it, but this fanaticism was often directed against those rulers who, because they were struggling to operate an empire, tended to be more liberal and cosmopolitan in their outlook, and thus, judged by the standard of devout Muslims, lacked proper Muslim fervor.

This brings us to another ingenious feature of jihad that makes it unique, the institution that scholar Bat Ye'or has called *dhimmitude*—the policy of offering "special" treatment to those whom Muhammad dubbed Peoples of the Book, i.e., Christians, Jews, and sometimes Zoroastrians. While normal pagans were given the choice to convert or die, Jews and Christians were offered the choice between conversion to Islam and the acceptance of an inferior status within the community of Muslim believers, who would themselves, of course, control every aspect of the public life of the Jews and Christians. Yet as the Koran itself had commanded, and as the classical Islamic scholars continued to insist, it was not enough that the Jews and Christians within Dar el-Islam accept the cultural hegemony of Islam with their lips and outward behavior—they must, as the Koran demands, "feel themselves subdued." Like children brought up as slaves, they must psychologically feel their own helplessness and inferiority.

Instilling this sense of submission in those who most stubbornly held on to their old faith was vital—it is necessary that Jews and Christians cease imagining that there could be an alternative to life under Islam. Islamic hegemony had to become second nature to them, so that they would not think of rebelling, but would go about their business with total resignation to the status quo achieved by Islam. Over time, this psychological submission would become an increasingly unattractive position for those who wished to be free of it—yet here again, there was a path to liberation from this state of mental dependence and servitude: conversion to Islam.

Andrew Bostom speaks of jihad as a "devastating institution," yet the evidence he provides demonstrates that jihad was also a devastatingly *effective* institution. It succeeded in transforming whatever cultural traditions fell before it. This is what accounts for its uniqueness, not the fanaticism and brutality with which it was systematically carried out. But in light of its devastating effectiveness we must return to the question that we asked at the beginning: Why would Muslims want to abandon an institution that permitted them to expand Dar el-Islam across so much of our planet? Why should they dismantle jihad so long as it continues to work for them?

The revival of jihad is the essence of radical Islam, and this revival indicates that those who follow the path of radical Islam are by no means ready to dismantle their peculiar institution. On the contrary, it would appear that they are vigorously working to adjust it to the circumstances of Western modernity. But the question is, Can they achieve their goal?

Let us put this question another way: Can the peculiar institution of jihad still be as devastatingly effective in the twenty-first century as it was during the centuries of Muslim conquest and expansion? Even if Muslims refuse to renounce the institution of jihad, even if they want to keep it alive, what difference would this make if jihad as an institution can no longer be effective in the modern world? The Mamlukes wished to keep their own military tradition of sword combat alive too, but the Ottomans liquidated the Mamluke tradition by deciding to forgo swords and fight with guns instead. So even if the Muslims don't relegate jihad to the trash bin of history of their own free will, might one not legitimately argue that history has already dumped it there? Haven't the superior technology of the West and its vast military might rendered classical jihad as obsolete as Mamluke sword fighting? How effective can jihad be in the modern age?

It is possible to look at the historical evidence that Bostom presents and say, Yes, yes—you have it right. You have described classical jihad to a T. But so what? As an institution, its day has long since passed away. There is no cause for us to get alarmed about those Muslims who regard themselves as engaged in jihad against the West. They are simply living in a fantasy world.

But are they?

Islamic jihad has demonstrated an astonishing adaptability to different historical and material conditions—and in the post-9/11 epoch, there is no reason to believe that the spirit of jihad cannot be adapted to the challenges of modernity.

The spirit of jihad first emerged out of the plundering raids of Arab camel nomads who, like all warlike bands, simply took whatever they wanted from those who were weaker. They attacked merchant caravans and took their loot. Yet as they grew bolder, they began to make raids into the settled and civilized populations of the Byzantine and Sassanian Empires—with the intention not to seize these empires for themselves but merely to rob them. Under Omar, however, a new project began. Seeing how weak and fragile these tempting empires were, it was decided that the warlike Arab bands would simply hijack the empires and control them for themselves. From that point on, the warlike bands lived off the labor of the peasants who had been the support of all the various empires that had emerged in the Levant since the time of the Assyrians. Yet the secret of the success of the Arab bands lay less in their own warlike qualities than in the weakness and decadence of the empires they overthrew—a similar attempt to conquer Abyssinia around the same time failed miserably; the Abyssinians were still far too warlike themselves.

For Arabic philosopher of history Ibn-Khaldun, the conquest by the warlike Arabs of more advanced, yet weak and decadent empires represented a deep historical pattern. When a civilization becomes too sedentary, too decadent, too forgetful of the struggle for existence that put it on top, it becomes ripe for conquest by those who are still warlike and driven by a fanatical sense of purpose. Thus, for Ibn-Khaldun, superior wealth and superior civilization were no guarantee that those who possessed them could hold on to them in the face of even small but determined bands of fanatics united by a sense of group feeling. In short, for Ibn-Khaldun, jihad can be devastatingly effective even when it is waged against a civilization that, defined in material terms, is far in advance of the jihadists.

Can the same thing happen again today—or over the course of the next few generations? Is such an idea even thinkable? Or should those who raise such questions simply be dismissed as "right-wing alarmists" and hysteria mongers?

Here we can see again the most serious flaw in the clash of civilization model. If jihad were being used simply as a means of carrying out Clausewitzian warfare, then jihad would indeed be a relic of the past, about which none of us in the West should worry overmuch. If Muslim civilization only decided to clash with ours, we could clash back, and with overwhelming military force. If we were confronting the armies of Omar or of Tamerlane, then there is little doubt which side would secure the victory—namely the West. But the objective of jihad is not Clausewitzian "politics carried out by other means." Its objective is the destruction and dissolution of politics as we have come to understand it in the West. The jihadists are not interested in winning in our sense of the word. They can succeed simply by making the present world order unworkable, by creating conditions in which politics as usual is no longer an option, forcing upon the West the option of either giving in to their demands or descending back into anarchy and chaos.

Consider the example of the Nazis' approach to the Weimar Republic. After the failed Munich putsch, Hitler resolved never again to try to seize state power by force. Instead, the Nazis elected to follow a policy designed to make the Weimar system incapable of governing through normal political channels. Just make the system unworkable; make parliament unable to handle crises; force the government to govern through emergency enabling acts; compel the head of state to assume more and more dictatorial powers—do all these things, and before long a situation is created in which liberal politics is no longer an option. At this critical juncture, the people, in desperation, begin to seek an alternative to the clogged and deadlocked machinery of the parliamentary system—just as they had done when Mussolini's Blackshirts, a tiny faction of fanatics, made their celebrated march on Rome and vanquished the Italian Republic for which so many nineteenth-century idealists had shed so much blood.

Had Hitler's aim been to gain power within the Weimar system, his approach would have been utterly irrational; but his aim was to destroy the system completely. For him and his fellow Nazis, the politics of nihilism made perfect sense. Hating the system itself, they had no qualms about destroying it.

Here again we have a pattern that follows our crash of civilization model: Those who take this approach want to destroy the status quo, and, because of this desire, there is nothing that the guardians of the status quo can do to bribe them or tempt them or seduce them from pursuing their goal. Hitler himself refused to be paid off with anything less than the appointment as chancellor of Germany—a position he used to liquidate the parliamentary system without which his party could never have come close to gaining the citadel of power.

It does not take a modern sophisticated army to bring down a fragile and delicately balanced political order. The German army, even under the restrictions placed upon it by the Treaty of Versailles, could easily have crushed the Nazi movement, if it had merely been a question of brute force—but those who controlled the German army did not want to risk the descent into chaos that such a move would have inevitably entailed.

The chief strength of any established order *is* order. Order means organization, and organization is always to the advantage of those who possess it when they come into conflict with mobs and paramilitary rabble, like the German stormtroopers. It is always in the interest of the established order to avoid risking disorder, yet those who have no interest in preserving this order, and who are eager to destroy it, will welcome disorder for the sake of disorder. It is by destroying order, by undermining the normal rules and regulations that preserve order, that those who wish to overthrow the status quo succeed. They do not need to achieve the same degree of organized and efficient force that is the monopoly of the established order. They only need to make the established order reluctant to use its great strength, out of the understandable fear that by plunging into civil war, the established order will itself be jeopardized in the process. This fear of anarchy—the ultimate fear for those who ascribe to the politics of reason—can be used by those who welcome anarchy for the purpose of paralyzing the political process until the point is reached where the established order is helpless to control events through normal political channels.

In the contemporary revival of the spirit of jihad, the weapons being used are not scimitars or swords, but acts of terror, such as 9/11, the Madrid bombings, the London bombing, and the assassination of journalists like filmmaker Theo van Gogh. But in addition to the lethal use of terror and intimidation by terror, the modern jihadists have a number of other factors going for them.

First, they have demographics—in Europe, the birthrate of the native Europeans continues to fall, while the birthrate among the

Muslim immigrants is explosive. Unfortunately, the carpe diem ethos of the liberal West is disinclined to look very much beyond the present, and this bias causes it to systematically ignore and neglect long-term trends whose ultimate result will be left for our children's children to face. Furthermore, because of the individualist ethos adopted by the liberal West, it is unthinkable for Western governments to try to control the reproduction of their citizens. No Western government can demand that Muslims have fewer children, nor can it compel non-Muslims to have more. Because the liberal West is made up of people who limit the number of children they have, it is difficult for Westerners to grasp the idea that the breed-and-multiply strategy can be an immensely potent weapon in the struggle for survival and supremacy among traditions. If you wish to overwhelm your enemy, simply outbreed them, and sooner or later you will dominate—a strategy that the liberal modern West simply has no effective way to counter.

Second, the modern jihadists are facing an enemy that has a superstitious awe of the very idea of democracy. To liberal Westerners, democracy is always a good thing. But this overlooks the fact that in the Muslim world, those who historically have been the most tolerant and cosmopolitan in their outlook have come from the ruling political class and the economic elite, while the religious class and the bulk of the population have been precisely those who are most fanatically opposed to Western ways, as Lane noticed in the Egypt of his time. Thus the spread of democracy in Muslim countries will end by empowering those who are most opposed to the very modernization that the West wishes to bring about in Islamic culture. Yet, as we saw, there is nothing distinctly Islamic about this fact. If King José had decided to hold free and fair democratic elections in Spain in 1808, the Spanish people would have voted for the return of Ferdinand VII and the Inquisition. During the democratic Third Republic in France, the socialist and radical parties refused to consider giving women the right to vote—they were convinced that if women had this right, they would support the parties of reaction. There is no magic that makes free and fair elections produce an enlightened electorate. Only an immense cultural transformation can achieved this end— a point on which the "utopian" Condorcet was far more realistic than is the Western leadership of today.

Third, radical Islam has an enemy who remains utterly oblivious of the fact that the future of their own cultural traditions are being threatened by the current wave of neo-jihadism. Both the ruling elite of Europe and America, like the dominant elite of all imperial powers, have long since abandoned as a relic from the dark age the very concept of cultural protectionism. Multinational capitalism, with the mantras of globalization, free trade, and no borders, has condemned the idea of economic autarky and cultural protectionism to the trash bin of history. Multiculturalism, as the creed du jour of the intellectual elite, has played a similar role in encouraging Westerners to feel ashamed of their own cultural traditions. While Muslim children are taught to look upon their own traditions as binding and mandatory, as the fountain of all truth and goodness, the children of the liberal West are taught that they should free themselves from the traditions of the past, and learn to think for themselves. "Free your mind, and the rest will follow" is the theme song of modern education in the liberal West.

Fourth, radical Islam has an enemy, i.e., the modern liberal West, which from its point of view has succumbed to cultural decadence. In the modern West, *decadent* has become a word that is mainly used to describe the flavor of a particularly rich coffee or ice cream. In the past, however, the concept of decadence paid a critical role in the thinking of both historians and philosophers of history. At the beginning of his monumental history of Rome, Livy (59 B.C.–A.D. 17) explains that his goal in writing his work has been "to trace the progress of our moral decline, to watch, first, the sinking of the foundations of morality as the old teaching was allowed to lapse, then the rapidly increasing disintegration, then the final collapse of the whole edifice, and the dark dawning of our modern day when we can neither endure our vices nor face the remedies needed to cure them." For Livy, the cause of Roman decadence was self-evident: "Of late years wealth has made us greedy, and self-indulgence has brought us, through every form of sensual excess, to be, if I may so put it, in love with death both individual and collective." By virtue of its very worldly success, Roman culture was flirting with cultural suicide because the Romans no longer found any need to maintain the old original Roman virtues that had brought them so much success in the first place. Similarly, Americans today have little need for the virtues of the pioneer and the frontiersmen; instead, such virtues strike us now as uncouth, primitive, and even barbaric. We forget that we can only afford to despise these virtues because we, like the Romans, have temporarily escaped the jungle in which the survival of the group depended upon them, and where it was the duty of each generation to hand down "the old teaching" to the next generation so that they could learn to survive in the jungle too.

To say that a society has become decadent, in the sense that I am using this word, does not imply a moralizing value judgment. On the contrary, by the standard being offered here, a society may well become more decadent *and* more moral. A culture in which everyone maintains a rigid and lofty standard of moral rectitude may well be a culture that is unable to defend itself against those who seek to destroy it. Thomas Huxley expresses this painful paradox when he writes in "Evolution and Ethics" that "Strictly observed, the 'golden rule' . . . is the refusal to continue the struggle for existence. It can be obeyed, even partially, only under the protection of a society which repudiates it. Without such shelter, the followers of the 'golden rule' may indulge in hope of heaven, but they must reckon with the certainty that other people will be masters of the earth." Thus, according to Huxley, tolerance, kindness, and the golden rule may have a far more pernicious effect on the survival of a culture than dancing girls and orgies.

Yet Livy was clearly right in associating decadence with material prosperity and security. As the Romans discovered, decadence is hard to avoid once you have become rich and powerful—especially once you dominate the world around you, and fall into the illusion that you no longer need the harsh, prohibitive, and self-denying code that created the men who created the power that created the wealth. Why continue to honor a tradition that forces you to deny yourself a desirable pleasure? Relax the shaming code and people will get more fun out of life.

Yet what happens when there is no shaming code to inhibit what Huxley called our "innate tendency to self-assertion"? Obviously this tendency will not be checked, and as the shaming code is relaxed, then people will naturally become more interested in following their own bliss or seeking out their own aims in life. If the shaming code is no longer useful to the survival of the group, why keep it? If you have reached the end of history, where there will be no more crashes of civilization—such as the crash of our own—then why should anyone regret losing the moral fiber that made our pioneer ancestors so tough? We agree that they needed to be tough—they had hostile natives to deal with. But we don't. We Americans are living in paradise—and in paradise, as the Bible reminds us, there is no need for shame.

It is pointless to try to blame anyone for this. The Romans didn't set out to become decadent, and neither did we. We simply did what came naturally to people who have achieved security and plenty—we stopped worrying about tomorrow. Cooperation could be organized around the individual's enlightened self-interest, hence we began to dispense with those aspects of the shaming code that are geared to produce an intensified group feeling. Duty was no longer based on a visceral imperative that made many of our more rigid forbearers slaves to duty. The watch-words for us have been "rights" and "empowerment"— and this is a far cry from the nineteenth-century English philosopher F. H. Bradley's stern conception of "my station and its duties."

The questions we must face are: How much more liberated can we get? Is there a limit? And can we know when we've reached it—or is this one of those facts that only comes to light in the midst of a very unpleasant surprise?

The carpe diem ethos has encouraged us to be intensely indi-vidualist, absorbed in the present moment, hostile to all forms of traditional religion and authority, champions of materialism, con-sumerism, and hedonism. Furthermore, we are under the intel-lectual control of a powerful central media that systematically celebrates the carpe diem ethos and bashes all inherited traditions as irrational superstitions that children should be gently weaned away from by a benevolent enlightened elite. We are throwing away the heritage of our past in search of a future filled with toys and baubles. It is a mindset virtually everyone picks up simply in the process of adjusting to Western modernity. The only ones who can escape its influence in the West are those who opt out of modernity altogether, like the Amish. In the West, to become normal is to be modern, and to be modern is to embrace the carpe diem ethos.

We in the modern liberal West must recognize that it is possi-ble, and even quite natural, for Muslims to resent us for our power, and to fear and loathe us for our decadence. The Iranian Revolution has been so radical to us precisely because it wished to eliminate all Western influence, and chose to resist modernity tooth and nail. They feared that if Western influence came to predominate in the Muslim world, their culture would fall prey to Western decadence.

To recognize a fact does not imply that you wish the fact were so. To accept how the Muslim world feels about us is not to say that they are justified in having these feelings. It is simply to be realistic. It is like saying to a person, Don't pet that dog—he will bite you. The comment is just a word of caution, a realistic appraisal; it does not imply that the person deserves to be bitten by the dog, or that the dog is right to bite.

Keeping Ibn-Khaldun in mind, in Part Five we will ask the painful questions, Have we become so decadent in the West that we will be unable to maintain Western supremacy? Or are we simply so wealthy and powerful that we do not need to worry about tomorrow?

Part Five

14

CAN CARPE DIEM
SOCIETIES SURVIVE?

In Robert Kagan's book *Of Paradise and Power* he describes America and the West in the same terms once used to describe the Polynesian Islands—they are paradises, and certainly, when viewed against the bloody and brutal background of history, there are good reasons for so describing them. Yet there is a profound problem with any paradise—it tends inevitably to drift toward a carpe diem ethos, in which the individuals of the current generation are far more concerned with maximizing their enjoyment of life than in sacrificing their present happiness for the good of future generations. Indeed, in an extreme carpe diem society, children are raised without being given any sense that they have a transgenerational duty to the as yet unborn—the duty to leave them a better world. Each child, in a carpe diem society, is encouraged "to follow his bliss," as Joseph Campbell puts it. He is free to choose whatever lifestyle suits him, and he is encouraged to break with the tribal traditions that still linger in isolated backwaters of America and Europe. Children are taught a great deal about their rights, but very little about their duties.

The term *capitalism*, like the term *democracy*, has become a hindrance to understanding the reality of our world. The capitalist ethos that began to flourish in Italy several hundred years before the Protestant Reformation and spread to so many parts of Europe and America, began as a transgenerational project in which capitalist fathers trained their sons to deny themselves the pleasures of the moment in order to save money to invest in business ventures. As Werner Sombart argued, even the Catholic Church's restrictions on usury were, paradoxically, a part of this original capitalist ethos—it argued that usury was wrong when the money was lent to spendthrifts whose only interest in it was the maximization of their immediate pleasure, without a thought for tomorrow. Don't give money to those who practice the ethos of carpe diem; only lend it to those who will do something productive with it.

Today, however, the word *capitalism* is used to describe a radically different ethos from the original ethos of delayed gratification and sacrifice for future generations. The whole point of consumerism is to live for the moment and to seize the day. Henry Ford refused to sell his cars on credit, because he sincerely believed that the use of credit would undermine the original capitalist ethos that required people to make sacrifices in the now in order to save up for a better future. If you gave it to them now, without their earning it, you would be reinforcing the human weakness that naturally seeks out instant gratification: I want it now!

The carpe diem ethos that has developed in America and the West has infected every aspect of our cultural and political life. Indeed, the end of history thesis, like its companion, the myth of modernity, is the perfect ideology for a carpe diem society: Why worry about the future? Things will naturally take care of themselves. Soon everyone else in the world will be living in a culture like ours—all we have to do is sit by our swimming pools and wait for them to come along.

Today in America we want religions that make us feel good, and flee from those that make demands on us. Even in politics, instead of looking at the world realistically, we prefer to follow our bliss. Those who would like to live in a peaceful world think it is enough to visualize world peace. Those who don't want anyone telling them what to do vote libertarian. Indeed, American politics is threatening to become an exercise in fantasy ideologies—we pick the party line that, like our religions, makes us feel good about ourselves. To see this, it is enough to visit any number of the blogsites that are devoted simply to reaffirming the point of view of those who follow the blog. The result is what might be called "blog-blindness," a pathology in which the only facts one notices are those that reinforce our own preconceived notions, and the only opinions we read are those of people who think exactly like ourselves.

The carpe diem ethos has much that is charming about it. It is happy with its Live and Let Live approach to life. Yet what happens to such a society when it is confronted by a culture whose motto is, "You must live as we live." How does it defend itself?

In other words, how long can a paradise stay in power if it succumbs to its own hedonistic impulses, seizing the day, but giving no thought for the morrow?

In the West, this is not a question that is even raised within the paradigms of Fukuyama or Huntington, and the explanation of this is quite simple: We in the West do not believe we have to worry about tomorrow because we are under the most dangerous delusion that a carpe diem society can entertain: that power is a permanent position of those who have gotten their hands on it.

J. William Fulbright spoke of the danger of arrogance of power; but in the West today, and especially in the United States, this arrogance has taken a particularly suicidal turn. We have come to believe that we are invulnerable, that we have accumulated such power and wealth that it is unimaginable that our dominance could be challenged. So what if there are those—multitudes of those—who bitterly resent our hegemony and who would like to bring us down? Let them try—they can't harm us.

In the fairy tale, there is an old sorcerer whose wisdom and magic wand allow him to command great powers, though being a wise man he is aware of the dangers that come with such enviable power. Unfortunately, his apprentice is fascinated only by the wonderful result of having so much power under one's wand, and so one day, when the sorcerer departs on an errand, his apprentice picks up the priceless wand and commences to use its magic in order to relieve himself of the daily drudgery to which he, as a lowly apprentice, is assigned. In the Disney cartoon version, featured in *Fantasia*, the apprentice is Mickey Mouse, and his magic consists of bringing to life mops and buckets to clean and sweep the sorcerer's shop. Yet, alas, the poor apprentice, though he has the wand in his hands, is not sufficiently versed in the wisdom of sorcery to know how to get the animated mops and buckets to stop once he has started them going, and, before long, the shop is flooded by an endless procession of self-willed buckets and overrun by maniacally mopping mops. The apprentice, though he has so much power at his fingertips, lacks the one thing he needs, namely the sorcerer's wisdom.

America and the West today are very much like the sorcerer's apprentice in the fable. The supremacy of America and the West was not the achievement of our own generation, but of the many generations who went before us, and who worked hard and made enormous sacrifices so that their heirs could benefit from their labor and dedication. Those who created the basis of America's world power were also shrewdly realistic men—men who were often capable of playing the most cynical games in order to further the interest of their nation. Today, however, this great heritage of power has been taken up not by master sorcerers, but by those who can only be compared to the sorcerer's incompetent apprentice.

The leadership of the present generation, from George W. Bush to Tony Blair, from Bill Clinton to John Kerry, have all been raised to believe that cultures of reason will naturally triumph over cultures of the tribal mind. They have all bought into the myth of inevitable progress that was a cardinal tenet of all socialist visionaries of the nineteenth century, from August Comte to Karl Marx. For all these visionaries, it seemed self-evident that mankind's trajectory had to follow that of the individual. Just as the child eventually outgrows his tendency to throw tantrums, so too mankind must eventually outgrow the appeal of tribal fanaticism. Yet, as I have argued in this book, there is absolutely no reason to hold such a view—the group mind will always remain a threat because popular fanaticism is, in and of itself, a formidable source of power, and if properly directed, can be used as a lethal weapon against precisely those cultures that have most thoroughly eliminated all vestiges of fanaticism from their midst.

Robert Kagan, in an influential article published in *Policy Review* titled "Power and Weakness," the basis of his later book *Of Paradise and Power*, made the claim that Americans and Europeans did not see eye to eye because America had power, whereas the Europeans no longer possessed it. Yet in light of the aftermath of the intervention in Iraq, it is tempting to present the difference between America and Europe not in terms of power and weakness, but power and wisdom. True, America had the power to intervene in Iraq, but it lacked the wisdom to recognize that waves of popular fanaticism would render null and void the noble but naïve hope of creating the ethos of a liberal democracy by means of "free and fair elections."

American policy makers, despite their noble intentions, made the fatal error of confusing populism with liberal democracy, thereby overlooking the fact that populism has almost invariably been the enemy of liberal cultures of reason, not only in the Muslim world, but in the West. Populism is the politics of the tribal mind, whereas liberalism is the politics of the rational actor.

The two leading Viennese politicians at the end of the nineteen century, Karl Lueger and Georg Schönerer, were both famous for their command of the masses. Both were bitterly anti-Semitic, and both became role models for Adolf Hitler, who was himself perhaps the greatest populist demagogue of all time, and who learned the lesson that anti-Semitism was the key to creating popular fanaticism. As Ian Kershaw has pointed out in his biography of Hitler, from the period of his rise to power well into the midst of the Second World War, Hitler was the most beloved and popular leader in Europe and even the world. Thus, populism and liberalism are not just different phenomena—they are more often than not the bitterest of enemies.

Yet herein lies the quandary of the West. It was our ancestors who began the struggle against popular fanaticism—our Enlightenment was not imposed on us from without, but arose from within. On the other hand, in those societies like early-nineteenth-century Spain, where Enlightenment was brought in with the aid of a foreign army, it was bitterly resisted by the popular fanaticism of those who wanted no part of it, and who wished to see a return of the Inquisition and of Bourbon absolutism. The moral: If a culture is to be enlightened, it can only come about from within. It cannot come about at the point of a bayonet, as the Spanish rebellion of 1808 proved. Nor can it come about by having people read our speeches and writings, and examine our proofs and demonstrations. What is required is an immense social transformation of the kind that swept over Europe with the Protestant Reformation, the rise of the middle class, and the coming of the Enlightenment. In short, there is no easy way to create a culture of rational actors.

Nevertheless there have been many intellectuals in the West who have sought reliable methods by which Islamic cultures could be modernized in a hurry. Basically, they boil down to three: conversionism, assimilationism, and seductionism.

First, consider conversionism. This has been the approach taken by Bush and the neoconservatives in their attempts at reconstructing Iraq. The premise was that, with the aid of military force and the institution of democratic reforms, we would be able to start converting Muslims from their traditions of popular fanaticism and turn them into liberal and secular-minded moderns, like ourselves. Like the Protestant missionaries of the nineteenth century who set out to convert the heathens, the neoconservatives believed that if we could only show them the light they would immediately accept it and turn away from their heathen path. Yet while the Protestant missionary approach worked well with certain cultures, like the Polynesian Islanders, it failed miserably when it came up against Islam—and the reason for this failure has already been explained in an earlier chapter. The Muslims are, from an early age, indoctrinated into a shaming code that demands a fanatical rejection of anything that threatens to subvert the supremacy of Islam. Both Protestant and the often far more subtle Catholic missions to the Muslim world have always failed miserably in their efforts to entice Muslims away from their fanatical devotion to their faith—they simply could not be converted. The new secular missionaries sent to Iraq under the Bush administration, for analogous reasons, have also failed miserably. The moral: We can reconstruct the buildings, pipelines, and infrastructure of an Islamic society, but we cannot reconstruct the collective shaming code of the group mind. Culture matters. Thus, conversionism has proved itself to be a false promise.

Second, take assimilationism. This assumes that Muslims when they emigrate to a new culture, like the Muslims who have moved into Europe, can be gradually assimilated into their new liberal secular environment. But the problem with this approach is that, if we look at the facts, the Muslim emigrants, by and large, do not show any inclination to assimilate themselves. Instead, when they move into a different culture, they quickly begin to demand that the culture start to transform itself to accommodate them.

In comparison, when Eastern European Jews moved to the United States around the turn of the nineteenth century, they were invariably eager to accommodate themselves to their new home. Rather than insisting that Americans should adopt their Old World ways, the Jewish immigrants struggled to master the ethos of the New World. They wanted, like all good Americans, to fit in—and fit in they did. The Muslim immigrant, on the other hand, reacts in two quite different ways. First, he may insist on claiming an exemption for himself from the customs of his new home, for example, by asking for courts of law based on Shari'a, as has occurred in Canada. Second, he may insist that his new home should change its customs to suit his own cultural traditions. In the aftermath of the cartoon riots, for example, many European Muslims demanded that the West should pass laws criminalizing any kind of disrespect toward Muhammad or his religion.

At a deeper level, however, the problem with assimilationism is that it ignores a law of great importance: Fanatics drive out non-fanatics. An intolerant ethical code will always end by trumping a carpe diem ethical code. Today in the West, where people are ashamed to be fanatical about anything, those immigrants who bring with them deep-set traditions of fanaticism are able, by virtue of their insistent and repetitive fanaticism and their willingness to go to extremes, to get virtually whatever they ask for. Thus assimilationism offers another false promise: In fact, rather than the Muslims assimilating themselves to us, we in the West seem to be assimilating ourselves to them.

The third approach I will dub seductionism. To use the language developed in this book, this approach argues that the rigid and prohibitionist Muslim shaming code will ultimately loosen its grip on those Muslims who have been exposed to Western societies with their carpe diem ethos. Muslims will be seduced into becoming modern, simply because by doing so they will be able to get away with doing all those things that they have been trained to look upon with visceral horror. Both Goebbels and Hitler, for example, felt that it had been a terrible mistake to permit German soldiers to spend time in Paris—the free-and-easy laissez faire of French decadence was too much of a temptation. It ended up corrupting them by loosening the rigidity of the far sterner and more puritanical shaming code by which they had been brought up. Or, to put it in the American vernacular, "How do you keep them down on the farm after they've seen Paree?"

Of course, this is always one possibility, but the problem is that Mohammed Atta and the other 9/11 hijackers had, themselves, been seduced by our carpe diem culture. They searched the Web for pornography and went out drinking at strip clubs. Yet that did not keep them from sacrificing themselves in order to bring down the World Trade Center. Indeed, it is tempting to speculate that it may well be those Muslims who have been most tempted by the carpe diem culture of the West who are most committed to the

violent effort to destroy it. Iconoclasts are often motivated by the
desire to destroy those images that stir up impermissible emotions in themselves—emotions that defy their own puritanical
shaming code. A man may decry pornography not because he was
revolted by it, but precisely because he was helplessly attracted to
it. And the same may be true for many Muslims who feel tempted
by the carpe diem culture of the West, but who are revolted by
their temptation. They find the only solution to their dilemma is
to destroy the icons of the culture that both fascinates and repels
them. The Yorkshire Ripper serial killer, it should be recalled,
confessed that he killed the prostitutes because they tempted him,
and the only way he could overcome his temptation was to kill
the temptress.

Yet if Islam cannot be modernized by any of the above meth-
ods, what else can be done with it? If Muslim fanaticism contin-
ues to pose a threat to our own carpe diem ethos in the modern
West, perhaps we can just destroy the threat by destroying the
Muslims with our overwhelming military superiority—a view,
never expressed publicly, but often expressed privately, that says,
"Oh well, if things get really grim, we can always annihilate the
Muslims with our nuclear weapons."

The objection to this approach is that the West cannot decivi-
lize itself to fight fanaticism with its own weapons of ruthlessness.
By this I am not saying that it should not do this as a matter of
ethical principle; I am saying that it cannot do it as a matter of
fact. It cannot violate its modern liberal code of decency and tolerance. In the Second World War, the Americans and the English
were capable of fire-bombing Dresden; the Americans had no
qualms using atomic bombs on the civilian targets of Hiroshima
and Nagasaki. Our "finest generation," as it has been called, was
capable of perpetrating acts no one in the West today can ever
imagine themselves doing. Thus, those who seek to find a radical

solution in repaying Islamic terrorists in their own coin are engaging in a fantasy of their own invention. The only way that the liberal West could be decivilized to this degree would be through the process of a world historical catastrophe, in which the law of the jungle has compelled all parties to return to the basic struggle for survival.

15

OUR NEW WORLD DISORDER

Wwhat undercuts the various attempts to pretend Muslim fanaticism is not a threat is the fact that today Muslims are using the politics of fanaticism to do what fanatics have always done best, namely to seize the historical momentum.

What do I mean by historical momentum?

A player on the stage of history has historical momentum so long as he is the one who is making the moves, while everyone else is in the passive position of simply reacting to these moves. Hitler's rise to power, for example, and his great triumphs until the invasion of Russia were all due to the fact that he grasped the importance of historical momentum. He did the moving and shaking, and everyone else had to figure out how to respond to him. Today, United States policy in regard to Iraq has been reduced to one of pleading for the Iraqi leaders to come together, settle their differences, and establish a government of national unity. Bush's foreign policy in Iraq, which set out as a bold bid at regaining the historical momentum after 9/11, has been reduced by the course of events and by the administration's own naïve folly into a policy of issuing vain and pointless exhortations to the Iraqi to behave themselves. John Ruskin, as a very little boy, once ascended a pulpit to deliver one of the world's shortest sermons. He said, "People, be good."

No doubt young Ruskin meant every word he said, and perhaps he expected his exhortation to transform the lives of those who heard his uplifting words. But in the case of the Bush administration, such vacuous homilies, accompanied by an occasional schoolmarmish shaking of the finger, are all that remain of what began as a "world-historical gamble" by the United States to gain control of the historical momentum, both in the Middle East and in the world.

The West is now in the position of the player in a game of chess who finds himself constantly on the defensive, waiting for the move of the far more aggressive player that he is pitted against. We have completely lost the historical momentum—it is now in the hands of others, though which others we cannot quite know.

Like a chess player on the defensive, we no longer have the option of forming our own strategy: We have our hands full in reacting to the unexpected moves of our opponent. It is this fact, more than any of the objections that were raised above, that makes all the various approaches to dealing with the Muslim world exercises in futility. We no longer have the luxury of constructing a policy toward the Muslim world; we can only wait and wonder what will happen next.

Yet, though it is apparent that the West has lost the historical momentum, it is not quite clear exactly who has seized it.

Here we encounter one of the most baffling of the problems presented by the new world disorder. So long as the various nations of the world went about their ordinary business, selecting their leadership in the same old corrupt or not so corrupt ways, it was quite easy to predict what figures would play a role on the world stage. Like the revolving door of leadership during the various parliamentary crises of the French Third Republic, new governments might be formed, but those that formed them were always the same old familiar faces. Similarly, in the United States, no one expects either the republicans or the democrats to pick a candidate for the next election whose name is not already a household word. The deck may be reshuffled, but it still contains the same old cards.

The same, however, cannot be said of the Muslim world. Boiling over with populist agitation, no one can confidently predict who will be ruling Iraq or Pakistan or Iran two or three years from now—no one can even be confident that the leadership of Muslim nations may not be turned over to men whose names are now completely unknown to us—as the name of the current president of Iran was unknown until his stunning electoral triumph and his equally amazing capture of the world's limelight. In addition, as populism secures triumphs in South America, the same thing is happening there—it throws up wild cards and jokers, making it difficult to predict the course these nations will take in the near future. Will they be our allies or our bitterest enemies?

This fact poses two problems for the West. First, there is the obvious problem of uncertainty. Since we do not know who will ultimately govern Palestine or Iraq or any other Muslim country in the coming years, it becomes extraordinarily difficult even to hedge our bets. The horse we back this year may be gone the next—as happened in Iraq, first with Chalabi, and then with Allawi. So all bets are off, and once again we are in the position where all we can do is wait and see.

But there is a second even graver danger to us in the puzzle of who will lead Islam. Precisely because of the populist turmoil in the Middle East—a turmoil that the Bush administration fecklessly encouraged in the mistaken belief that populist turmoil was proof of a desire for liberal democracy—the next leaders of the Muslim world will almost certainly be self-made men who have struggled hard to gain power in their countries, and who will have the common touch—they will be men of the people who, like all populist leaders, will feel the shaming code of their people operating in their own viscera. They will therefore be wily and cunning; they will be familiar with the politics of the mob; they will be demagogues and rabble-rousers; but most of all, due to their own tough struggle to achieve power, they will have a far more profound appreciation of the laws of the jungle than our own leadership.

On the other hand, the leadership of the West is made up entirely of men and women who have obtained positions of authority not by seizing it after a bitter power struggle, but simply by following a routine procedure acknowledged as legitimate by their society. For example, in both the United States and in European democracies, there are long-established and immensely powerful political parties whose support is essential if a candidate has any hope of achieving high office—or even relatively low ones. Those who are able to achieve high office are therefore men and women who have abided by the rules and conventions of the system. They would not be permitted to come close to positions of authority if they had not shown themselves to be reliable representatives of the party that decides to back them. Thus, the political parties of the West are solely responsible for screening and selecting those who they can trust to hold power. They will, obviously, wish to field a candidate who is popular enough to win votes. But it is still the established party that chooses the candidates, and not the people themselves. The people, therefore, are only asked to express their preference among the choices that have been given to them by the established political parties.

Herein lies the danger of the Western crisis of leadership: As our current crisis drifts aimlessly toward a world historical catastrophe in which policy is no longer an option and our leadership is forced simply to react to the events initiated by others, the people will become increasingly cynical and angry at the failure of their leaders to lead and to control events. More and more they will regard their established political systems as being inherently incapable of producing genuinely popular and charismatic leaders—leaders that are able to inspire the confidence of their followers. Consequently, as the system seems more and more inept, the search for radical alternatives will intensify.

The danger here is that the established political systems of the United States and Western Europe will face the kind of crises of confidence that lead to the dissolution of the rule by parliamentary democracy in Europe between the end of the First World War and the beginning of the Second World War, accompanied by a search for new and charismatic leaders who will emerge not from the established political parties, but from among the people themselves. These populist crusaders, unlike the established leadership, will be able to speak directly to the hearts of the people because they feel the same rage and anger and betrayal that the people themselves feel. They will share their tribal code. For this is the essence of all populist leadership—the leader must be seen as someone who is loyal first and foremost to the people, and not to some higher abstract ideal, however noble. They must be willing to act like the chief of a tribe, and not like the chair of the board of a multinational corporation.

Whether America and Europe will see the dissolution of their own established political systems is, of course, an open question that can only be answered by the unfolding of history over the next decade or two. But there is one thing that we can be sure of—in the collapse of the corrupt regimes in the Middle East, under the mounting waves of populist fanaticism, the men who will emerge as the new leaders will be those who are willing to play the role of the tribal chieftain. As noted above, they will be well versed in the brutal struggle for power that is the only way to get ahead in a society that no longer has a routine procedure for obtaining positions of authority. And above all they will represent their tribe fanatically, because it is only by their own fanatical loyalty that they can expect their tribe to remain loyal to them.

This is one of the most important features of the dissolution of the politics of the status quo. When legitimate authority self-liquidates, it leaves a power vacuum—unable to fill this power vacuum with the inner members of the old order, new leaders emerge who are able to seize power through cunning or ruthlessness, or by fanatical determination. These people, precisely because they have come to power by moving outside the established channels and routines, will normally possess a far better grasp of the popular sentiment than the established insiders. By virtue of being outsiders, they will be able to relate and feel in sync with the emotions and visceral reactions of the people.

In a world in which the Cosmic Process is again getting the upper hand over the Ethical Process, the tribal/group mind will play an increasingly significant role, not only in Muslim nations, but in the West as well. The struggle for survival will again create the Us versus Them mindset necessary to success in a life-and-death struggle, and in such an environment, the liberal internationalist will increasingly be looked upon as a traitor to his tribe. Nor does it make any difference whether the liberal internationalist is pushing the globalist agenda of multinational capitalist corporations, or the cosmopolitan agenda of the multicultural Left. From the point of view of the tribal mind, both forms of internationalism will represent a betrayal of the interests of the tribe.

Indeed, this is one of the great vulnerabilities of the modern liberal West. As we observed earlier, in Islam the intellectual and spiritual elite, represented by the mullahs and the clergy, are virtually never at odds with the popular sentiment of the Muslim faithful. They articulate the tribal visceral code that they share with the masses—a fact that is often baffling and infuriating to the West, especially when the spiritual leaders of Islam either ignore or endorse what we regard as acts of sheer terrorism. But in the West, from the time of the Enlightenment, the intellectual elite have tended to see their role not as spokesmen for popular sentiment, but as critics of it. As we saw in our discussion of Condorcet's theory of education, it was the mission of the Western enlightened elite to eradicate the prejudices, superstitions, and intolerance of the masses—and not to confirm and support them.

This fact has momentous consequences for the future. Radical Islam, as a mass movement, will not be held back by the scruples or qualms of an intellectual elite, nor of a political leadership that has a vested interest in working toward global and international cooperation. Rather, both the clerical elite of Islam as well as the populist leaders who come to the fore will, instead of restraining the mass fanaticism of the people, incite it and thrive on it. Thus while the reemerging tribal mind of the West will become increasingly frustrated at a leadership that continues to espouse liberal and internationalist values, the Muslim world will be unified behind a leadership that has completely renounced and repudiated these same values.

To say it once again, the specter that looms before us is not the clash of civilizations, but the crash of Western civilization. Radical Islam cannot hope to defeat us through superior military technology, but it can aim at seizing the historical momentum. It can force the West to respond to events completely beyond its control until the point is reached where the West abandons the defense of the tottering status quo, and reverts back to the brutal struggle for existence.

Furthermore, because we in the West are reluctant to depart from our carpe diem ethos, we are unwilling to think in terms of the very long long run that comes quite naturally to those peoples who are fanatically committed to holding on to their traditions, and who are intent on spreading them to the rest of mankind. While we think little further than our retirement, they think in terms of centuries—what, however, do centuries mean to us anymore? In the long run, we're all dead—so who cares about the long-term fate of the West? Finally, while we raise our children to have contempt for the very traditions that created the Western cultures of reason, they are raising their children to be willing to die to keep their traditions alive. In the long run, whose traditions will triumph? In the long run, whose children will inherit the earth?

In the liberal West of today we have virtually eliminated fanatical intolerance, and we think, by doing so, that we have done a great thing. In fact, we *have* done a great thing—we have created cultures of reason in which fanaticism is a thing of the past. We have allowed the Ethical Process to triumph over the Cosmic Process, created societies peopled with rational actors, rather than tribal actors. Yet fanaticism remains a powerful weapon in the Cosmic Process, so that those human beings who are most fanatically committed to retaining their cultural traditions will inevitably be the ones who are most successful in passing them on to future generations. Thus, ultimately, the root cause of fanaticism is none of the things that we in the West have imagined— the root cause of fanaticism is the Cosmic Process itself, and as long as human beings remain as they have always been, those who are able to use fanaticism as a weapon in the struggle for survival will have a good and reliable one.

Of course, we can express our moral outrage and condemnation of the acts of Muslim fanatics. No doubt, the Mamluke swordsmen were just as outraged by the decision of the Ottomans to use the gun instead of the sword with which the Mamlukes were far superior. But the danger of moral outrage is that it deludes us into thinking it has any appreciable effect on the inevitable. It doesn't. No doubt those Frenchmen who in 1940 were horrified at the lightning advance of Hitler's blitzkrieg felt moral outrage that Hitler had not played the rules of the game as these rules were understood by the French high command. But did that make any difference to the outcome? Even the most morally indignant Frenchman had to accept the total and catastrophic defeat of France—both as a great military power, and as a state that could exercise the national independence that Frenchmen had always valued above all else.

No one expected the sudden collapse of France. No one ever seems to suspect when a great established order is about to fall. How many people predicted the implosion of the Soviet Union? The French historian Pierre de la Gorce says that in the weeks before Louis Philippe was chased off the throne in France, no monarchical status quo appeared to rest on such solid and substantial foundations.

The fact that people cannot foresee the coming collapse of a great established order should make us suspicious of those who predict the end of history in our time. Indeed, it is quite possible that we should always heed the message of those who declare the end of history, not because they are right, but because they are unwittingly warning us that catastrophe is waiting right around the corner. On the other hand, those who believe that we are experiencing a clash of civilizations need to reflect seriously on Ibn-Khaldun's theory of the historical cycle. If one of the civilizations has lost its warlike spirit, its sense of self-evident superiority, while its adversary is still intensely animated by these exact qualities, then in the long run it makes little difference whether the self-doubting civilization has toys—or guns—superior to those of the fanatically committed. Eventually, the fanatics will become king of the mountain.

Is this an example of historical inevitability, or is there something we can do about it? Will the devastatingly effective institution of jihad, adapted to new circumstances, be able to transform the entire world into the realm of Dar el-Islam? No. But it may well be able to destroy the world that Western liberalism has made. And that is something to think about.

Muslim fanatics believe that by destroying the Western status quo they will be ushering in a golden age of human happiness. This illusion mirrors the neoconservative faith that destroying corrupt and despotic regimes in the Middle East will lead to the triumph of global democracy. In fact, the conflict between the two, if it continues, will not end in the victory of one side over the other; it will lead to a process of decivilizing that is already evident on both sides.

The ultimate outcome of such a process is impossible to predict. Who will emerge triumphantly out of the struggle is something none of us can now foresee. All that we can know with certainty is that the decivilizing process will come at a high cost: It will entail the dissolution of the established order dubbed the Pax Americana.

It is true that the Pax Americana fell far short of the "true perfection of mankind" envisioned by Condorcet. It is equally true that the Pax Americana did not quite come up to the end of history as imagined, both on Right and Left, by our utopian intellectuals: brilliant men and women, to be sure, but brilliant men and women who bicker endlessly about how to design the gates of Paradise, without worrying overmuch whether anyone will ever live to open them.

The Pax Americana represented one of the rare and precious periods in human history in which the forces of the Ethical Process were able to triumph, more or less, over those of the Cosmic Process. With the dissolution of the Pax Americana, there will come what Arnold Toynbee called a time of troubles, what we have dubbed the return to the law of the jungle.

Yet there is still a ray of hope—and one that may prove our best defense against our new world disorder. The threatened return to the law of the jungle may wake us up—and wake us up in time to defend ourselves from it. The crisis that is now threatening may have a therapeutic effect on the West by shocking us into a sharp awareness of both the uniqueness and the nobility of our own traditions. Those who have been forced to defend a tradition that represents a higher stage of civilization against one representing a lower stage are not as apt to be forgetful of the difference between the two. The Dutch, in order to maintain their independent Republican tradition, had to create a nation out of the sea bed. They had to be prepared to flood their own country in case of attack, as they did when the armies of Louis XIV tried to occupy Holland in the Dutch War (1672–78). The Dutch thus were perfectly aware that their independence was an anomaly—it no more represented the natural order of things than their own landscape did, a landscape which, without the powerful system of dykes, would by nature have been a seascape. For the Dutch, civic liberty, freedom of thought, the essence of their culture of reason—these were all things that had to be bitterly fought for. How long could the Dutch have survived if they, like us, had been convinced that we all want the same things, and taught their children to respect the culture of those who were trying to crush their freedom?

The modern liberal West must take its cue from the Dutch: We must be prepared to defend our own unique and rare cultures of reason as ferociously as they defended theirs.

CONCLUSION

Paradoxically, America can only help the world if it remembers how profoundly different from it we are. By assuming that other nations can copy us, we are forgetting that we are, in every sense of the word, inimitable—the product of an exceptional set of circumstances that occurred in one spot of the globe at one particular moment in the history of humankind. That is why any foreign policy that refuses to recognize our own uniqueness is inevitably doomed to failure.

Yet Americans, in addition to understanding their own historical exceptionalism, must also realize that it is this very quality that has provided our wealth, stability, and power. Republican constitutionalism could flourish here, but only because it did not have to contend with cultural predators like empires and migrating barbarian hordes. Perhaps even more importantly, the settlers in North America had to work for themselves. They could not set themselves up as a ruling class whose job was to exploit to the utmost a docile peasantry they had simply inherited from the previous conquerors. The culture of such a ruling class will always be aristocratic, in contrast to the democratic liberalism natural to a community in which everyone is expected to provide for himself by his own hard work. The tradition of Protestant dissent also made mandatory a high degree of religious tolerance of sectarian differences. Voltaire, in his *Letter on England*, wrote that a society that has only one church cannot be tolerant, while a society with twenty-six different churches must be.

American exceptionalism proves nothing whatsoever about the inevitable triumph of liberalism or democracy throughout the world. Indeed, few illusions could be more fatal to the survival of the United States than the alluring belief that our tolerant liberalism has succeeded in dominating so much of the world because tolerant liberalism is a superior adaptation to the real world than rival systems, such as the intolerant fanaticism of Islam, or Oriental despotism, or the rule of military fraternities. In America, tolerant liberalism survived only because it had no natural predators in the form of empires, and no natural temptations in the form of a peon class.

The position that America is unique due to unusual historical and geographical circumstances is called American exceptionalism. But in fact the modern liberal West is itself an exception that has been built on the creation of the stubborn and libertarian communities that spontaneously arose in the United States, Canada, and Australia. There would be no modern liberal West if it were not for these three nations, and the freakish conditions out of which they emerged historically. To see the truth of this, simply ask yourself, What would twentieth-century history have looked like if there had been no United States or Canada or Australia? What, for example, would have been the outcome of the Second World War? Both Australian and Canadian troops spilt vast amounts of blood defending England—so disproportionately, in fact, that Joseph Goebbels made a point of it in his propaganda campaign: "The British would fight to the last Canadian and Australian." (After 1941, he added, "To the last American.") The cost for England of the Second World War was the loss of most of the empire. If the United States had not existed, who would have inherited the pieces of this empire? Would a successful Soviet Union have respected the territorial integrity of Iran? Would it have reconstructed Japan as a liberal democracy, or West Germany? Who could have saved France, either from the Nazis or from the Soviets? If one hadn't devoured her, the other would have, assuming that they had not made a temporary agreement to divide up Europe, as they did in the case of Poland. How much liberalism would there be in the world today if the United States, Canada, and Australia had never existed?

In short, the success of the modern liberal West is totally derived from the freakish nature of the Protestant libertarian communities of stubborn pioneers who left their homeland in the Old World in search of a place where they could start their lives afresh. What Hegel said of North America could also be said about Australia—the settlers who came there could "abandon the ground on which world history has hitherto been enacted." Yet by abandoning the historical past of the Old World, these English-speaking colonies were subsequently able to rescue the Old World from plunging back into the rule of brute force and the Cosmic Process.

There is no one, however, who will come to our rescue if we in the modern liberal West are plunged back into the universal struggle for existence. Today there is no place on earth where human beings can go to escape the burden of too much history, in order to start a new historical cycle. There are no more lands of the future. There are now only lands of the past.

At the end of the nineteenth century, the American historian Frederick Turner announced the closing of the American frontier.

It took much less time to reach this point than Hegel had thought it would—though, as we have seen, Hegel anticipated the logic behind the Turner thesis by nearly eighty years. Libertarian "civil societies" could only exist as long as there were outlets by which those who were resentful or discontented with the status quo could go off and create their own communities, and establish their own lives on their own terms. Otherwise there would simply be too many contenders for the position of king of the mountain— and as the number of contenders rose, the intensity of the competition would inevitably increase, threatening a return to the age-long struggle for survival and supremacy, accompanied by its normal ghastliness.

The carpe diem ethos has helped to ameliorate this effect. If you can spread around enough toys, then perhaps everyone can have his share. By urging ambitious males to focus on trying to accumulate better and neater toys, a society can turn would-be rebels into hard workers. Crass materialism can become the outlet for those discontented with their status.

Capitalist utopians have argued that the carpe diem ethos could be extended to all mankind. Everyone could get enough toys to keep them happy and quiet. But there are two problems with this solution.

First, in large parts of the world there are entrenched elites that have absolutely no interest in sharing their toys with anyone else. Those on top will resist any efforts to create genuinely free market societies because the free market is seen as a threat to their own supremacy. Hernando de Soto has compiled astonishing statistics that display the obstacles, in terms of red tape and bureaucratic rules and regulations, that face anyone enterprising enough to want to start his own small business in many of the nations of the Third World. Why not simply cut out all this fuss and hassle, de Soto asks—and, of course, he is right, it should be eliminated. Yet why isn't it?

The answer is simple. If you are the owner of a flourishing business, do you want new competitors? And if there is a way to nip competition in the bud before it has a chance to get started, wouldn't it be in your obvious self-interest to do this? Werner Sombart observed that Americans were happy with the capitalist system because it worked for them; but in the Third World it only seems to work for those who are already rich, and in many cases for those whose families have long been rich because they were the descendants of a ruling elite whose customs and instincts had been shaped by their experience of exploiting a servile population—a hard habit to break once acquired. But a ruling class that has been accustomed to dominating a servile class will not be likely to abandon its privileges. What strikes us as irrationalities in the economic systems of Third World nations, such as the red tape documented by de Soto, is not irrational at all from the point of view of the dominant elite: It is part of what keeps them dominant. With enough red tape, they can stay king of the mountain forever. The result is that those who are kept down by this system will despair of a free market that has been permanently closed to them, and, filled with resentment, will turn to populist demagogues who will promise them at least revenge.

The second problem with trying to spread the carpe diem ethos globally is the resistance of Muslim fanaticism to it. Radical Islam is a revolt against what it sees as the decadence of the West. It is often said that they hate us for our freedom; it might be truer to say that they fear us for our carpe diem ethos, because they rightly see that the spread of this ethos in Muslim societies would quickly undermine the foundations of Islam. The shared puritanical visceral code of the Islamic faithful would be threatened by a rising generation who wanted to seize the day for themselves and get more fun out of life. The community would dissolve into an association of diverse individuals, free to create their own unique lifestyles. Islam would become simply one option among others. To the followers of radical Islam the best defense against creeping carpe diemism has been a revival of the virtues of the Heroic Age of Islam. If boys are taught to be holy warriors, brought up in a strict code of fanatical and unthinking loyalty to the traditions of Islam, then they will be far harder for the West to seduce. They will be instilled with hatred of the West and made to feel ashamed of any desire to adopt Western ways and values.

The question that ultimately faces us is, Will radical Islam be able to create a new Heroic Age? Will it end in channeling the high-testosterone energy of its boys and young men into becoming holy warriors who, like the jihadists of the past, aim at conquering and subduing those they regard as infidels? And if so, will the West be able to produce boys and young men who are able to stand up to them?

Many people today are familiar with Francis Fukuyama's book *The End of History*, but not everyone remembers its full title: *The End of History and the Last Man*. For some reason, the second part of the title dropped off, and the book came to be referred to as *The End of History*, period. Few pay any attention to the phrase *the Last Man*; fewer still can tell you what it means. Yet Fukuyama's argument only makes sense if we grasp the meaning of the curious phrase, "the Last Man."

The phrase "the Last Man" might seem to imply that there will be no more males at the end of history, but this clearly is not what Fukuyama intends. He means, to put it bluntly, that there will be no more "real men." Indeed, this is essential to grasping Fukuyama's logic. Alpha males are aggressive; their aggression is responsible for causing human conflict. With no alpha males around, there would be no struggles, no fights, no battles, no wars. But in a world without struggles, fights, battles, and wars, there would also be no more history. Of course, years would continue to pass, human beings would continue to grow old, but they would all be destined to die peacefully in their own beds, since they would be living in a world without aggression. Because all the alpha males had been eliminated, no one would have what Fukuyama calls "the irrational desire to be recognized as greater than others." Everyone would be satisfied to be recognized as equal. No one would think that they were better than anyone else and demand that their superiority be acknowledged. The world would be organized on strictly egalitarian lines. At the end of history, there may be baboons and chimpanzees and gorillas and wolves that are alpha males; but there will be no more human beings who fit this description. They will have all died out, or given up. In short, the end of history is predicated on the end of testosterone.

The problem is not that Fukuyama is dead wrong; the problem is that he is half right. Unfortunately for us, the wrong half.

In the West, we are perilously getting down to *our* last man. Liberal democracy, among us, is achieving the goal that Fukuyama predicted for it: It is eliminating the alpha males from our midst, and at a dizzyingly accelerating rate. But in Muslim societies, the alpha male is still alive and well. While we in America are drugging our alpha boys with Ritalin, the Muslims are doing everything in their power to encourage their alpha boys to be tough, aggressive, and ruthless. We teach our boys to be good students, to aim at getting good jobs with large, safe corporations, to plan prudently for their retirement. They want their boys to become holy warriors. We are proud if our sons get into a good college; they are proud if their sons die as martyrs.

To rid your society of high-testosterone alpha males may bring peace and quiet; but if you have an enemy that is building up an army of alpha boys trained to hate you fanatically and who have vowed to destroy you, you will be committing suicide. It may take years or decades before you realize what you have done, but by that time it will be far too late to reverse your course.

The end of testosterone in the West alone will not culminate in the end of history, but it may well culminate in the end of the West. Testosterone still matters. Radical Islam knows this. Indeed, radical Islam represents a revolt of the unbridled alpha male within Islam itself. It is a return to the spirit of the original Arab band of brothers that toppled sedentary empires, and spread Islam through the Levant and across north Africa and into Spain. The fanaticism of militant young alpha males, bound together by the artificial tribe created by Islam, was an unbeatable weapon when it was first forged during the period of Arab conquests, and its revival today is the fundamental challenge to the survival of the rational actor.

If the modern liberal West is to survive, it must begin by recognizing the laws of power that govern the jungle. Even if it does not wish to obey these laws, it must know them. For example, it must clearly understand that our own liberal and popular cultures of reason are serendipitous exceptions to these laws; they must not be taken as evidence that the laws of the jungle are destined to wither away. Where the tribe is a person's only guarantee of security and defense, men will continue to rely on their tribes, and they will act as tribal actors because it is the rational thing for them to do. On the other hand, the rational actor cannot exist unless his whole society has managed somehow to escape the laws of the jungle; hence, the rational actor must recognize that if he is to remain a rational actor, he must be willing to defend at all cost the traditions and institutions of the society that permits him this option. If he is deluded into believing that all men are rational actors by nature, then he will be clueless when confronted with the tribal actor, whose conduct and behavior will make no sense to him. Worse, because the rational actor will be tempted to dismiss the tribal actor as behaving irrationally, the rational actor will fail to see that it is the tribal actor, and not himself, who is acting rationally in terms of the universal struggle for survival and supremacy.

Let me end by offering two political paradigms, one conservative and one liberal, both of which begin by recognizing that there is no reason why reason should prevail; no reason why fanaticism should disappear. Both accept as their premise the view that the modern liberal West is a historical fluke, and not the inevitable wave of the future. Both are keenly aware that there is no guarantee that any social order will be permanent. Both realize that there is no illusion more dangerous than the belief that human beings can put an end to history or to evil, to resentment or to the struggle for survival and supremacy. The conservative paradigm will be dubbed "enlightened tribalism," the liberal paradigm, "critical liberalism."

Enlightened tribalism is the attempt to give intellectual coherence and clarity to the visceral feelings of those Americans who wish to see severe restrictions on immigration, a return to a policy of America First, a curtailment of the outsourcing of American jobs, a hardnosed and realistic approach to foreign policy that relentlessly puts American interests above all other considerations, and that repudiates any claim that it is the mission of America to abolish the law of the jungle as it tragically operates in far too much of the world even today.

Many Americans today "feel" that these positions are right, but they are often at a loss to explain why they are right. Yet if America is a historical fluke, an exception to the rules that have brutally governed most of humankind, then those conservatives who wish to defend our unique traditions can justify themselves by telling their liberal opponents: It is America that has made the world safe for liberals like you. If America does not retain its core traditions and values, then the historical epoch known as the modern liberal West will come to an end—perhaps not in the next decade, but over the next few generations.

Enlightened tribalism retains the tribal distinction between Us and Them, but the basis of this distinction is that our artificial tribe is made up of people who are determined to preserve our own historically unique popular culture of reason. All the members of our tribe agree to abstain from fanaticism; they agree to bind themselves to universally respected and impersonal rules of reasonable behavior in resolving their disputes and differences. They refrain from the use of violence and mob hysteria in order to achieve their political objectives; they agree to disagree, and they respect the point of view of others in their own community, even when it is personally objectionable to them. They try to see the other guy's side of the story. But precisely because all the members of our tribe are willing to impose on themselves these universal standards of reasonable conduct, they will be keenly aware of their difference from those cultures whose members refuse to respect such a universal code of reasonable conduct, and who feel free to use violence, intimidation, riots, fanatical intolerance, and terrorism in order to achieve their own particularistic and divisive agendas. Thus our tribe will be guided by its own self-conscious sense of its world historical exceptionalism; it sees itself as ethically superior to those tribes in which fanaticism runs wild, where individuals hate and murder other members of their own community because of race, ethnic origins, or sectarian affiliations. Furthermore, because of this awareness of its own exceptionalism, enlightened tribalism will not be seduced by forgetfulness into thinking that culture doesn't matter or that all men really want the same things—they may want the same things, but many are all too willing to use violent and barbarous methods to obtain them, and it is these methods that our tribe has forbidden any of its members to use, on pain of being evicted from the tribe.

The second paradigm, critical liberalism, is a form of liberalism that has put away all utopian schemes of spreading the ethos of liberalism throughout the world by a quick fix, such as the staging of "free and fair" elections. It will be a liberalism that has become aware of its exceptionable historical origins—a liberalism that realizes that laws and forms do not create a liberal society made up of reasonable men. Rather, reasonable men are the result of a visceral code that must be implanted within them from an early age. Furthermore, it will be a militant liberalism that refuses to extend toleration to those who are unwilling to tolerate others. In addition, it must be a liberalism that recognizes that it has a sacred duty to instill its own ethos in the next generation, which is another way of saying that it must repudiate the drift within the West toward the creation of a carpe diem culture in which the individual is given no higher aim than to follow his bliss. It must be a liberalism that assigns duties, and does not merely hand out rights. In short, it must be a liberalism that has overcome its nemesis, namely forgetfulness.

Critical liberalism, however, should not be looked upon as the antithesis of enlightened tribalism. It too begins with the recognition that a popular culture of reason is an exceptional achievement;

it too will emphatically demand that all the members of our community play by the same universal rules of reasonable conduct. And it will avoid the suicide of reason by insisting that no one who is not willing to play by the rules of tolerance will be tolerated. It too will make no excuses for fanaticism or an appeal to violence and intimidation. But where it differs from enlightened tribalism is in its own deep conviction that the universal rules that govern the behavior of our tribe, although historically unique to our culture, ought to be extended as widely as possible, in the hope that one day all cultures will be governed by the same universal obligation to behave according to the canons of reasonable behavior. Thus, while enlightened tribalism is content with simply protecting and defending its own exceptional culture of reason, critical liberalism will be inspired by a missionary impulse to construct a cosmopolitan culture of reason to which all men and women on the globe will one day, perhaps in the distant future, be willing to bind themselves.

A historical example might help to make this distinction clear. In the debate over slavery that began in the eighteenth century and that culminated in the nineteenth century, there were two basic antislavery positions. First, there were those communities, represented by the slave-free states of the United States, that were emphatically opposed to slavery within their own territory, but that were willing to accept the peculiar institution of slavery in the Southern states. No one could own slaves in the free states—this was a universal rule that was absolutely obligatory on all the citizens of the Northern states. Yet even though these same Northerners might personally abhor the slavery of the American South, they were content to live with it, provided the South did not try to impose its own slave culture on the North.

Second, there were those radical abolitionists, like Wilberforce in England, who lived in a nation that had abolished slavery within its own territory, but who, not content with this achievement, worked tirelessly to see slavery eliminated throughout the whole globe. At the time they commenced their great work, these radical abolitionists were perfectly aware that in many parts of the world slavery had been an immemorial cultural tradition. None of them believed that their own antislavery beliefs were universally recognized truths agreed to by all members of the global community—quite the contrary, they knew all too well that tolerance of slavery was far more common in the world than intolerance. But what they did emphatically believe was that their own antislavery convictions *ought to be* universally respected by everyone on the planet, and they felt that they had the duty to try to create a world in which their own profound moral intuitions would one day be shared by the entire world community. For the radical abolitionists, the universal condemnation of slavery was thus looked upon as a project. For them the empirical fact that slavery had not *yet* been universally condemned was a challenge, and not a reason to conclude that the attitude toward slavery taken by a slave-holding culture should be respected and tolerated on the basis of a misguided multiculturalism.

Though enlightened tribalism and critical liberalism may disagree on the feasibility of expanding their own historically specific popular culture of reason across the globe, they will not clash over the necessity of protecting their own unique culture of reason from being subverted or undermined through an abstract ideal of tolerance that forces tolerant men and women to tolerate those who have no interest in tolerating others. They will, in this respect, be like a group of boys who are playing a game of baseball, where each of the boys has internalized the rules of the game and where all of them are prepared to resolve their disputes and conflicts in accordance with those impersonal and universally binding rules. Because they have all pledged to acknowledge these rules, they will all act vigorously to expel from the game any new player who insists on exempting himself from the rules that all the other players have committed themselves to obeying. They will do this, not because they have a personal antipathy for the new player, but because they all know that if one player is allowed to make up the rules for himself then the game of baseball will be quickly subverted through the will to power of this one player. He will always insist on getting his own way, bending or breaking the rules as he sees fit, and before long, what was a classic game of baseball will become a naked power struggle in which the refusal of the one player to play by the rules will end in a melee in which no one will play by the rules, and where each will be forced either to assert his own will to power, or to submit to the will to power of the strongest and most ruthless rule-violator.

In short, those who ascribe to enlightened tribalism and critical liberalism must all be like the boys in the game of baseball who know that if there is to be a game of baseball at all, all the players must follow the same rules, and all must insist that every player must follow these rules as well. Similarly, if there is to be a popular culture of reason, then those who are fortunate enough to be members of this culture must be equally emphatic in their insistence that everyone else must obey the same universal and impersonal rules that govern them, since if exemptions and exceptions are permitted, what started as a culture of reason will quickly degenerate into a naked struggle for power, where the most ruthless, and those most contemptuous of the rules, will inevitably end by winning, and in their victory they will destroy the very culture of reason that so foolishly permitted them to violate those ground rules. In short, for reason to tolerate those who refuse to play by the rules of reason is nothing else but the suicide of reason—and with the suicide of reason, mankind will face the dismal prospect of a return to the brutal law of the jungle that has governed human communities for the vast bulk of both our history and our prehistory, and from which certain lucky cultures have miraculously managed to escape—and, even then, only by the skin of their teeth.

September 1, 2006
Stone Mountain

INDEX

Abbe St. Pierre, 49
Abolitionists, 179, 276–277
Abyssinia, 228
Aché people, 105
Afghanistan, 71, 209, 211
Afrikaners, 179, 181
Al-Ghazali, 82
Allawi, Iyad, 255
Alpha males, 121–122, 123, 196, 271–272
Al-Zarqawi, 224
America First, 273
American Civil War, xi, 29, 43, 44, 181
Anarchy, 32, 33, 61, 64, 67, 74, 107, 112,
    118, 126, 130, 190, 229, 230
Anti-Americanism, 37
Appeasement policy, 34, 35, 47, 62
Arago, Francois, 152
Aristotle, 82
Arrogance of Power, The (Fulbright), 39, 52
Assimilationism, 248–249
Assyrians, 180
Atta, Mohammed, 249
Auschwitz, 182
Australia, 96, 104, 266, 267
Autonomy, xv, 127, 154, 188
Aztec civilization, 9

Babylonians, 180
Back-woodsmen/pioneers, 165, 166,
    167–168, 170, 174, 177, 182, 234,
    267

Bagehot, Walter, 102
Balance of power, 56, 57, 220
Balkans, 206
Baptists, 171, 209
Baylen, battle of, 69
Berserk warriors, 25
Beveridge, Albert, 165, 166, 167, 170
Bible, 170, 172, 173, 176, 235
Bin Laden, Osama, 37
Blogsites, 243
Boer War, xiii
Bonaparte, Louis Napoleon, 192
Bonaparte, Napoleon and Joseph, 68
Born-again Christians, 11, 43–44
Bostom, Andrew, 216, 219, 221, 223, 224,
    226
Bourbons, 42, 68, 107, 191, 192, 246
Bradley, F. H., 236
Braudel, Fernand, 7
Brown, John, xix–xx, 29
Bryan, William Jennings, 190
Buber, Martin, 218
Buddhism, 80
Bush, George, H. W., 46
Bush, George W., 16, 26–27, 42, 43–45,
    48, 49, 50, 52–53, 224, 247
    Bush administration, 15, 51–52,
        74–75, 210, 213, 248, 253–254,
        255–256
    as born-again Christian, 43–44
Bushmen, Australian, 96

Businessmen, 187, 190, 193, 268–269
Byzantine Empire, 9, 180, 206, 219, 228

Cake of custom, 102
Calvin, John, 81–82, 211
Campbell, Joseph, 12, 71, 241
Canaanites, 224
Canada, 104, 248, 266
Capitalism, ix, 5, 187, 188, 189, 190, 233,
    268, 269
  original ethos of, 242
Carpe diem ethos, 6, 7, 8, 10, 11, 12–13,
    232, 236, 241–243, 249, 260,
    268–270, 275
  and instant gratification, 242
Cartoon riots, 209, 210, 248
Catherine the Great, 138
Catholic Church. See Roman Catholic
    Church
Cedar Revolution (Lebanon), x
Centralization, 191, 192
Chabot, Francois, 146
Chalabi, Ahmed, 255
Chalotais, René de le, 142
Chamberlain, Neville, 36
Charles I, 107
Chechens, 7, 8, 130
Chénier, Andre, 65, 66
China, 46, 80
Chomsky, Noam, 41, 70
Christian Crusades, 42, 220
Christian fundamentalists, 209–210
Churchill, Winston, 47–48
Civil society, 176–177
Civil war, 231
Clash of Civilizations, The (Huntington),
    55–59
Clash of civilizations model, 9, 55, 56, 58,
    221, 229, 262
  and crash of civilization model, 230,
    235, 259
Class issues, 176. See also Middle class;
    Ruling class; Working class
Clausewitz, Carl von, 56
Code of honor, 96–97, 112

Cold War, 39
Collective denial, 33, 61
Collective identity, 95
Collective psychology, 18
Comte, August, 245
Comte de Segur, 223
Concentration camps, xiii, 182
Condorcet, Marquis de, 49, 67, 132,
    139–154, 157, 161–163, 164, 168,
    170, 171, 186, 193, 196–197, 200,
    201, 212, 233
  on barbarians and savages, 148–149
  death of, 152
  and historical pessimism, 139–140
  See also Reason, Condorcet on
Condorcet and the Rise of Liberalism
    (Schapiro), 143
Conflicts, ix, xi, xii, 18, 31, 32, 56, 58, 161,
    271
Confucius, 80, 81
Conquistadors, 180
Conscience, 90
Consumerism, 194, 195, 196, 236, 242
Contracts, 176, 187
Cooperation, 95, 97–98, 103, 111, 127,
    187–188, 235
Core values, 195
Cosmic Process, 91–92, 93, 96, 111, 122,
    130, 131, 132, 258, 260, 263, 267
Cowardice, 16, 22, 114
Crimean War, 56
Crusades. See Christian Crusades
Cults, 29, 175
Cultural Other, 26
Cultural protectionism, 208, 233
Cultural success, 5–7
Cultural suicide, 234
Cultural survival, 4, 5
Culture of reason, xi, xviii–xiv, 13, 83, 104,
    137, 139, 158, 160, 161–162, 170,
    189, 192, 245, 246, 260, 274, 275,
    276, 278
  of the Dutch, 263–264

D'Alembert, Jean-le-Rond, 140, 141

Danzig, 34
Darwin, Charles, 86, 87–91, 92, 93, 95, 118
Dawkins, Richard, 101, 102, 207
Death squads, x, 73
Decadence, 233–234, 235, 237, 249, 269
Decivilizing process, 58–59, 115, 250, 262
Declaration of Independence, 44, 49, 50
De la Gorce, Pierre, 261
Democracy, 5, 31, 40, 41, 49, 166,
        171–172, 191, 232–233, 266, 271,
        275
    for Middle East countries, x, 18, 44,
        62, 71, 72, 74–75, 246, 262
    and populism, 246, 256
    stubborn individuals as precondition
        for, 171
Democracy in America (de Tocqueville), 171
Demographics, European, 231–232
Denmark, 209
Descent of Man, The (Darwin), 88–89
De Soto, Hernando, 268–269
De Tocqueville, Alexis, 171, 174, 191–192
Devçirme process, 120–122
Dhimmitude, 226
Diderot, Denis, 86, 138, 141
Diversity, 194. See also Multiculturalism
Divine right of kings, 106–107, 114, 115,
        126, 192
Dogs, eating by Hawaiian Islanders,
        163–164
Dutch Calvinists, 179
Dutch War, 263
Dutch West Indies, 47

Edict of Nantes, 174
Education, xi, 137, 164, 186–187, 196, 199
    educated/intellectual elite, 197, 198,
        212, 259
    of Iraqi children, 213
    as mental training, 159
    as propaganda/indoctrination,
        169–170, 197–198
    public secular education, 139,
        142–145, 158, 168, 170, 186, 193,
        212

Egypt, 3–4, 102–103, 206, 209, 218, 232
Ellul, Jacques, 220
Empowerment, 236
End of history, ix, x, 9, 10, 31, 32, 38, 54,
        55, 58, 59, 72, 235, 242, 261,
        262–263, 271
End of History, The (Fukuyama), 154
    full title of, 270–271
England, 34, 40, 46, 54, 104, 107, 142, 147,
        153, 160, 162, 163, 187, 193, 207,
        267
    abolitionists in, 179, 276–277
    Civil War and interregnum, 106–107,
        110
    Glorious Revolution, 125
Enlightened despots, 138
Enlightenment, xi, 4, 8, 35, 54, 83, 86, 89,
        132, 133, 137, 162, 169, 200, 208,
        212, 213, 246, 247
Essay on Integral Calculus (Condorcet), 140
Essay on National Education (Chalotais),
        142
Ethical Process, 91, 93, 111, 122, 130, 131,
        132, 258, 260, 263
Ethiopia, 46
Ethnocentricity, 10, 212
Eugenics, 118
Eunuchs, 180
Evans-Pritchard, Edward, 85, 100
"Evolution and Ethics" (Huxley), 91, 93,
        118, 234–235
Evolutionary theory. See Darwin, Charles;
        Huxley, T. H.

Fadl, Khaled Abou El, 217
Falwell, Jerry, 70
Fanaticism, xvii–xviii, xix, xx, xxi, 55, 57,
        120, 129, 144, 145, 146, 185, 189,
        200–201, 230, 245, 248–249, 273,
        274, 275
    of artificial tribes, 128
    collective/popular, 207–208, 246, 258,
        259
    of converts to Islam, 225—226
    denial of, 15–27

Fanaticism, *continued*
  as epiphenomenon, 41
  eradication of, 159–160
  essence of, 159
  logic of, 205–213
  Muslim, 3, 4, 200, 205–211, 215, 262,
      269–270
  politics of fanaticism, 58, 253
  and resentment, 31–38, 61–62
  role in history, 30–31
  root cause of, 260
  and struggle for existence, 261
  uncanny quality of fanatics, 25–26
  and willingness to die, 7–8, 16, 20–23,
      23–24, 61, 133, 260, 272. *See also*
      Suicide-bombers
  See also under Reason
Fantasia, 244
Fatah, 18
Fear of death, 112, 113, 114, 123
Fenelon, 117
Ferdinand VII, 68, 69, 232
First World War, 33–34, 35, 49, 54
Fish, Stanley, 16
"Follow our bliss," 71, 241, 243, 275
Ford, Henry, 191, 194, 242
France, 34, 46, 54, 73, 104, 116–117, 147,
    163, 188–189, 193, 207, 267
  collapse of, 261
  Festival of Reason in, 64–66, 81
  Franco-Prussian war, 55–56
  French Revolution, 29, 42–43, 51, 62,
      63, 64–67, 74, 107, 117, 141, 142,
      145, 153, 162
  Paris, 249
  Second French Revolution, 191–192
  Third Republic, 232–233, 255
  See also Condorcet, Marquis de
Franklin, Benjamin, 184
Frederick the Great, 138
Freedom, 6, 50, 72, 105, 154, 167, 182, 192
Free market, 269
Fukuyama, Francis, 39–40, 55, 72, 154,
    243, 270–271

Fulbright, J. William, 39, 52, 244
"Future of Tradition, The" (Harris), 83

General Motors, 194
Germany, 189, 229–230, 267. *See also*
    Hitler, Adolf
Girondins, 145, 151
Gladstone, William, 71
Globalization, 233, 258
Gobineau, Arthur, 148
Goebbels, Joseph, 19–20, 36, 47, 249,
    266–267
Golden rule, 234–235
Gordon (General), 224
Gorgias, The (Plato), 110—111
Gossec, François-Joseph, 65
Gramsci, Antonio, 212
Grant, Ulysses S., 181
Greeks (ancient), 20–21, 105–106, 110,
    114, 137, 158
Grunebaum, Gustave E. von, 128
Gulf War, 45, 47, 48, 53

Hadza people, 84–85
Halliburton, 43
Hamas, 18
Harper's, 16
Hawaiian Islands, 163
Hebrews, 129, 218
Hegel, Georg Wilhelm Friedrich,
    171–172, 174, 175, 176–177, 186,
    267, 268
Herder, Johann Gottfried von, 86
Hinduism, 151, 211
Hiroshima, Japan, 250
Historical momentum, 253–254, 259
History of Christian Missions (Latourette),
    206
History of the Hebrew People (Renan), 129
Hitler, Adolf, 34, 35–36, 48, 52, 223,
    229–230, 246, 249, 253, 261
Hobbes, Thomas, 98, 105–110, 112–115,
    123–125, 126
Holland, 263–264

Höss, Rudolf, 183
Hume, David, 81–82
Hunting Ape, The (Stanford), 84–85
Huntington, Samuel, 55, 56, 57, 243
Hussein, Saddam, 17, 46, 53, 73. *See also*
    Gulf War; Iraq
Huxley, T. H., 91–96, 98, 100, 103, 108,
    110, 118–119, 234–235

Ibn-Khaldun, 31, 98, 132, 139, 206, 228,
    229, 237, 262
Ideology, 80, 170, 189, 196, 242, 243
Idolatry, 65, 172, 173, 176
Immigration, 231–232, 248–249, 273
Imperialism, 222
India, 211
Indians. *See* Native Americans
Individuality/individualism, 95–96,
    102–103, 105, 154, 160, 168,
    174–175, 178, 232, 236, 245
Indoctrination, 170, 197–198
Inquisition (Spanish), 68, 69, 232, 246
Internationalism. *See* Liberal
    internationalism
Interregnum periods, 114, 115, 116. *See
    also* England, Civil War and
    interregnum, 106–107, 110
Iran, 37, 236–237, 255, 267
Iraq, 73, 74, 255
    education of Iraqi children, 213
    Iraq war, x, 17, 43, 44, 45, 48, 52–53,
        54, 62, 64, 172, 245–246,
        253–254
    reconstruction of, 247
    See also Gulf War; Hussein, Saddam
Islam, 3, 37, 55, 72, 81, 133, 151, 162, 184
    apostates from, 210, 211, 247–248
    as artificial tribe, 128, 129, 224, 272
    assimilation of Muslim immigrants,
        248–249
    birthrate among European
        immigrants, 231–232
    conversions to, 128, 129, 211, 222,
        224, 225–226

expansion/conquests of, 4–5, 30, 206,
    216, 218–219, 222, 272
future leaders of, 255–256
hadith about farming, 182
Heroic Age of, 270
Islamic great thinkers, 80
modernization of, 8–9, 41, 208, 211,
    213, 232, 247, 249
Muslim celebrations for 9/11 attacks,
    17, 18, 40
as revolt of unbridled alpha males, 272
Shi'a vs. Sunni Muslims, 73
See also Fanaticism, Muslim; Jihad;
    Ottoman Empire
Isolationism, 54
Israel, 17, 18
Italy, 46, 184, 207, 230

Jacobins, 145, 146. *See also* France, French
    Revolution
Janissaries, 119, 120–123, 127–128, 196
Japan, 22–23, 46, 47, 123, 250, 267
Jefferson, Thomas, 171, 176, 178
Jesuits, 142–143, 196. *See also* Roman
    Catholic Church
Jewish immigrants, 248
Jihad, 213, 215–237, 270
    effectiveness in twenty-first century,
        227–228, 262
    nonviolent interpretations of, 217,
        218, 219
José (Spanish King), 232
Joseph II (emperor), 139
Josephus, 22
Joshua (biblical), 224
Just war concept, 220–221

Kagan, Robert, 241, 245
Kamikaze pilots, 24
Kant, Immanuel, 49
Kershaw, Ian, 246
Keynes, John Maynard, 7
Khartoum, siege of, 224
Koran, 226

!Kung people, 84–85, 105
Kuwait, 46, 48, 54

La Mettrie, Julien de, 86
Lane, E. W., 3–4, 208–209, 212, 220, 232
Langrange, Joseph, 140
Language Instinct, The (Pinker), 12
Latourette, Kenneth, 206
Law of the jungle, ix, xiv, xv–xvi, xvi–xvii,
        xx–xxi, 8, 9, 18–19, 34, 35, 40, 59,
        61, 64, 68, 96, 98, 129, 131, 132,
        221, 251, 256, 263, 272–273
    and suicide of reason, 278–279
Leadership, crisis of, 257
League of Nations, 34, 45, 46
Lebanon, x
Leftists, 12, 43, 52, 209, 210, 258
Legacy of Jihad, The (Bostom), 216, 219,
        221, 223
Letter on England (Voltaire), 266
Levant, 174, 228, 272
Leviathan, The (Hobbes), 107, 108
Liberal internationalism, 34, 45–46, 49,
        50, 53, 258
Liberalism, 4, 7, 16, 53, 71, 98, 103–104,
        112, 115, 140, 141, 186, 196,
        198, 208, 210, 212, 246, 262,
        266, 267
    bourgeois liberalism, 189
    critical liberalism, 273, 275–278
    exceptionable historical origins of, 275
    French liberalism, 188–189
    vs. populism, 246
Liberation metaphor, 42–43, 52, 69, 73,
        213, 236
Libertarians, 12, 243
Libertarian societies, 184–185
Lincoln, Abraham, 43, 44–45, 49, 181
Livy, 233–234, 235
Locke, John, 125, 184, 185
Louis XIV, 174
Louis Philippe (citizen king), 117, 188,
        192, 261
Louis XVI, 73, 74, 107, 116–117

Lowery, Rich, 17
Lueger, Karl, 246

McVeigh, Timothy, 29
Madison, James, 166
Malthus, Thomas, 93
Mamlukes, 227, 261
Marat, Jean-Paul, 145
Marshall, John, 165
Marx, Karl, 72, 80, 186, 188, 189, 245
Masada, 22
Materialism, 268
Media, 236
Mehmed II (sultan), 116, 121
Memes, 102, 207
Memoirs (Comte de Segur), 223
Memoirs (de Tocqueville), 191–192
Michelet, Jules, 64–66, 67
Middle class, 184, 186–189, 192, 193, 247
Militias, 167, 177–178, 185
Mill, John Stuart, xiii, 71, 102, 141
Missionaries (Christian), 163, 206–207, 247
Modern Egyptians (Lane), 3, 220
Modernity, 8–13, 27, 38, 40, 41, 129, 132,
        133, 137, 227, 228, 236, 242. *See
        also* Islam, modernization of
Mongols, 150
Montaigne, 24
Mormonism, 173
Muhammad, 226, 248. *See also* Islam
Multiculturalism, 70, 71, 148, 193–195,
        210, 212, 222, 233, 258, 277
Muslims. *See* Islam
Mussolini, Benito, 230

Nagasaki, Japan, 250
National Review, 17
Nation-states, 56
Native Americans, 9, 23, 167, 177–178,
        178–179, 179–180
Nazis, 30, 34, 54, 224, 229–230. *See also*
        Hitler, Adolf; Second World War
Neoconservatives, x, 62, 63, 64, 71–73, 74,
        247, 262

Nevins, Allan, xi
New world order, 32, 36, 46, 53, 57
    new world disorder, 253–264
Nigeria, 209
Nihilism, politics of, 230
9/11 terrorist attacks, 24, 55, 231, 249
    American response to, 37, 40–42, 215,
        253
        9/11 terrorists as cowards, 16
        See also Islam, Muslim celebrations for
            9/11 attacks
Norse warriors, 25
North Korea, 37
Nuclear weapons, 37, 250
Nuer people, 85, 100

Of Paradise and Power (Kagan), 241, 245
Oil, 43, 46, 47, 54
Omar, 228
On the Admission of Women to the Right of
    Suffrage (Condorcet), 141
Original sin, 93–94
Origin of Species (Darwin), 90
Otchakof (Ottoman city), 223
Ottoman Empire, 9, 115–118, 130,
        195–196, 207, 223, 227, 261. See
        also Janissaries
Outsourcing jobs, 273

Pakistan, 255
Palestinians, 18
Papoulia, Vasiliki, 120, 121
Parliamentary system, 230
Pax Americana, 72, 75, 262–263
Peasants, 180, 181, 182, 188, 228
Peloponnesian war, 106, 110, 112
Peoples of the Book, 226
Persia, 180, 206, 211, 219
Philosophes, 138, 143. See also Condorcet,
    Marquis de
Pinker, Steven, 12
Pioneers. See Backwoodsmen/pioneers
Pipes, Daniel, 8
Plato, 110–111

Poland, 30, 267
Policy Review, 83, 245
Political correctness, 198, 213, 217
Political parties, 256, 257
Polynesian Islanders, 247
Populism, 246, 255–256, 257, 258
Pornography, 249, 250
Postmodernism, 16
Potemkin (Prince), 223
Poverty, ix, 31, 176
"Power and Weakness" (Kagan), 245
Prejudice, 138, 139, 147, 148, 168, 169,
        199, 212
Progress, myth of, 245
Property rights, 186
Protestantism, 30, 140, 161–162, 163, 184,
        186–187, 211, 212, 217, 247, 267
    doctrine of God's grace, 218
    Protestant Dissenters, 160, 170–171,
        172–173, 174, 179, 266
    Protestant work ethic, 179, 183
    See also Reformation
Prussia, 55–56
Puritans, 184

Racism, 197
Radical Other, 24–25, 130
Rational actors, xi–xxi, 5, 7, 10, 23, 25, 26,
        27, 59, 63, 64, 67, 71, 73, 83, 86,
        91, 97, 109, 112, 127, 129–130,
        164, 178, 190, 246
    and hegemony of middle class, 189
    produced by shaming code, 101
    and strong states, 192
    survival of, 272–273
    virtues of, xvii
    See also Reason
Reason, 4, 8, 40, 50, 106, 131, 144, 145,
        146, 170, 273
    Condorcet on, 148–149, 150,
        152–153, 154, 158–159
    and consensus, 67
    critical reason, 80–82
    as cultural tradition, 75, 83

Reason, *continued*
    demystifying, 75, 79–104
    exaggerated confidence in, xxi, 59, 63
    and existence of God, 80
    fanaticism of, 61–75
    and historical pessimism, 139
    as innate, 11, 75, 79, 82, 83, 88
    limitations of, 36–37, 81, 164
    politics of reason, 35, 36, 75, 123, 125,
        126, 130, 131, 188, 231
    and Protestant Reformation, 161–163
    reasonable behavior and shame,
        91–102, 111
    as religion, 65, 154
    suicide of reason, 276, 278–279
    See also Culture of reason; Rational
        actors
Rebellions, 68–69, 122, 125, 126, 177, 211,
    247
Red tape, 268, 269
Reformation, 30, 161, 247
Renan, Ernst, 128–129
Revenge, 31, 100
Revolutionaries, 63, 71, 73, 74, 145. *See
    also* France, French Revolution
Rhineland, 48
Rights, xii, 6, 44, 67, 70, 108, 112, 125, 141,
    158, 165, 166, 185, 236, 242, 275
    property rights, 186
Riots. *See* Cartoon riots
Robespierre, Maximillien, 145
Roman Catholic Church, 30, 65, 82, 142,
    143, 184, 206, 211, 212, 242, 247.
    See also Jesuits
Roman Empire, 22, 137, 219, 222,
    233–234
Rousseau, Jean-Jacques, 124
Rule of law, ix–x, xxi
Rules of conduct, xvi–xvii, 276, 277–278
Ruling class, 121, 180–181, 225, 232, 233,
    265–266, 269
Ruskin, John, 254
Russia, 37. *See also* Soviet Union

Samurai, 22–23

Sassanian Empire, 9, 180, 211, 219, 228
Schapiro, J. Salwyn, 143, 144
Schönerer, Georg, 246
Second Treatise on Government (Locke), 125,
    184
Second World War, 19–20, 22, 24, 36, 42,
    45, 46, 47–48, 53, 249
    Australian and Canadian troops in,
        266–267
    fire-bombings of German cities, 40,
        250
Self-assertion, 108, 109, 235
Self-government, 166
Self-interest, xii, xx, 5, 7, 56, 57–58, 80, 90,
    97, 109, 112, 113–114, 124, 125,
    127, 155, 177, 178, 187, 188, 236,
    269
    individual vs. collective, 111
Self-liquidating legitimacy, 73–74
Selim III (sultan), 120
Sepoy rebellion, 211
Seppuku, 22–23
Servants, 166–167
Servetus, Miguel, 211
Seven Years' War, 223
Shame, 83–84, 85, 86, 95–102, 110, 111,
    123, 128, 163, 164, 186, 198, 199,
    200, 235, 236, 247, 249, 256. *See
    also* Reason, reasonable behavior
    and shame
Shari'a, 248
Sicily, 206
Sincerity, 50–51
Skepticism, 159, 172
Sketch of the Intellectual Progress of Mankind
    (Condorcet), 146–147, 151
Slavery, xix, 179, 181, 276–277
Sloan, Alfred, 194
Smith, Joseph, 173–174
Social contract, xix, 98, 113, 124, 125, 126,
    127, 130
Social Darwinism, 92, 111, 118–119, 122,
    129
Social engineering, 72
Socialism, 37, 189, 190, 232–233, 245

Socrates, 81, 82
Sombart, Werner, 184, 189–190, 242, 269
Sorcerer's apprentice fable, 244–245
Sorel, Albert, 62–63, 191
South Africa, 179
South America, 37
Soviet Union, 19, 20, 30, 37, 39, 46, 261,
    267
Spain, 9, 68–69, 180, 206, 232, 246–247,
    272
    Madrid terrorist bombings, 231
Sparta, 123
Speidel, Michael P., 25
Spencer, Herbert, 92
Spengler, Oswald, 132
Spinoza, 81
Stanford, Craig B., 84–85
State of nature, 185
Status quo, 31–33, 37–38, 41, 52, 61, 62,
    71, 72, 74, 130, 177, 188, 190,
    221, 226, 230, 262
    and anarchy and terror, 74
    and clash of civilization model, 55–59
    dissolution of politics of, 258
    fanaticism as, 207
    and just war concept, 220–221
    and order vs. disorder, 231
"Stay the course," 51
Steinmetz, Charles, 118
Struggle for existence, 92–93, 95, 99, 104,
    114, 116, 118, 119, 122, 126, 131,
    154, 174, 175, 187, 195, 200, 234,
    251, 258, 261, 267, 273
Stuarts, 106, 107
Sturlusson, Snorri, 25
Suicide-bombers, 15. See also Fanaticism,
    and willingness to die; Terrorism
Superstition, 138, 139, 145, 146, 147, 148,
    151, 168, 185, 212, 236
Syria, 180, 219

Taliban, 210
Taochi tribe, 20–22
Tartars, 150
Ten Commandments, 209

Terence, 24
Terrorism, 7, 64, 130, 231, 259
    9/11 terrorists as cowards, 16
    See also 9/11 terrorist attacks
Thinking for oneself, 157, 168, 169, 170,
    173, 197, 233
Third World, ix, 268, 269
Thoreau, Henry David, xx
Thucydides, 105, 106
Tierra de; Fuego, 88, 89, 90–91
Time, x
Tolerance, 163, 184, 198–200, 222, 235,
    249, 250, 260, 266
    of the intolerant, 275, 276, 277
Torture, 22, 23
Toynbee, Arnold, 132, 263
Tribal actors, xii–xiii, xv, xvi, xvii, xviii, xx,
    xxi, 7, 8, 10, 27, 73, 86, 96, 127,
    154, 163, 178, 197, 205, 246, 257,
    259, 272–273
    artificial tribes, 127–128, 224
    enlightened tribalism, 273–275, 276,
        277, 278
    and internationalism, 258
    and shaming code, 102
Turgot, 141
Turkey, 223
Turner, Frederick, 191, 267

United Nations, 46, 53, 54
United States, 104, 153, 160, 162, 163,
    193, 266
    fundamentalism in, 209–210
    and historical exceptionalism,
        175–178, 265, 274
    See also 9/11 terrorist attacks
Usury, 242
Utopian socialism, 12

Van Gogh, Theo, 231
Vernet (Madame), 146
Versailles Treaty, 33–34, 47, 48, 230
Vico, Giambattista, 86, 132, 139
Vietnam War, 23–24
Vikings, 219

Visceral code, 83–86, 95, 101, 128,
        163–164, 256, 259, 269, 275
Voltaire, 138, 141, 266

Warrior elites, 177, 187, 188
Wealth, 5, 38, 52, 176, 190, 234, 235
Weapons of mass destruction, 4. *See also*
        Nuclear weapons
Weber, Max, 34
Weimar Republic, 229–230
Wilberforce, William, 276
Wilson, Woodrow, 33, 45, 49
Wolfowitz, Paul, 17, 41

Women, 44, 141, 195, 233
Working class, 183, 189, 190
"Work makes freedom," 182–183

Xenophon, 20–21

Yahweh, 218
Ye'or, Bat, 226
Ynglinga Saga, 25
Yorkshire Ripper serial killer, 250

Zealots (ancient), 22
Zoroastrianism, 206, 211